Agambe

Agamben

Claire Colebrook and Jason Maxwell

polity

First published in 2016 by Polity Press

Polity Press
65 Bridge Street
Cambridge CB2 1UR, UK

Polity Press
350 Main Street
Malden, MA 02148, USA

ISBN-13: 978-0-7456-5310-5
ISBN-13: 978-0-7456-5311-2(pb)

A catalogue record for this book is available from the British Library.

Library of Congress Cataloging-in-Publication Data

Colebrook, Claire.
Agamben / Claire Colebrook, Jason Maxwell.
Malden, MA : Polity, 2016. | Series: Key contemporary thinkers |
  Includes bibliographical references and index.
LCCN 2015039100| ISBN 9780745653105 (hardcover : alk. paper) |
  ISBN 0745653103 (hardcover : alk. paper) | ISBN 9780745653112
  (pbk. : alk. paper) | ISBN 0745653111 (pbk. : alk. paper)
LCSH: Agamben, Giorgio, 1942-
LCC B3611.A44 C645 2016 | DDC 195–dc23 LC record available at
http://lccn.loc.gov/2015039100

Typeset in 10 on 11.5 pt Palatino
by Toppan Best-set Premedia Limited
Printed and bound in the United Kingdom by Clays Ltd., St. Ives PLC

For further information on Polity, visit our website: politybooks.com

Contents

Introduction

Agamben and the Present

Why read Agamben today? At first glance it would seem that the dominant themes addressed by Agamben's already extensive corpus deflect attention away from the most urgent questions of the twenty-first century. In an era of mass media and information overload, what sense does it make to think about poetry and the emergence of humans as speaking beings? And why, when working on questions of sovereignty and life, does Agamben turn to theological problems and the history of Church government? As the irreversible and catastrophic effects of climate change become increasingly evident, and as more racialized forms of violence mark a world of neoliberal expediency, are Agamben's stated goals of community and practical thinking only going to intensify anthropocentric myopia at the expense of a life beyond organisms? One of the most scathing and often-cited objections to Agamben's work is that his unified theory of power as sovereignty (or the "top-down" model of power over life and death) precludes us from understanding the specific and acute problems of different power operations that occur throughout historically, culturally and institutionally unique and dispersed sites (Rabinow and Rose 2006). Although Agamben is critical of the sovereign paradigm, he nevertheless – against the work of Michel Foucault – sees sovereignty and its negativity as still dominant not only in politics but also in some of the twentieth century's most radical theorists.[1] Sovereignty is not only a political paradigm but intersects in Agamben's work with some fundamental concepts and experiences, including time, language, happiness, and life.

Indeed, both the difficulty and value of Agamben's approach lie in what we might refer to as his politicization of ontology (Abbott 2014): sovereignty *is* a political structure but is expressive of a deeper rupture of negativity.[2] One might say that Agamben's work is fruitful because of its attention to the political forms taken by our abstract experiences of language, being, time, and what it means to be human; but one might *also* object that this grounding of political events in grand abstract motifs (such as potentiality) has the tendency to generate a catastrophic monomania, where *the* overarching and non-negotiable focus of the present must be toward modernity's most extreme point of despair which is, in turn, the outcome of a history of thought and being going back at least as far as ancient Greece (Whyte 2013). Agamben is committed to a critique of contemporary biopolitics (or the reduction of human political being to formless "life") *and* to a diagnosis of biopolitics that grounds the present in fundamental concepts of Western philosophy and theology.[3]

For this reason, despite the seemingly distinct focus of Agamben's books – from language and poetry to Auschwitz and the narrative of Pontius Pilate – each work uses a slightly different lexicon to explore different ways of thinking about the relation between the relational and non-relational, or a politics that will "put the very form of relation into question" (HS 29).[4] One way of thinking about sovereignty is not so much as a specific political form – where there is a single top-down and centered power – but as a modality of thinking about what *is* (or has form, identity, and a proper way of being and acting), and that which is merely or barely existent until it takes on form. Here, too, Agamben's work appears oddly divided between arguing for a primacy of language (where all problems of politics and ethics come down to man's distance from life because he speaks) and his criticism of those who focus only on the constitutive power of language, without thinking about language as a milieu, medium, or *medio* that humans at once occupy but that divides everything without any division being graspable. As Alexander Garcia Duttmann notes:

> One will wonder, however, whether attaining communicability is a question of touching upon the limit of a "sublime hesitation", a limit at which the exteriority of communication disappears and continues to manifest itself, or whether it is a question of establishing an integral actuality of language, an actuality without hesitation, an actuality that would no longer betray a separation between potentiality and act, between possibility and reality, between essence and existence, between communicability and communication, between the midst, the milieu, the medium, the "between" in which philosophy and poetry come to stand. (Duttmann 2008: 30)

Language is at once the first of all things – the "thing itself," because it is by way of language that there *is* anything at all, or a relation, and yet language is given only in relations: "The thing itself is not a thing; it is the very sayability, the very openness at issue in language, which, in language, we always presuppose and forget, perhaps because it is at bottom its own oblivion and abandonment" (P: 35). This strange doubleness of language that simply is, and yet also gestures to something not itself – this strange immediacy that we live only in mediating and communicating – is played out in various registers by Agamben, including art, politics, theology, animality, and law.[5]

In each case Agamben occupies a "scission": there is a split between two terms, but this is not the division of some prior unity; it is by way of splitting that distinction comes into being, and this scission then creates the milieu or medium that appears as the ground of the split. Language seems to be privileged by Agamben as exemplary of the operation of the scission, a process that divides and differentiates but is also haunted by the indifference that it discloses and from which it seemed to emerge. Language appears frequently in Agamben's work as the first of all things, and just as frequently as that which "we" must think beyond. In part one might explain this ambivalent relation to language as a shift of emphasis in his work and method, moving from an interest in language, toward law and politics. But one might also say that his work is defined by an under- and over-investment in language as such. On the one hand, everything in Agamben's work seems to turn back to the emergence of language, or how it is that life becomes relational, able to take up a distance and relation to itself by way of voice; and, on the other hand, this problem *of language* is possible because of something that language intimates but can never itself grasp. As an example of this hyper- and hypo-linguistic tendency in Agamben's thought, one might consider the significance he grants to gesture:

> gesture is not absolutely a linguistic element but, rather, something closely tied to language. It is first of all a forceful presence in language itself, one that is older and more originary than conceptual expression.... Linguistic gesture [is] the stratum of language that is not exhausted in communication and that captures language, so to speak, in its solitary moments. (P: 77)

Agamben grants a pre-linguistic importance to gesture, thereby challenging the primacy of language's formal and systemic difference, and yet he refers to *linguistic gesture*, suggesting that beyond language as a system of formal or sovereign difference language is itself something like a movement or bringing into being of relations.[6]

One might say that only language as a system of differences and relations allows us to think of the world in terms of distinct identities; but, for Agamben, simply accepting language as differential and constitutive fails to confront the threshold of language. For some readers of Agamben, it is this question of language and its outside that is *the* motivating drive of Agamben's work (and this would explain why so much time has been devoted to comparing Agamben to Jacques Derrida and deconstruction and the limits of language (Attell 2009; Fiovoranti 2010)). In *Homo Sacer*, Agamben reiterates an observation about language that marks his earliest work, whereby language seems to generate what is other than itself: "Hegel was the first to truly understand the presuppositional structure thanks to which language is at once outside and inside itself and the immediate (the nonlinguistic) reveals itself to be nothing but a presupposition of language" (HS: 21). Language is therefore like sovereign power, requiring and producing what is other than itself. But language is also akin to a dominant way of thinking about the divine, as a force that generates (but is never definitively other than) what it brings into being. Language is at once full actuality – that which simply *is* – and also potentiality or virtuality (it gestures to what is not itself, and which is always marked as known or defined *by* language). It is this "sovereign" structure of language that Agamben will increasingly criticize, and that allows him to connect abstract conceptions of difference and existence to politics and theology. One might say that God creates the world according to distinct essences (what something *is*) and that it is life that brings essences into existence, or allows something potential to become actual; but, for Agamben, the division between essence and existence, and potential and actual, covers over a deeper and more profound problem of "pure potentiality," or a mode of existing that is not exhausted by essence or proper form (P: 251).[7]

The question of potentiality has, as often as language, been identified as Agamben's primary concern (and reading Agamben this way situates the value of his work in an abstraction from language and *actual* politics for which he has been criticized (Power 2010)). Or one might say that there is only a polity because of a sovereign domain of law, and that without law life would fall back into chaos and indistinction; but thinking life beyond law is one of Agamben's often stated goals. To render law inoperative would require recognizing that the very notion *that there is law* is generated from all those figures who claim to guard the gate of law. What needs to be overcome is precisely the notion that one cannot think or act beyond the systems of speech, sovereignty, or theology that seem to be in command of the terrain over which they reign. The gate or door of law – sovereignty as instituted – needs to be rendered inoperative. Writing on Kafka, Agamben argues:

> The door of the law is the accusation through which the individual comes to be implicated in the law. But the first and supreme accusation is pronounced by the accused himself (even if in the form of self-slander). This is why the law's strategy consists in making the accused believe that the accusation (the door) is destined (perhaps) precisely for him; that the court demands (perhaps) something from him; that there is (perhaps) a

trial underway that concerns him. In reality there is no accusation and no trial, at least until the moment in which he who believes he is accused has not accused himself.

...It is a question, not of the study of the law, which in itself has no guilt, but of the "long study of its doorkeepers"...to which the man from the country uninterruptedly dedicates himself in his sojourn before the law. It is thanks to this study, to this new Talmud, that the man from the country – unlike Josef K. – succeeded in living to the end outside the trial.

What might become of the high and the low, of the divine and the human, the pure and the impure, once the door (that is, the system of laws, written and unwritten, that regulate their relations) has been neutralized...(K: 26)

For many defenders of Agamben's work it is this aspect of his writing (of "pure law" or "law beyond law") that opens the possibility of a new politics beyond simply accepting constituted traditions (Crockett 2011: 114; Prozorov 2014). To think of what lies outside the law as indistinct and non-relational is to accept a negativity that, for Agamben, marks everything from an understanding of language (as formal differentiating structure) to twentieth- and twenty-first-century death camps.[8] In concrete terms, one way of thinking about the difference between humans and animals is that animals are so bound up with their environment that they do not bear a relation to the world, whereas humans are at a distance from their world and have the freedom to think and speak. But rather than accept or reject this distinction, Agamben's work renders the difference between relational and non-relational being problematic (O: 60). How does such a distinction come into being, and how might we think about moments when such a distinction is *not* so distinct? So, rather than accept a binary between the differential systems of law or language, and the supposedly lawless or undifferentiated worlds that can only be known as other than (or as the negative of) law and language, Agamben looks to experiences of law and language that are inoperative, or that expose the threshold of indifference between difference and its other: "The messianic end of history or the completion of the divine oikonomia of salvation defines a critical threshold, at which the difference between animal and human, which is so decisive for our culture, threatens to vanish" (O: 21). If it is the case that it is the non-relational or indifferent that needs to be thought, then *no* division – human/animal, law/life, actual/ potential, language/life – can be the starting point for theory. Instead, Agamben takes his lead from a quite different type of method, whereby one takes up an inscribed figure that seems to mark out a difference, and then looks at the ways that an apparent differentiation conceals a complex history that is given in further distinctions and insecure divisions. For all his philosophical and theological learnedness, it often seems that Agamben, as he himself suggests, is most indebted to the work of Aby Warburg, where artworks are neither works of individual artists nor representations of the world but "signatures of things," or vestiges and remnants of an inherited archive that can *and must* be illuminated:

> The history of humanity is always a history of phantasms and of images, because it is within the imagination that the fracture between individual and impersonal, the multiple and the unique, the sensible and the intelligible takes place. At the same time, imagination is the place of the dialectical recomposition of this fracture. The images are the remnant, the trace of what men who preceded us have wished and desired, feared and repressed. And because it is within the imagination that something like a (hi)story became possible, it is through imagination that, at every new juncture, history has to be decided. (N: 79)

It is possible to discern a regal aestheticism and catholicism to Agamben's work whereby every text and problem needs to be taken from the domain in which it currently resides, or torn out of the art gallery of the present, and then set alongside a completely different set of figures and inscriptions so that a past that was never present might be created, or – to borrow a term from Simone Weil, the subject of Agamben's doctoral dissertation – "de-created" (Ricciardi 2009).

Agamben is as critical of the present and its failure or abandonment of anything that lies outside law and language as he is of pre-modern conceptions of absolute power and the sacred that grant law a constitutive function. Rather than accept that law brings order into being and allows life to be lived in a human and political manner, Agamben theorizes a new form of politics that would not begin with the polity (as a structure) nor with some constituted form of the individual or person, but with a life that can constantly be experienced as the potentiality *for form*, as allowing form to come into being – and where each member of this community experiences each other *not* by way of some law or form but as nothing other than a potentiality for forming: "what is a life outside the law, if it is defined as that form of life which makes use of things without ever appropriating them?" (HP: 144). In order to break with a present where "life" is increasingly nothing more than the bare means through which power secures its ends, it is not sufficient to turn back to some golden age of communitarian politics, for although Agamben *does* insist that the present has lost all sense of a life lived according to its own form, most conceptions of formed political being have operated by way of a relation to the formless and supposedly non-relational. Communitarians and neo-Aristotelians argue that it makes no sense to speak of a self outside its social and shared form (MacIntyre 1981), while liberal individualists insist that the only fair social form is one that each individual would imagine as rational for any other individual (Rawls 1972). Agamben sets himself apart from both these traditions, and instead defines a "new politics" that would not rely upon any single term such as the polity or the self:

> There is politics because human beings are argōs-beings that cannot be defined by any proper operation – that is, beings of pure potentiality that no identity or vocation can possibly exhaust…politics might be nothing other than the exposition of humankind's absence of work as well as the exposition of humankind's creative semi-indifference to any task, and might only in this sense remain integrally assigned to happiness. (MWE: 141–2)

Agamben's historical work looks back to the earliest stages of Roman law and Christian theology, and even to ancient conceptions of sacrifice and oaths; but this is not so much to find an outside to the present as to discern something already harbored within the tradition that has never been realized. If his work is messianic this is not because it focuses on a future that is always "to come," but rather because the present already harbors the potentiality for redemption if only redemption be seen *not* as radically at odds with life (Attell 2014: 214). The question is, then, not so much how abandoned and bare life might be redeemed, but how the distinction between life and its supposedly other state of blessedness might be rendered inoperative. How might life be lived in its natural sweetness without accepting all the divisions and moral oppositions that have marked notions of nature?

It is precisely this problem of curious divisions and contrary tendencies that Agamben's entire corpus confronts and works through. His investigations at once concern the curious relations among law, magic, and religion alongside acute contemporary crises. To take perhaps the most prominent example: the most pertinent theme throughout Agamben's work is the "state of exception," where sovereign powers suspend the constituted law. This is at once highly relevant to current uses of state power that fly in the face of law and constitutional limits at the same time as it requires us, Agamben argues, to consider the origin and ambivalence of the sacred: "The principle of the sacredness of life has become so familiar to us that we seem to forget that classical Greece, to which we owe most of our ethico-political concepts, not only ignored this principle but did not even possess a term to express the complex semantic sphere that we indicate with the single term 'life'" (HS: 66). The main claim of his major work, *Homo Sacer*, is that the untheorized conception of the sacred still inflects politics and must be dealt with in order to reconfigure politics; interestingly enough, certain dimensions of Agamben's own political thought remain similarly untheorized. One of Agamben's translators and most astute commentators recently made the audacious claim that, "if and when Guantanamo is closed down

permanently, it will in no small measure be due to the thought of
Giorgio Agamben," and yet it is only pages later that Timothy Campbell laments the extent to which in some respects Agamben remains
indebted to an almost nostalgic conception of a proper language that
would heal the gap between human beings and alienated writing: "The
uncomfortable conclusion that emerges from this reading of Agamben
would be its deep indebtedness to a Heideggerian ontology of proper
and improper writing" (Campbell 2011: 41).

One could make sense of the political trajectory of Agamben's work
by noting a shift of emphasis from earlier works on poetry and language, through a middle period concerned more with law, to the conclusion of the *homo sacer* project that focuses increasingly on the relation
between abandoned life and life that is able to be lived in relation to
(rather than outside) form and that is exemplified in Franciscan monasteries. Agamben's relation to language, and to life and the proper,
shifts dramatically from his earlier to later work; if there is, as Campbell
notes, an apparent yearning for language to be authentically emergent
from the world and *not* operating at some sovereign and negating
distance, Agamben's work moves progressively away from an attention on language toward finding a new mode of practical politics that
is not so much restorative as it is oriented to a future quite different
from a history of thought grounded in loss or negativity.

The entirety of Agamben's work, and the responses it has provoked,
are marked by ambivalence, and by being at once directly engaged
with striking issues of twenty-first-century power, while at the same
time operating with such a wide historical sweep that questions of race,
class, sexuality, and historical difference are occluded.[9] The points of
deepest despair in Agamben's work – such as the modern condition
where "we" are all reduced to bare life and subjected to the immediate
force of the state (where the state is a law unto itself) – is also intrigu-
ingly close to the redeemed future where there will be no law opposed
to life, and life will be experienced in its singular "thisness," without
requiring the sanctification of rights and personhood.[10] "Life," then,
when it is known and managed as bare life (or a life outside the law,
or at odds with our communicative political being), is a symptom of
an ongoing and intensifying negativity in Western thought:

> The first act of investigation was therefore the identification of bare life
> as the first referent and stake of politics. The originary place of Western
> politics consists of an *ex-ceptio*, an inclusive exclusion of human life in
> the form of bare life. Consider the peculiarities of this operation: life is
> not in itself political, it is what must be excluded and, at the same time,
> included by way of its own exclusion. Life, that is, the Impolitical
> (*l'Impolitico*), must be politicized through a complex operation that has
> the structure of an exception. The autonomy of the political is founded,

in this sense, on a division, an articulation, and an exception of life. From the outset, Western politics is biopolitical. (DP: 2)

However, it is also life – not as differentiated but as *indifferent* – that increasingly provides an opportunity for a post-biopolitical future. This would not be a life set apart from politics and form (mere animality), nor a fully formed political life, but a life that experienced its relations with others as an ongoing potentiality, as a "form of life" (Bailey, McLoughlin, and Whyte 2010). If biopolitics operates by managing a bare life that it posits without law, then it is life conceived beyond negativity – life as the threshold from which law and language emerge but which can never operate with the systemic force of sovereignty – that promises a new future. If it is a redeemed relation to language that seems to hold promise in Agamben's early work, it is life that increasingly becomes the focus of the threshold of indifference or indistinction that will take politics beyond its oppositional mode; such a new mode would be immanent, where the form of life is not something toward which life is oriented (as though life had some proper end of which it was the mere means), but life's own potentiality that is also exposed in impotentiality (or the absence of any proper or necessary form):

> It will be necessary...to embark on a genealogical inquiry into the term "life." This inquiry, we may already state, will demonstrate that "life" is not a medical and scientific notion but a philosophical, political, and theological concept, and that many of the categories of our philosophical tradition must therefore be rethought accordingly. In this dimension, there will be little sense in distinguishing between organic life and animal life or even between biological life and contemplative life and between bare life and the life of the mind. Life as contemplation without knowledge will have a precise correlate in thought that has freed itself of all cognition and intentionality. *Theōria* and the contemplative life, which the philosophical tradition has identified as its highest goal for centuries, will have to be dislocated onto a new plane of immanence. It is not certain that, in the process, political philosophy and epistemology will be able to maintain their present physiognomy and difference with respect to ontology. Today, blessed life lies on the same terrain as the biological body of the West. (P: 239)

As Agamben's work develops over decades, certain motifs that he originally endorses (such as Friedrich Nietzsche's concept of "eternal return," in which one might live the present liberated from any negative or mournful distinction between the world as it is and the world as it is ideally represented) are subsequently seen as symptomatic of an unworthy nihilism. It is the same Nietzsche whom Agamben targets for having elevated the will (and therefore act, force, and power) to a supreme principle, thereby losing all sense of a more profound conception of power that would be intertwined with *not-doing* or inoperativity (ER; Thurschwell 2004; de la Durantaye 2009: 273–4).[11] Rather than see the shifts and reversals in Agamben's work as just another instance of a change of opinion, it is possible to see such dynamism as expressive of the problem that unites his corpus. What unites early work on language's negativity (or the irreducible distance between word and world) with sovereignty (or the law's creation of itself as a power that transcends life), with ongoing but intensifying interests in visual experience and gesture, and what it might mean to live well without following a rule, is an attempt not only to *think* outside the moral divisions of Western thought, but to make thought *practical* rather than disembodied, logical, or propositional.

Throughout this book, while moving back and forth from Agamben's early to later work, the focus will be on *indifference*, not as an affective state of not caring but – on the contrary – of taking what appear to be the most arid topics and demonstrating their urgency for how "we" experience ourselves. Rather than think of indifference as a loss of distinction, which is one way in which we might despair the modern tendency to reduce all human being to bare life without any sense of the political life of humans, we might – after Agamben – focus on indifference as a liberation from the moral distinctions that have always located human happiness in some sphere beyond this life. In overcoming the subjection of "life" or "humanity" to something other than itself (including the concepts of life and humanity), Agamben seeks to find a way beyond the generality that negates singular existence, and accordingly uses the term "whatever" to think a new mode of indifference:

> Whatever is constituted not by the indifference of common nature with respect to singularities, but by the indifference of the common and the proper, of the genus and the species, of the essential and the accidental. Whatever is the thing *with all its properties*, none of which, however, constitutes difference. In-difference with respect to properties is what individuates and disseminates singularities, makes them lovable (quodlibetable). Just as the right human word is neither the appropriation of what is common (language) nor the communication of what is proper, so too the human face is neither the individuation of a generic *facies* nor the universalization of singular traits: It is whatever face, in which what belongs to common nature and what is proper are absolutely indifferent. (CC: 19; see also Sayeau 2013: 238; Doussan 2013: 32)

Sometimes this "coming philosophy" (P: 220) requires going back to moments in textual history to reconsider conceptual divisions (in Agamben's work on Greek thought, Roman law, and Christian theology), but it also requires thinking about thresholds between humanity and animality, and between what is seen and what is (or might be) meant. Looking backward historically is a way not so much of restoring the past as of finding a past that was never fully lived, in order to construct a more open future, one *not* delimited in advance by inherited divisions and negations.

Agamben's work gained purchase in the anglophone world with the translation of *Homo Sacer* in 1998 (published in Italian in 1995); the September 11 terrorist attacks on New York City and the Washington, DC, areas occurred three years later, and seemed to provide a perfect instance of the politics of "bare life" that emerges in supposed states of emergency. An example of such a "state of exception" would be the USA's 2001 "Authorization for Use of Military Force" or AUMF, a joint resolution of Congress that granted the then President George W. Bush the power to use all "necessary and appropriate force" against those nations, organizations, or persons he determines "planned, authorized, committed, or aided the terrorist attacks that occurred on September 11, 2001, or harbored such organizations or persons." The resolution is still in force today and enables the President to circumvent the usual constitutional procedures that would be required to initiate attacks on persons suspected of terrorism. The usual rule of law, which at first glance seems to limit the powers of the sovereign, can be suspended by the sovereign; it is at that point – when there is no longer a consti-tuted law *through which power is exercised and mediated* – that power operates directly and takes hold of bodies who can become what Agamben refers to as "bare" life.

Although sovereignty and bare life are only two of Agamben's key concepts, the structure of sovereignty – its negativity, systematicity, and mode of creating itself by excluding its posited outside – inflects the way in which Agamben generates his more positive conceptions of immanence, *and* the way in which his ambiguous relations to other authors and concepts play out over the course of his career. One of the clearest instances of Agamben's relation to the past and present is his seemingly minor but significant ongoing engagement with Jacques Derrida's deconstruction which, at its simplest, insists both that we cannot reduce justice or law to any of its inscribed actualizations, and yet that we can also only think of justice from the limits of inscription. Justice, for Derrida, would always be "to come," and would therefore be radically different from or beyond the law, even if only given as beyond the law (Cornell, Rosenfeld, and Carlson 1992). For Agamben, deconstruction, far from being a radical departure from metaphysics, repeats what sovereignty exposes in concrete politics: what has been forgotten or abandoned is anything that is not caught up with, or negated by, constituted differences and relations. What needs to be thought, for Agamben, is indifference and the non-relational. This unthought zone can be as arcane as thinking a potentiality that is not yet the potentiality to do any specific act, or as pertinent as thinking about life that is not already subjected to managerial or efficient modes of power (a life beyond will, self-actualization, and yet not the bare life that is the mere substrate of personhood). "Life," then, in Agamben, operates across his corpus as a way of thinking a series of thresholds; this project of rendering distinctions inoperative ranges from the most well-known and ongoing project of *Homo Sacer*, where life has been increasingly abandoned as nothing more than the bare substance managed by politics, to his early work on language where the event of speaking exceeds the already constituted differences of a linguistic system, to his later work on theology and duty and conceptions of "a" life as an ongoing actualization of a style or figure, rather than a willing subject who decides upon his own moral law. What unites these phases is a path charted between negativity (or abandoning life to what can only be known as other than language and politics) and will (or the assumption that language, law, and culture are pure self-constituting systems without remainder). In relation to contemporary politics and culture this means that one neither accepts the political terrain as constituted, but one also has no normative ground – such as the self, humanity, justice – to which one can appeal as a simple outside factor. When Agamben does refer to happiness it is critically rather than negatively; happiness is not what has been set outside politics, but is a way of thinking a politics that is not structured by law and its managed outside.

In the recent United States practice of targeted killings, humans are executed without trial; both the individuals who are the targets of military drone strikes, and the population that is threatened, become instances of life to be managed (Brennan 2012). In *Homo Sacer* Agamben discusses the case of Karen Quinlan, whose sustained existence on life support exposes life as *zoē*:

> We enter the hospital room where the body of Karen Quinlan or the overcomatose person is lying, or where the neomort is waiting for his organs to be transplanted. Here biological life – which the machines are keeping functional by artificial respiration, pumping blood into the arteries, and regulating the blood temperature – has been entirely separated from the form of life that bore the name Karen Quinlan: here life becomes (or at least seems to become) pure *zoē*. When physiology made its appearance in the history of medical science toward the middle of the seventeenth century, it was defined in relation to anatomy, which had dominated the birth and the development of modern medicine. And if anatomy (which was grounded in the dissection of the dead body) was the description of inert organs, physiology is "an anatomy in motion," the explanation of the function of organs in the living body. Karen Quinlan's body is really only anatomy in motion, a set of functions whose purpose is no longer the life of an organism. Her life is maintained only by means of life-support technology and by virtue of a legal decision. It

is no longer life, but rather death in motion. And yet since life and death are now merely biopolitical concepts, as we have seen, Karen Quinlan's body – which wavers between life and death according to the progress of medicine and the changes in legal decisions – is a legal being as much as it is a biological being. A law that seeks to decide on life is embodied in a life that coincides with death.

The choice of this brief series of "lives" may seem extreme, if not arbitrary. Yet the list could well have continued with cases no less extreme and still more familiar: the Bosnian woman at Omarska, a perfect threshold of indistinction between biology and politics, or – in an apparently opposite, yet analogous, sense – military interventions on humanitarian grounds, in which war efforts are carried out for the sake of biological ends such as nutrition or the care of epidemics (which is just as clear an example of an undecidability between politics and biology).

It is on the basis of these uncertain and nameless terrains, these difficult zones of indistinction, that the ways and the forms of a new politics must be thought. (HS: 104)

Life is not the life of *someone* whose intentions, personality, and ongoing mode of behavior are evaluated and judged – as when, in earlier forms of sovereign power, a citizen is tried for having violated a constituted law and must appear before a jury and deliberating judge. In targeted killings humans are immediately executed, sometimes without any sense of who is being killed, as drones target groups or bodies whose movements indicate possible terrorist affiliations. Further, the population protected by these drone strikes, targeted killings, extraordinary renditions, and enhanced interrogation procedures is also posited as "bare life." Rather than thinking of the political order as unfolded from the potentiality of life and its generation of relations, political power operates as immediate force in relation to life that itself is deemed to have no force or order other than that bestowed by the law. It is life that – in its relation to law – is deemed to be non-relational, "bare." The politics of this "life" is a form of negative biopolitics, one that deprives life of any relation to the law by establishing life as non-relational. This bare life is a life *stripped* of relations (and is definitively other than sovereignty); it cannot be challenged by – say – thinking that there is no life other than that which is known through language or power. Bare life is the constitutive opposite of a system of force that is experienced as fully actual, immediate, and requiring nothing other than itself in order to operate; law is nothing other than pure operation. Against this, one might consider the inoperativity of *mere life* – not as that which is nothing more than operation, but which exceeds and allows for (but does not guarantee) relations and operations. In a tradition that runs from St. Paul to Kafka, Agamben identifies a form of "redemption" that is quite distinctive from one of fulfillment, achievement, realization, and arriving at a lawful blessedness; it is not the re-inclusion of life within law, so it is not a granting of rights, freedoms, or humanity to those who had been abandoned by law. On the contrary, it is the rendering inoperative of law, such that *this life in its immanence* need not be seen as other than law:

> ...the ambiguity of the angelic powers, like that of the law and of every power, resides in the fact that what had been given provisionally and for sin pretends to be valid absolutely....
>
> The angels, as a cipher for the divine power of government of the world, also represent the dark and demonic aspect of God, which, as such, cannot simply be expunged.
>
> Pauline messianism must be seen from this perspective. It acts as a corrective to the dynamic hypertrophy of angelic and human powers. The Messiah deactivates and renders inoperative the law as well as the angels and, in this way, reconciles them with God...
>
> The theme of the law no longer applied, but studied, that in Kafka's novels goes hand in hand with that of the constantly inoperative angelic functionaries, here reveals its messianic pertinence. The ultimate and glorious telos of the law and of the angelic powers, as well as of the profane powers, is to be deactivated and made inoperative. (KG: 166)

This mere life, rather than abandoned and negated bare life, would be not-yet relational and yet would bear the potentiality to generate relations and difference: not two distinct powers or realms, but an expression of glorification *from which* a sense of a divine power is generated (KG: 166). This seems a highly abstract concern, but is for Agamben the only way that the presently pervasive biopolitical horizon might be transformed. What might once have been exceptional – a life that was set outside the law and not even worthy of being able to speak or articulate itself at trial or within the polity – has now become the standard in a world of governmentality that is increasingly acting directly on a body or biological existence.

Procedures such as drone strikes and the means used to execute them are not deliberated by the polity, but situate the body politic as an object of immediate bureaucratic control; the primary imperative of security and life reduces the protected population to a managed mass. The US citizenry has accepted increasingly intrusive degrees of surveillance, monitoring, screening, and documenting, all for the sake of avoiding terror. "Life" thus becomes defined and managed in relation to its fragile border with an always-potential death. The bodies in the polity are not so much citizens as they are "*zoe*" – bare life defined by capacities of the organism rather than the self-organizing practices of speech and reason: "the syntagm *homo sacer* names something like the original 'political' relation, which is to say, bare life insofar as it operates in an inclusive exclusion as the referent of the sovereign decision" (HS: 85).

As already mentioned, *Homo Sacer* was translated in 1998, three years after its publication in Italian, and was not only prescient in being applicable to the emergency measures introduced after 9/11, but has become ever more salient given the modes of political intervention in the twenty-first century. The contention of this book will be that the manifest immediate pertinence of Agamben's theory of the state of exception is both strengthened and undermined by other strands of his corpus. On the one hand, Agamben's criticism of sovereignty and negativity as running throughout the entire course of Western metaphysics and politics requires and justifies his focus on theological, philological, and aesthetic history; at the same time, once urgent political concerns are tied to grand questions of potentiality and language we seem to be faced with paralysis.[12] One might even say that paralysis, or the practice of *not doing and not acting*, becomes so celebrated in Agamben's work as an opposition to sovereignty that genuine revolution becomes no longer possible, and we are left with quietism (Oliver 2013: 239). Agamben's focus seems poised between lamenting bare life – life stripped of all force – and appealing to a mere life that would oppose sovereignty by way of passivity. Why, we might ask, does life abandoned from the polity become the point from which a new politics might be thought, rather than – say – a body that takes hold of the power to operate and actualize itself? Here Agamben's work is in marked contrast with other theorists of biopolitics and modern capitalism, who would see activism and a full actualization of life as revolutionary; Hardt and Negri's influential *Empire* (2000), also written from a standpoint critical of the global reach of managerial capitalism, is adamant that living labor needs to become the self-present and self-actualizing force of a unified humanity. Agamben, by contrast, sees not working and remaining in potential, without self-actualizing, as the more radical mode of resisting the ways in which "life" has been reduced to nothing more than the medium through which sovereignty realizes itself (Coleman and Grove 2009; Mills 2014: 74).

Detention camps (such as Guantanamo) that reduce suspected terrorists to a condition of bare life are, increasingly, not the only sites where bodies are merely managed as "life" and as so much possible threat to the population (which is also no longer a citizenry that has excluded biological existence so much as a mass of bare life). Life is now set apart from the operation of law and treated as manageable by technical expertise in institutions ranging from refugee camps and immigration detention centers to schools, universities, and hospitals, which are now focused on achieving targets generated from population statistics and quantitative research. Under the guise of healthcare and "wellness initiatives," workplaces are increasingly monitoring employee biometric data; this shift of focus, from a politics that concerns citizens who argue for policies and procedures, to a government that operates on populations by means of knowledge, statistics, and surveillance, has become known as "biopolitics," even though just what this term means depends on how one traces the history and future of sovereignty. Agamben takes this term from Michel Foucault, who saw it as the hallmark of modernity; but while agreeing that bio-politics *is* modern, Agamben argues that its rationale goes back to the hidden origins of Western thought. Further, Agamben's claim that bio-politics is an intensification of Western metaphysics' ongoing accept-ance of negativity ties his political and historical work with the seemingly more "aesthetic" and early work on literature, or more spe-cifically language. As Colin McQuillan (2012) has argued, the notion of an original "fiction" ties Agamben's focus on language's creative quali-ties with his focus on sovereign power's production of itself, by exclud-ing a bare life that is mute before the law. What both sovereignty and language share – and what unifies Agamben's corpus despite some important shifts – is a unique sacrificial logic, where an inside/outside binary is generated by destructive exclusion.

It is for this reason that the extreme pertinence and timeliness of Agamben's work on bare life and the state of exception are combined with a highly untimely insistence on the need to examine such events via a reflection on a history of Western thought going back to Aris-totle, ancient Roman law, medieval theology, and pre-modern juris-prudence. *Homo sacer*, Agamben argues, is the current potential condition of every human on the globe, vulnerable as we all are to being reduced to nothing more than expendable life that may be exterminated on the basis of being perceived as a possible threat to the population. For Agamben, then, today's states of exception require thinking back to the condition of *homo sacer*. *Homo sacer*, in turn, derives from ancient Roman law but expresses an ontological problem that goes back at least as far as Aristotle, and before that to concep-tions of the sacred, which "is necessarily an ambiguous and circular notion" (LD: 105).

This directs Agamben back to a genealogy of some manifestly arcane questions, including the theological problem of the divine governance of the world, the relation between God's being and acting, the relation between the monasteries and ecclesiastical government, and the dis-tinction in ancient Greek thought between *bios* and *zoe*. If the present requires us to look back at ancient Roman law and *homo sacer*, this is because ancient Roman law is already indebted to what Agamben frequently refers to as a fracture in Western thought – a split or impos-sible divide between being and acting; between a complete and abso-lute life opposed to a life subjected to governance; between a God who requires no other being in order to be, and a God whose glorification explains the history of the world (or a relation *to* God) (KG: 53); between a politically formed life (*bios*) and a life that is prior to self-actualization (*zoe*); and between a recognized and legally protected citizenry and an abandoned or bare life of *homo sacer*.

These last two oppositions of *homo sacer*/citizen (from Roman law) and *bios*/*zoe* (from ancient Greek philosophy) at first seem to provide the seeds for a narrative that will structure Agamben's entire corpus. Originally, Agamben argues, the Greeks had two words to refer to life: *bios*, or the formed life that was the outcome of decisions taken with regard to other members of the polity, and *zoe*, or the life that simply is and does not set an end or form for itself. This understanding of life as having two distinct potentialities was, for Agamben, decisive. That is, a certain distinction that we can now read in ancient philosophy has implications for the way we think and act to this very day. Agamben suggests that this linguistic distinction expresses a specific way of thinking, acting, and governing; it would seem that he is committed to the idea that language is the way it is because of pre-linguistic prob- lems, and this is where he would depart from theories of textual or linguistic construction of reality. However, there is also in Agamben's work an overwhelming sense that distinctions in language are founda- tional, such that language itself has a force that determines life and thinking. So, rather than say that Agamben sees language as determin- ing the way we think, *or* that he sees the way we think as generating the vocabularies and grammar that we have, he questions the threshold that passes from what is (being) to how we say what is (language), and within language itself he focuses on the difference between the physi- cality of voice, and then the systemic structure that enables the voice to be heard as speech, or that enables sound to be other than itself. For Agamben, that very problem of whether language causes or reflects thinking is itself indicative of the deeper problem of what he constantly refers to as an original indistinction or threshold. Like a series of other distinctions (*bios/zoe*, human/animal, praxis/*poiesis*, potential/actual), Agamben argues that the relation between language and life needs to be thought in terms of a different mode of relation, one that does not place one term as the cause or ground of the other, and one that neither accepts the distinction nor posits some prior unity. In the beginning is indistinction: writing on "philosophical archaeology," Agamben sug- gests that we do not trace terms back to a present past, nor accept that we cannot think beyond the systems of the present; rather, the present itself is haunted by an origin that is non-original, intimating what is not fully distinct and differentiated from within an existing set of distinctions:

What happens when archaeological regression reaches the point where the split between conscious and unconscious, between historiography and history that defines the condition in which we find ourselves is produced? It should now be obvious that our way of representing the moment before the split is governed by the split itself. To imagine such a "before" indeed involves, following the logic inherent in the split, presupposing an original condition prior to it that at a certain point divided itself. In this case, this is expressed by the tendency to represent the before or beyond of the dichotomy as a state of happiness, a kind of golden age devoid of repressions and perfectly conscious of and master of itself.... On the contrary, before or beyond the split, in the disappearance of the categories governing its representation, there is nothing but the sudden, dazzling disclosure of the moment of arising, the revelation of the present as something that we were not able to live or think. (ST: 99)

Here, again, we can note Agamben's timeliness, given that theory and philosophy are reacting negatively to the supposed dominance of "linguistic" models, where language is seen as a limit beyond which thinking cannot go. But Agamben is also quite untimely in that he is no simple new materialist, realist, or even an advocate of ontology. Rather than say that language constructs life *or* that life naturally extends itself into language, Agamben will insist that we confront these oppositions with the awareness that such binaries can neither be fully explained by one term, nor resolved by referring to some explanatory origin. For Agamben, neither is it sufficient to remain within the terms of one's language, as though there were no way out of an already constituted system of differences; at the same time, he is increasingly insistent that stepping outside language is not something we can do at will. The emergence of human beings *into language* (or the creation of the impossible threshold within which we exist) is something we have become less and less able to confront. The task of the future, he insists, lies in thinking the emergence of distinction precisely because our present world is one in which we have lost all relation to a language that now appears as mere circulating system without ground. In *Means Without Ends* (the title of which indicates that we might think of language not as a way of relaying information but as something that is a potentiality not subordinated to some present end), Agamben describes our contemporary "uprooting," but also sees that failure to experience language as an opportunity – finally – to face up to language's strange groundlessness:

What prevents communication is communicability itself; human beings are kept separate by what unites them. Journalists and the media establishment (as well as psychoanalysts in the private sphere) constitute the new clergy of such an alienation of the linguistic nature of human beings... Even more than economic necessities and technological development, what drives the nations of the Earth toward a single common destiny is the alienation of linguistic being, the uprooting of all peoples from their vital dwelling in language. But exactly for this reason, the age in which we live is also that in which for the first time it becomes possible for human beings to experience their own linguistic essence – to experience, that is, not some language content or some true proposition, but language *itself*, as well as the very fact of speaking. Contemporary politics is precisely this devastating *experimentum linguae* that disarticulates and empties, all over the planet, traditions and beliefs, ideologies and religions, identities and communities. (MWE: 84–5)

It is this particular way of thinking about oppositions and relations that organizes each one of Agamben's interrogations and marks his work as distinct from either structuralism or post-structuralism. He refuses the idea that language constructs the differences through which we think, but he is equally opposed to the notion that one might simply grasp some pre-linguistic and pristine reality. Instead, he insists that *the* distinction we need to focus upon is the experience of language, *but* that experience is never something that we can simply represent, and is always ungraspable in terms of presence and denotation. It is, ultimately, not a thing that "we" experience but a threshold. This, in turn, requires us to ask quite distinct forms of questions that differ from both structuralism and post-structuralism. Structuralism, broadly speaking, had argued that we experience the world as mediated through systems of difference; language organizes reality, and the ways in which languages divide the world create the different worlds of different cultures. Post-structuralism (and especially the deconstruction of Jacques Derrida) seems closer to Agamben's method insofar as it approaches a seemingly causal hierarchy (where being precedes language), and then argues for its undecidability: we only know being *through* language, and only know language as that which signifies a being or reality it can never fully grasp. For Derrida, these oppositions and hierarchies are necessary and impossible. The classic example is that of speech and writing. We imagine that speech is the direct and immediate expression of our own experience, and that we then use systems of writing to record and transfer those expressions in our absence (and such written texts can then be repeated out of context or misinterpreted). But Derrida argues first that all the features that seem secondary and parasitic about writing – that it operates without the presence of the speaker, and that it relies on an already marked out structure of differences – are exactly what make speech and experience possible. The seeming effect – a differentiated system for repetition and recording – is what makes the original condition of experience possible. The origin is already marked by everything we took to be secondary. For this reason, whatever seems to lie outside and before difference is an effect of difference (Derrida 1978). Ethically and politically, for Derrida, this means that certain seemingly foundational ideas, such as justice, freedom, and democracy, cannot be seen as universal truths that we strive to actualize, but are always "to come": we are never given justice as such; nor is our idea of justice an example of something that is fully present but inaccessible, for it is the very nature of experience and language to be dependent on a past it does not master and a future it can only anticipate. This essential non-presence grants all speech and experience a promissory quality. Experience always consists of an anticipated presence that transcends the subject, while language is always repeatable beyond any context or instance and opens to a future that is always "to come."

The key point, at least for Agamben's criticism of deconstruction, is that – for Derrida – we are always within difference, and any notion of an origin that precedes difference is always given by way of some instance of difference. For Derrida, there is no transcendental ground, and we are essentially and necessarily alienated; there is no proximity to the origin, precisely because what we think of *as original* is effected by way of an initial difference. For Derrida, then, there are quasi-transcendentals that allow us to imagine, provisionally, some force that generates and disrupts any differential field. We could think of "writing" not just as actual written text, but as a way of thinking a differential force that generates speech, writing, and the difference between them. If we wanted to sum up deconstruction in an overly simplistic manner, we might say that "in the beginning there is difference," and that any beginning is always imagined or thought from within difference.[13] Derrida argues, then, for a *grammatology* precisely because he sees voice and proximity as having been privileged over the necessary differential force of writing. By contrast, Agamben includes Derrida within a history that has privileged differential force and system over voice; what needs to be thought is the proximity of voice that has the potentiality to take up a relation to itself but does not have any necessary relation or end or actualization toward which it is destined.

For Agamben, the differences of a language presuppose a distinction between language and its outside, and it is for this reason that he questions deconstruction's hesitancy to theorize the genesis of difference: "Language is the sovereign who, in a permanent state of exception, declares that there is nothing outside language and that language is always beyond itself" (HS: 21). Accordingly, rather than think of something like difference as primordial, and as a system that operates as a limit beyond which we cannot think, the greater political and historical task would be to think the passage from indifference to difference, or from a non-relation to relation. In concrete terms, this would be the passage from something like a silent, mute life that has no sense or formation of itself (yet) but bears the potentiality for form – mere life – and then the ways in which we imagine that life as radically different from formed life (as bare life): from indifferent or non-relational life that has the potentiality for relations, we take up a relation that establishes an opposition between *bios* and *zoe*.

The failure to think through these distinctions, which we have inherited but no longer examine, often appears the most pressing problem of the present for Agamben. Although Agamben stresses the extent to which the present has changed radically since the time of these early Christian and Greek articulations, and that it suffers from a loss of the sense of these distinctions, he does not want to retrieve the opposition, but instead poses the task of examining how the linguistic dimensions emerge from a zone of indistinction that has never been fully thought through. Today's loss of a once-meaningful opposition, and an increasing crisis in our conception of (and relation to) life, pose two opportunities for Agamben. First, what is life such that it is possible for it to be conceived both as a formed, meaningful, and relational life – lived according to an ongoing time of decided and individuating projects – and as a non-relational, mute, impersonal, or "animal" life? Second, this problem of life has been articulated, in the Western tradition at least, as a theological and ontological problem. How can we understand either God or being – something that *is*, and is complete and fulfilled – and then explain the actions it goes through? For Agamben, the West has been marked by a "fracture" between being and praxis (which is not the same as, but is related to, formed complete life and mere life): "Ethics in a modern sense, with its court of insoluble aporias, is born, in this sense, from the fracture between being and praxis that is produced at the end of the ancient world and has its eminent place in Christian theology" (KG: 54). If something is alive then it must go through both change and a relation to an outside world, and yet the ideal of divinity is one of complete and closed perfection – of being rather than becoming. In the case of God, the very conception of a perfect, divine, complete, and absolute being would seem to rule out the idea of any need for action or becoming, so how do we explain God's relation to the world if we do not want to regard our world as godless? How do we see life as anything other than lack or evil if we define the good as that which is complete and self-sufficient? Would it be possible to think of life as potential, without thinking of potentiality as a privation or (worse) an evil in relation to full and complete being? For Agamben, this problem of life then cashes out into a problem of transcendence and immanence, or two notions of the good (both of which can be read in early Christian and Aristotelian thought): a good that would be transcendent and placed as a sacred end beyond this life, *or* an immanent blessedness that accepts this life as it is. For all the simplicity of this immanence, however, thinking its possibility today must confront two difficulties: a modern politics that relies on the bareness of life as something to be managed, and a history of theology and philosophy that is dominated by a series of oppositions that preclude a thought of life beyond logics of the sacred.

Agamben therefore not only makes a claim for the relevance of ancient thought but insists that the *only* way to deal with the present is to confront problems that have their origin in the history of Western philosophy, jurisprudence, and – most importantly and increasingly – theology. Agamben frequently argues that we will not be able to alter the course of what he diagnoses as an alarming historical trajectory of increasing political subjection (and the loss of genuinely political questions) unless we reconfigure our modes of thinking and experiencing, including the conception of what counts as politics and redemption. Agamben is committed to a notion of the West as a single history (with shifts and contradictions) that is grounded on ontological problems. The dominant ontological problem of the relation between being and acting – or what is and what we ought to do – does not simply characterize philosophy and theology, but bears directly on twenty-first-century politics. In his more recent work, Agamben therefore explores a theological lexicon that is ultimately ungrounding: that is, there is in Christianity *both* a complete and fully actualized God, *and* Christ who provides a way of thinking about God's administration or action in the world. For Agamben, this problem of *oikonomia* explains – to this very day – the problem of how action in this world relates to the good, and it also allows for a hidden potentiality of anarchy. Christ must be thought of as *anarchia*, or not simply reducible to God's being:

> The fracture between being and praxis, and the anarchic character of the divine oikonomia constitute the logical place in which the fundamental nexus that, in our culture, unites government and anarchy becomes comprehensible. Not only is something like a providential government of the world possible just because praxis does not have any foundation in being, but also the government – which, as we shall see, has its paradigm in the Son and his oikonomia – is itself intimately anarchic. Anarchy is what government must presuppose and assume as the origin from which it derives and, at the same time, as the destination toward which it is traveling. (KG: 64)

For Agamben, the present moment requires a confrontation with the *ontological* genealogy of our basic concepts and premises, the most significant of which is the fracture between being and praxis, or what is and what becomes, and this is most evident in the precedence of the concept of "will." The ways in which we have privileged will in art, politics, and understandings of life depend upon an ontology and theology of being, or the idea that something *is* only if it fully realizes or actualizes itself:

> If being is something that must be realized, if it necessarily implies a putting-to-work, it will be necessary to presuppose a will that renders it possible. This demand is already embryonically present in Aristotle, in whom the concept of will appears for the first time in an ontological context precisely to explain the passage from potential to act.... The ontology of command and the ontology of operativity are therefore closely bound: as a putting-to-work, the command also presupposes a will.... Will is the form that being takes in the ontology of command and operativity. If being does not exist, but must actualize itself, then in its very essence is will and command; and vice versa, if being is will, then it does not simply exist but has to be. The problem of the coming philosophy is that of thinking an ontology beyond operativity and command and an ethics and a politics entirely liberated from the concepts of duty and will. (OD: 128–9)

This concept at once points back to what Agamben deems to be *the* two theories of being that characterize the West – the ontology of being, versus the ontology of "having to be" – at the same time as it explains some of our most horrific contemporary problems. There was, Agamben argues, a transition from a "classical" ontology that acknowledged some sense of being that was distinct (however problematically) from acting – a distinction between being and praxis – toward a modern ontology of operativity or effectuation, where being is nothing other than its fulfillment or unfolding. Christian thought had always maintained a relation of mystery toward the distance between God and his action or ministry, but this difficult distinction is increasingly covered over and being becomes nothing more than operation or effect:

> One can say then that what is at stake in both the conception of the Trinity as an economy and that of the liturgy as a mystery is the constitution of an ontology of the *effectus*, in which potency and act, being and acting are distinct and, at the same time, articulated through a threshold of indiscernibility. To what extent this effective ontology, which has progressively taken the place of classical ontology, is the root of our conception of being – to what extent, that is to say, we do not have at our disposal any experience of being other than operativity – this is the hypothesis that all genealogical research on modernity will have to confront. (OD: 55)

One of the claims of Nazi Germany's SS officers was that their commitment of war crimes followed from simply doing their duty; it is as though *who they were*, or their being (an officer), was identical to a will that accepted the duties by which it was defined. It is as though being and acting require the acceptance of an external or transcendent form and law. At a more everyday level we might think that the horror of the twenty-first century lies in the notion that who we are is defined by what we do, and that a good life is one in which one dutifully obeys the implicit imperatives of one's job: "I was only doing my job..." We also tend not to value life that is not operational (abandoning "the" unemployed, persons without papers, or those who do not possess a distinct identity), and yet this bare life is increasingly exposed and pervasive. All humans now potentially experience themselves precisely as bare life, as nothing more than substance that has no form unless it is recognized as worker, citizen, or some other proper human mode of being. How is it that we have come to think of ourselves as defined by what we do, with our will in turn being commanded to follow who we are? We become nothing more than *operations* or functions of the office we hold. To think of totalitarianism and the genocides of the past 100 years as having nothing to do with the Western tradition of theology and politics is, for Agamben, a laziness that could cost us our future. To think of the same atrocities as opposed to modern democracy and consumerism is similarly erroneous: democratic hedonism, and the notion of each individual in the polity becoming what he ought to be by maximizing his potential, has the same unthinking commitment to will as the totalitarian structure that defines individuals as nothing more than beings who exist to fulfill the duty of "the law." The law, increasingly, becomes less and less about *what* is deemed to be lawful and instead becomes something like pure law, acting only to maintain itself without any end outside itself. Submission as such – or simply *that there be law* – becomes an end unto itself:

> what is at stake is to understand that if the aberrant idea of an action carried out only for the sake of duty (that is, in obedience to a command, and not for the sake of natural inclination) was able to penetrate into ethics and impose itself there, this is only because the Church, by means of a centuries-long praxis and theorization, had elaborated duty or office as a model of the highest human activity. (OD: 112)

Agamben's questioning of the will as that aspect of the self that defines us by making us necessarily become who we ought to be is not only opposed to a Western philosophical and political tradition committed to a privileging of the full actualization of force; it also provides a stark contrast with many forms of contemporary theory and popular culture. Postmodernism – both in theory and popular culture – frequently celebrates the self as being nothing other than pure performance, or the roles freely adopted and taken to be definitive of who one is; one might say that both identity politics (where one speaks "as a" decided upon persona), modern advertising that exploits each of us becoming who we want to be by fully exercising consumer freedom, and the increasing power of a law that has no definitive being, and no relation to definitive being, other than exercising itself, are all aspects of what Agamben defines as an operative ontology. What something *is* is what it ought to become; the passage to actuality or achievement of an end that is nothing but that full actualization is all that matters (doing one's duty, obeying the law, being a self-willing subject). For Agamben, the question for the present is not simply one of retrieving some completely other space or utopia outside this problematic relation between being and acting, but rather of embracing the problem as a problem. Could we imagine a new polity or community, *not* as a collection of wills that produces a social whole in one actualizing force of pure self-creation, but a polity that could be poised *between* being and coming into being? What if we were *neither* impelled to maximize our full potential (become the willing, self-creating beings we ought to be) *nor* simply managed or determined as beings who were already fully realized (as in the worst cases of genetic or biological determinism)? Agamben tries to find a way between liberalism (where we are nothing but pure will, and where the only valuable life is one of work and efficiency) and the crisis of liberalism (where we are nothing but mere life subject to the force of law that manages us as so much living substance, and where we become nothing more than passive spectators).

The overall grand claim we need to confront in Agamben's work is the necessity of *thinking*, and then the restoration of thinking to a life that is no longer set outside the will or the mind as mere means. What appear to be the most brutal events of the twentieth and twenty-first centuries – ranging from the Nazi death camps to Guantanamo Bay – cannot be truly understood without an analysis of the ways in which our political values have been generated from a past that we have yet to comprehend. The rethinking of the present requires a confrontation with a theological past, but this is not because of some texts that happen to have a dominant influence. Agamben is not claiming that we maintain ideas, ideologies, or beliefs from a past that we simply need to reread critically; he is not making a claim for an analysis of Plato, the Bible, or the supposedly founding texts of liberal political theory. On the contrary, often the sources Agamben draws upon are seemingly minor, but they express an ongoing problem or aporia that is continually articulated because of a deeper political problem of the human being as an animal *who speaks*. Speaking is at once our essential condition, and yet this "essence" both distances us from ourselves and places us in relation to our own animality, which can never be rendered meaningful or fully articulated:

> uniquely among living things, man is not limited to acquiring language as one capacity among others that he is given but has made of it his specific potentiality; *he has, that is to say, put his very nature at stake in*

language. Just as, in the words of Foucault, man "is an animal whose politics places his living being in question," ... so also is he *the living being whose language places his life in question.* (SL: 68–9)

Agamben is not the first thinker to say that the essence of human being is that "we" have no essence, but he is unique in regarding language's capacity to create a split in the self – more specifically, a split between the self who speaks and the self who is spoken about – as an ongoing problem with the very animal life of ours that makes speaking possible.[14]

So his claim is quite different from that of Marxism (which would argue that we are primarily determined by conditions of labor, along with the ideologies that maintain the relations of divided labor); indeed, Agamben has been criticized by the Italian Marxist Antonio Negri for not seeing active life as a positive productive power that has been diminished by capitalist systems of exchange. Whereas Agamben seeks to theorize life as enigmatically silent and possessing a capacity for inactivation or impotentiality (which would be a positive refusal of the working mechanisms of power), Negri regards Agamben's "life" as a passive acquiescence as long as it cannot be activated and rendered revolutionary:

And where does he want to lead us then? In a world in which singularity is in any case definable neither as work (and not even as a refusal of work), nor as resistance (and not even as struggle)? *Without being theologians we can realize that the effort to comprehend production (creation) in the theological circle need not result in impotence and sterility, but rather in resistance and activity.* (Negri 2008: 98)

Agamben's claim for life as a form of *im*potentiality that resists being brought into full actuality and representation is, as already mentioned, insistently different from the deconstruction of Derrida who defined metaphysics as the valorization of presence. For Derrida, what lies outside writing and systems of difference is not some form of silent presence, and certainly not some singular power of speech (which for Derrida is as differentially structured as writing). For Agamben, what speech offers is not some self-present silent subject who precedes systems, but rather a potentiality *to speak, to enter into language.* When speech does occur it emerges from an always possible silence or impotentiality. Further, the voice that is articulated by way of language is always the voice *of* this singular subject, never fully captured by the general system of signs. Any act of speech is therefore split between the event of this singular saying, and then the generality of what is said; anything referred to in language is always split between this specific and singular gesture of speech (or the act) and then the present world that it signifies. For Agamben, the reason why politics and theology have constantly circled around, while never resolving, the problem of the relation between the act of speech (saying) and what *is* (being) cannot be dealt with by abandoning what lies outside language, law, or meaning; he disagrees with the broadly post-structuralist tendency to accept that we cannot think outside systems of differences.

Agamben *does* focus his analysis on texts, but this is because what texts express is a deeper problem that might be defined broadly as the problem of the human being as a speaking animal. Humans are animals, but their capacity to speak (and *not* speak) divides them from other animals. At the same time, this act of speaking or existing in language places humans in relation to their animality, which is at once deeply intimate while also resisting any full self-understanding. Our bodily, animal being is precisely that which never comes into full artic-ulation and yet it constantly reappears when speech breaks down, or when the fragile being of "bare life" appears as abandoned or outside the life of law, language, and articulation. So, rather than see *life* as simply positive and productive *or* as some silent biological raw mate-rial that needs political form, *or* as some illusory outside generated by law and language, Agamben argues that life is given in *non-relation as the potentiality for relation*. Or rather, from a given system of relations – such as the legal system, the world of actual beings, language, rela-tions among persons, or the relation between humans and animals – there can (and should) be an experience of life other than that which is simply assumed as external or negative. The potentiality *for relations* is not grasped by moving back to some silent origin, but in the experi-ence of impotentiality.

In any system of relations there will always be a potentiality for relations that can never be fully experienced or articulated as such, but only given after relations have occurred as a remainder – as the pos-sibility of (also and always) *not* relating. Agamben cites the example of the Canadian pianist Glenn Gould, who cannot *not* play:

> Only a power that is capable of both power and impotence, then, is the supreme power. If every power is equally the power to be and the power to not-be, the passage to action can only come about by transporting (Aristotle says "saving") in the act its own power to not-be. This means that, even though every pianist necessarily has the potential to play and the potential to not-play, Glenn Gould is, however, the only one who can *not* not-play, and, directing his potentiality not only to the act but to his own impotence, he plays, so to speak, with his potential to not-play. While his ability simply negates and abandons his potential to not-play, his mastery conserves and exercises in the act not his potential to play (this is the position of irony that affirms the superiority of the positive potentiality over the act), but rather his potential to not-play. (CC: 36)

What does this mean? Agamben's remark about "irony" here displays his distance from modern conceptions of the self: selves are ironic if they remain distant from what they do and say, if they are *nothing* other than their act (no self lying behind words and deeds as some sincere intention). A postmodern subject speaks and performs an identity, all the while aware that they might have been otherwise, but *is* nothing other than the act. By contrast, Agamben rejects this privilege of the self as pure act, who might always have been otherwise; selves are not pure will or force, but are exposed in a *not doing*. I would be a truly great pianist, not simply if I held on to the idea that I might also have been a banker, writer, or athlete; to master the piano is to have arrived at a point where I can no longer be absolutely anything at all, and my relation to playing has now become something I no longer have the power to dissolve, and so I am intimately involved with the potentiality of not-playing all the while that I am playing. Most humans have the potential, technically, to play the piano; if there is some human who is playing the piano, then clearly they also have the potentiality both to play and to not-play. If they simply have to play, then playing would be automatic or something necessary, like breathing. By analogy, think of God as a being who *had* to create; if this were so, He would not be divine or supremely powerful. To be divine would be to create, but to do so in a way that was freely expressive of a power not to create; at each moment of creativity God would be in relation to not creating, and this would be fully creative. But Agamben defines the pianist by a different notion of supreme power, where one's potential *not to do* has been "extinguished." What makes the difference, for Agamben, is impotentiality or a relation to *not playing*. Gould is a pianist because when he plays he truly realizes the potential of playing precisely because he does not just happen to be playing, but is also positively extinguishing the potential not to play. He is, in this sense, the opposite of the modern conception of the individual who is nothing more than an activity that *is* their duty: the pianist who plays the piano with the most supreme power is always performing, but with an intimate relation to a power *not* to do that which also has come to define him.

In the situation of speech, to say that humans have the potentiality to speak means that their emergence as speaking beings contains a relation to not speaking (we are not silent, *not mere life…* and yet it is this mere life that remains virtually present as impotentiality when we speak, for something always remains that is not exhausted in an event of language). For Agamben, a new conception of relation needs to be forged, and this can only be achieved by confronting the threshold between humanity and animality, or the relation between our potentiality as speaking beings and the actuality of speech in the tradition of texts that have always hinted at but never resolved the strange "zone of indistinction" from which relations emerge. Agamben makes a series of suggestions throughout his corpus about how to approach this threshold: sometimes it is through art, sometimes through rereading legal, political, or philosophical texts, sometimes through poetry, and sometimes through simple experiences such as love:

> For precisely this is proper to mankind: writing a poem that escapes the communicative function of language; or speaking or giving a kiss, thus changing the function of the mouth, which first and foremost serves for eating. In his *Nicomachean Ethics*, Aristotle asked himself whether mankind has a task. The work of the flute player is to play the flute, and the cobbler's job is to make shoes, but is there a work of man as such? He then advanced his hypothesis according to which man is perhaps born without any task; but he soon abandoned it. However, this hypothesis takes us to the heart of what it is to be human. The human is the animal that has no job: it has no given biological task, no clearly prescribed function. Only a powerful being has the capacity not to be powerful. Man can do everything but does not have to do anything. (TC)

Agamben suggests that the main way in which this problem has been articulated (but never fully confronted) has been in theology, and then a subsequent tradition of jurisprudence that never fully detached itself from theology. (And even theology is articulated around a mystery or problematic that it never fully resolved.) This is why Agamben confronts highly contemporary problems, such as detention camps and refugees, by using ancient legal terms (such as the Roman *homo sacer*), which in turn require a conception of the sacred.[15] It is the notion of the sacred, or a holiness that would grant mere life its proper sense, that precludes us from thinking about life and law *immanently* or from this world as it is (without external redemption or justification).

Although Agamben deals with a range of concrete topics, one very abstract concept dominates (and is related to the overarching problem of being and acting): potentiality. This concept is primarily theological in its early articulation, precisely because it concerns the relation between what something is, in its state of perfect completion (being), and then what it may or may not do (its potentiality, or action). For Agamben, Western thought has always begun with some notion of a perfect and complete being (such as the infinite and absolute existence of God) and then had trouble explaining or conceiving how God relates to creation and becoming:

> According to the complex mechanism that...marks the relations between economy from the beginning – and, then, the functioning of the governmental machine – the two trinities, though intimately articulated, remain distinct. What is in question is rather the reciprocity of their relations.... Glory is the place where theology attempts to think the difficult conciliation between immanent trinity and economic trinity, *theologia* and *economia*, being and praxis, God in himself and God for us. (KG: 208)

If we begin with perfect and complete being, or define goodness in terms of absolute self-sufficiency and completion, then our way of thinking about *life* (or that which has to grow, become, and reach beyond itself) becomes highly difficult. There is also a tension between perfection and completeness; if something is perfect then it should not require anything else in order to be, but if something is complete it should include all possibilities and leave nothing outside itself. How, then, might we explain the existence of a perfect and complete God without setting certain possibilities (such as creation or the time and becoming of the world) outside his infinite divinity? This has direct implications for politics, for we tend to desire a polity that is regulated or legitimated by some stable and fully realized "good," but then this leaves the becoming of political life outside the founding presence of law and the good. We are, according to Agamben, left with a gap or aporia that cannot be resolved within the terms of the present. Political life would either be subject to some transcendent notion of "the" good, as in theological conceptions where this life is nothing more than a striving toward a complete goodness that lies beyond this world; *or,* politics just is pure becoming and self-realization, and so we are reduced to a world of pure force or will. Democracies imagine the law as being nothing more than the will of the people, but for Agamben this is perilously close to totalitarianism where there is nothing other than the force of law: and so, for Agamben, there needs to be a way of thinking beyond *either* a stable transcendent good *or* a world of nothing other than pure self-realizing force.

One of the questions that will concern Agamben is whether there might be a *profane* polity: one in which forces are neither redeemed by reference to some divine external good, nor seen as intrinsically good because they are capable of acting and fulfilling or realizing their own full potential (as in the contemporary attachments to free will, free speech, free trade, or free creation – as though there should be no question of impeding a force from realizing itself). Despite first appearances such contemporary commitments to the pure will or freedom of force remain within a logic of the sacred that Agamben seeks to overcome. The task will be to think in a way that appeals to neither side of the opposition of the sacred: the opposition between purity and impurity, or proper and improper. Further, Agamben seeks to theorize the sacred without referring to sacrifice: rather than see an offering to divinity as the original political institution (which would then derive law from some prior institution of religion or magic), Agamben places the exclusion of the unsacrificeable as the precondition for the political, and then for events such as sacrifice:

> sacredness is ... the originary form of the inclusion of bare life in the
> juridical order, and the syntagm *homo sacer* names something like the

originary "political" relation, which is to say, bare life insofar as it operates in an inclusive exclusion as the referent of the sovereign decision.
Life is sacred only insofar as it is taken into the sovereign exception, and
to have exchanged a juridico-political phenomenon (*homo sacer*'s capacity
to be killed but not sacrificed) for a genuinely religious phenomenon is
the root of the equivocations that have marked studies both of the sacred
and of sovereignty in our time. (HS: 85)

The sacred functions in Agamben's work, along with potentiality, as
a way of thinking about what he frequently refers to as the threshold;
if we exist in a world of political relations and oppositions, then we
need to think their emergence in order to find a new mode of relation
that would not assume already distinct terms (or the world as it actually is); instead we might think of this world *as it might be* (potentiality),
but without that potentiality being set in relation to something beyond
itself. This would be a world not of constituted relations but one, possibly, of non-relation or immanence. This would be a life that might
find happiness and blessedness in itself without awaiting redemption
from a world beyond. The sense of the fallenness of this life cannot be
overcome by considering everything in this world to be sacred, but by
abandoning the notion of a sacred that would be set beyond this immanent life.

Agamben comments critically on a long tradition that has noted the
"ambivalence of the sacred." Even before contemporary notions of the
sacredness of life became a means for managing and controlling life –
or controlling life by saving life – the sacred was never simply divine
but signaled a curious exterior. Law is a threshold or force that constitutes itself by setting itself outside mere life; and this is why the law
creates a domain over which it operates, while being necessarily exempt
from the legality and limits it prescribes. Because Agamben is focused
upon rethinking the relation between potentiality and actuality (or
breaking that relation by imagining a potentiality without any law or
actuality toward which it tends), he sees the problem of the sacred as
operating at the broadest of levels, well beyond religious and legal
thought. Indeed, the sacred is not something that can simply be
explained by turning back to religion, but is itself – as the creation of
a border between inside and outside, proper and improper – something
that requires explanation, and draws us back yet again to the thought
of a potentiality *for relation*. Here, again, rather than assume that potentiality is one side of a relation – and exists only in relation to actuality
– it is more productive, and urgent, to think of potentiality as that from
which relations may (and may not) emerge. This is why Agamben's
seemingly wide-ranging concerns – poetry, law, theology, animality,
politics – are not so much expressions of some underlying unified
vision as they are interrelated ways of thinking a curious problem of

non-relation, indistinction or thresholds. Agamben is not a thinker with a philosophical system or theory of being that might then be applied or related to other domains. Instead, he tends to focus on strange points of incoherence and, rather than draw particulars back to some prior unifying ground, he regards the possibility or potentiality for confusion, incoherence, enigma, or aporia as disclosing something radically unsayable (while not referring this silence to some mystical absolute or ground). If there is something that can *not* be said or grasped this is not because we are precluded from an absolute *nor* because there is only the world as we know it. Rather, the world as it is spoken about, or the world to which we relate as speaking beings, does not exhaust something that occurs in the very event or possibility of speaking:

> Language, which for human beings mediates all things and all knowledge, is itself immediate. Nothing immediate can be reached by speaking being – nothing, that is, except itself, mediation itself. For human beings, such an *immediate mediation* constitutes the sole possibility of reaching a principle freed of every presupposition, including self-presupposition. (LD: 47)

The following chapters and sections will weave back and forth between various motifs in Agamben's work. Although the many book-length works he has composed are ostensibly devoted to distinct themes – ranging from early work on poetry and language, to a multi-volume *homo sacer* project on the limits of law, a study on testimony and the death camps of Auschwitz, a brief but important book on animality, and a recent phase devoted ostensibly to theological topics of duty, sacrament, and the forms of life in monasteries – every book makes a continuing contribution to a long-term project focused on the threshold. Every topic or concern that we might delimit or focus upon can be understood not so much by appealing to a prior unified ground but to an "original" *indifference*. This is not to say that prior to the distinctions that we mark out in concepts and language there is some unified and undifferentiated absolute. Indifference, if anything, is *more different* than our world of differentiated terms: so that we might say that in addition to the oppositions through which we think, there are finer differences not captured by relations between terms. These finer differences (or "indifferent" differences) might be thought of not as differences between terms, but as potentials *to differ* from which relations emerge. *Indifference* is a term employed by Agamben to signal that the distinctions of our thought and language – with their seeming clarity – conceal something more profound. That profundity might be thought of as *life*, but not a life of some coherent self-present body that knows itself and is in command of itself; nor is this life a life of biology that might be known as some masterable substance or object. It is a life that Agamben regards as having been abandoned but that might be the milieu for a new "blessedness" or happiness that would not require the redemptive notions of a higher life or duty:

> This is why ethics has no room for repentance; this is why the only ethical experience (which, as such, cannot be a task or a subjective decision) is the experience of being (one's own) potentiality, of being (one's own) possibility – exposing, that is, in every form one's own amorphousness and in every act one's own inactuality...The only evil consists instead in the decision to remain in a deficit of existence, to appropriate the power to not-be as a substance and a foundation beyond existence. (CC: 44)

1

Language

On the one hand, Agamben's philosophy appears to be profoundly textual and linguistic, given his focus on retrieving terms from ancient sources and then exploring their use and etymology (the *homo sacer* motif is a case in point). Further, Agamben seems to substitute language's power to be nothing more than itself – or the power from which relations emerge – for earlier notions of God as the only being who can truly be said to be without presupposing relations: "there is being whose nomination implies its existence, and that being is language" (LD: 41). We can talk about all other beings and those beings may or may not be present, but talking about language (or anything) necessarily places us in language. On the other hand, Agamben is highly critical of what he takes to be the defining approach of poststructuralism: that all we have is a system of linguistic differences or forces, with any sense of an outside or meaning being an effect of relations from which we cannot exit:

> Although we must certainly honor Derrida as the thinker who has identified with the greatest rigor...the original status of the *gramma* and of meaning in our culture, it is also true that he believed he had opened a way to surpassing metaphysics, while in truth he merely brought the fundamental problem of metaphysics to light. For metaphysics is not simply the primacy of voice over *gramma*. If metaphysics is that reflection that places the voice as origin, it is also true that this voice is, from the beginning, conceived as removed, as Voice. To identify the horizon of metaphysics simply in that supremacy of the *phone* and then to believe in one's power to overcome this horizon through the *gramma*, is to conceive of metaphysics without its coexistent negativity. Metaphysics is always already grammatology and this is *fundamentology* in the sense that the *gramma* (or the Voice) functions as the negative ontological foundation. (LD: 39).

Agamben is therefore poised between two twentieth-century trends: the focus on language as the medium by which humans give themselves a world (a world of meaning and projects), and an almost opposing focus on life, or what resists inclusion in the systems that order, name, and denote our world. From the beginnings of twentieth-century philosophy and what has come to be known as the "linguistic turn," through movements like structuralism and (for Agamben) deconstruction, it has become a commonplace to assume that one could only think of what is other than language from within language, and that any notion of "life" would always be "life" as constructed or posited by language. The outside of language could only be grasped from within language, as *language's* outside. The clearest and most influential example of this conception is the work of Judith Butler, who argued that the idea of us having a biological "sex" that was then constructed by "gender" was itself an effect of the gender system. Rather than think of biological sex as that which is then coded by socio-cultural norms of gender, Butler argued that it is only from the system of gender that one supposes *that there must have been some prior pre-linguistic* sex. The body and life are what must be presupposed by linguistic and social systems, but can never be grasped as such (Butler 1990). Butler's work is a sophisticated version of a broader tendency toward linguistic or textual conceptions of the social construction of reality, and it is a trend that is now receiving much criticism (including from Butler herself).

The twentieth century's linguistic turn is now being responded to by various forms of realism, with an increasing attention paid to bodies, life, affect, and the inhuman. Agamben's turn back to life differs from contemporary vitalisms and materialisms in that it still grants language supreme importance for its capacity to articulate and render us as human subjects; indeed, his focus remains very human, even if he thinks that humanity can only be understood by thinking through its highly problematic relation to its own animality. Typically, as with so much of his work, Agamben is neither on the side of those who would declare human exceptionalism over, nor on the side of those who want to retain an essential humanity; instead, the more profound question is how – by way of language – humans render themselves exceptional. Something like a "state of exception" applies whereby the human is a speaking animal, but one whose animality is such that "man" sets himself outside the animal life that is his very being. For Agamben, what is required is not simply a forgetting of our humanity or of our potential to speak; rather, we need to begin from "man" as a speaking animal, and then explore the threshold between speaking and not speaking. We need to move beyond the notion of language as a system that constructs and negates its outside. Such a conception fails to attend to the *saying* of language; rather than accept the negativity of language and its silent other or outside, one might think about language when it says nothing other than itself – when rather than referring to what is not itself we might experience language as language, prior to its relational or communicational force. (Similarly, focusing on the existence of legal systems, or simply accepting their arbitrary or culturally constructed nature, fails to account for the coming into being of the law, and therefore the capacity for any legal system to be able to suspend itself.) For Agamben, we too readily accept language *as language* (or as a system). If we attended to moments when speaking occurs in the absence of language – when a traumatized individual is reduced to murmuring, or when poetry simply presents itself as having a power to name but without really denoting anything – then we are exposed to language as potentiality rather than system; but this is potentiality as impotentiality, as though in speaking we were remaining intimate with *not speaking*. Language is neither a system of force or difference beyond which we cannot think, nor a fixed set of terms naming our world in a straightforward fashion. Agamben suggests that it might be more interesting and closer to the life and being of language to think of speaking in terms of the event or saying of names that nevertheless miss capturing what they name; it is as though language were always a nickname, something provisional and unreliable rather than systematic:

> It is as if every word were preceded by an invisible "so-called," "pseudo-," and "would-be" … This referent is no longer nature betrayed by meaning, nor its transfiguration in the name, but it is what is held – unuttered – in the pseudonym or in the ease between the name and the nickname. (CC: 59–60)

Throughout his work, Agamben marks his distance from what he takes to be deconstruction's failure to think outside the constituted system of signs: language (like law) is too easily accepted as simply distinct from life, or arbitrarily imposed. For Agamben, such an acceptance of linguistic indeterminacy or language as structure is not only a theory of language; it also generates a conception of the subject. "I" am nothing other than a speaking subject. Potentiality is lost; we have nothing more than actual subjects, and to be a subject is to be nothing more than one's speech and actions. The modern self becomes a being in his performance of language, or his will to speak. His mere bodily being is taken to be a silent and presupposed substrate; and the threshold (or the coming into being of the human self as a speaking being) is left out of account. At its extreme (as we see increasingly in the self-help industry), the body's "life" is nothing more than that which is to be manipulated by an individual who, in turn, is nothing more than his will: we are our becoming, and we can – and should – be anything that we want to be. The flipside, then, is that when we encounter life outside this event of will all that remains would be abandoned as inhuman bare life. Such considerations of life as valuable only insofar as it arrives at sentience and will have allowed some philosophers to argue that infanticide for the profoundly disabled would be quite legitimate, while we would save and value forms of animal life that displayed complex sentience; not to do so would be a form of "species-ism":

> the fact that a being is a human being, in the sense of a member of the species Homo sapiens, is not relevant to the wrongness of killing it; it is, rather, characteristics like rationality, autonomy, and self-consciousness that make a difference. Infants lack these characteristics. Killing them, therefore, cannot be equated with killing normal human beings, or any other self-conscious beings. (Singer 1993: 182)

Although Agamben himself does not consider the implications of this ontology that divides humans as speaking systems from their animal life, one of the main areas in which his thought might be fruitful would be in the area of disability studies; if we can only define humans in terms of rationality and will, then we have no sense of the profundity and richness of other modes of human life that do not bring themselves into being through language. What occurs is a loss of potentiality in any profound sense. By focusing on humans as linguistic beings who are nothing more than their performance of a system of signs, we forgo a richer conception of human *life* in its capacity and incapacity to speak: language, for Agamben, sets the human outside itself, for there is at once the self of speech and relations, and then that which can never be captured by those relations other than in the singular event of each act of speech. We can name things outside the realm of language, and we can even refer to language by quoting or mentioning terms, but what we cannot objectify or render into a linguistic term is the passage or relation of naming that produces linguistic distance: "What remains without name here is the being-named, the name itself (*nomen innominabile*); only being-in-language is subtracted from the authority of language" (CC: 76–7). Language is tied closely to potentiality precisely by way of non-relationality: we live in a world of actual objects and relations, but the potentiality that brings those relations into being (like the naming that opens the being-named) itself has no name and is not something toward which we bear a relation without losing the "original" proto-relational potentiality.

As living, speaking beings we are never fully within relations and actual terms but always occupy a threshold where speaking and naming come into being. A living being does not (like some sort of machine) simply do what it is designed to do, but comes into being by way of fulfilling a potentiality that is always coupled with impotentiality. To say that something has potentiality is to say that it does not unfold like a programmed mechanism, and does not simply become what it already is (as though there were already a full and actualized blueprint). To have potentiality is to be capable of *not* becoming what one has the capacity to be. While this is true of all living beings – that going through life and time always places actuality and actualization at a distance that allows for a degree of freedom – Agamben regards language as definitively distinct insofar as it distances humans from their life, even if language's physicality and voice is also bound up with life. In turn, then, language should not be thought of as something that simply *is*, nor as something that constitutes subjects by way of the actual performance of speaking (with their life being a negated or abandoned outside). Life – the life that has the potentiality to be silent – is what makes language both possible and impossible, precisely because the coming into language of life can never itself be grasped by language.

Here, we can tie two key motifs that will be reiterated across Agamben's corpus: potentiality and singularity (both of which open from a consideration of law, language, and being). To think about potentiality as being *truly potential* (and not destined or determined to meet a set end), there must be the possibility of *not* actualizing itself. This is particularly or essentially so for humans, precisely because language opens them up to a world, history, and system that destroy any simple immediacy of life. For this reason, Agamben's work refuses to remain within language and linguistic performance, while also avoiding some naïve return to life, as though life were a simple substance, self-present or existing in itself, which might be expressed or represented seamlessly in language. Life is not some absolutely passive substrate that requires some imposed system (such as language) to grant it distinction, but life is also not determined to realize a specific form. Agamben would refuse both an evolutionary approach, whereby language is nothing more than an extension of natural survival mechanisms, *and* a post-structuralist approach, where we are always already within systems of relations and therefore incapable of thinking beyond relations and differences. Agamben is neither a linguistic determinist nor a biological determinist. He writes in the tradition of Aristotle, whereby it is our nature not to be determined by nature; but he adds to this tradition by stressing that the taking on of a second nature is fragile and always capable of *not being*. Further, rather than see the potential life as being good only insofar as it orients itself toward some proper end (such as the good, reason, or identity) Agamben stresses a new ethics and new relation to law and language whereby we might accept life as such, without valuing it only insofar as it strives toward realizing itself.

Life, then, is neither some absolutely silent "outside" that we only know through language, nor something that inevitably realizes or arrives at its proper moment when man becomes a speaking animal. Humans, as speaking animals, are not only realizations of a potential *to speak* (a potential that we witness as a refusal of silence, of not *not speaking*); speaking also discloses something singular about potentiality. Every speaking being at once enters the law or system of language, so that there is a move from language as a potential system to its actualization in speaking beings; but each speaker is always this singular speaker with *this* voice, and it is this singularity or remainder that perhaps reveals a different sense of potentiality. If we think of potentiality as nothing more than that which precedes actualization, and as properly coming into its own when fully actualized, then language is the realization of our being. But Agamben wants to say that potentiality is better thought of as *impotentiality*, so that speaking is not what must happen in order to reveal that I am a speaking being; I speak insofar as I do not remain silent. So the first thing we can say about potentiality in general is that it is not just the unfolding of what must be, but always – even when actualized – maintains a relation to not coming into being. But there is a further dimension to speech and potentiality that also has a deeper relation to the human, and to the problem of relations. It is by way of speech that we take up a relation to our singular being; it is through speaking that we are both brought into relation with each other, while at the same time it is speech – rather than the generality of language – that discloses each human body as singular. The singular voice with its pitch, timbre, cadence, accent, and rhythm is the threshold that enables the passage from a singular body as potential speaker to a speaking subject, but voice is not exhausted in the general structure or meaning of what is said. What we experience when we experience language, then, is not a common system but an experience of the passage from singularity to generality, and experience of the threshold. It is not the case that outside language there is real being (the thing itself), nor is language some type of thing or system; rather, language is something like an event that – when experienced profoundly – destroys generality and commonality, allowing "us" to experience singularity:

> Nothing immediate can be reached by speaking beings – nothing, that is, except language itself, mediation itself....There can be no true human community on the basis of a presupposition – be it a nation, a language, or even the a priori of communication of which hermeneutics speaks. What unites human beings among themselves is not a nature, a voice, or a common imprisonment in signifying language; it is the vision of language itself and, therefore, the experience of language's limits, its *end*. A true community can only be a community that is not presupposed. (P: 47)

There is something, Agamben insists, about this strange remainder or potentiality to speak (evidenced in a certain remainder and silence *in speaking*) that is akin to the structure of law, and akin to the structure of sovereignty. We could think of language and law as simply the final ground or presupposition for anything that is, *or* we might think about law and actual language as having emerged or come into being with some potentiality for not coming into being, allowing everything that appears as lawlike to be fragile and exposed. The *Idea of language* is not language as it is so much as the potentiality for language: "Pure philosophical presentation, therefore, cannot merely be the presentation of ideas about language or the world; instead, it must above all be the presentation of the *Idea of language*" (P: 47).

A system brings relations into being, and allows for potentiality to realize itself, but in doing so must pass from indistinction to distinction, and from a threshold of potentiality/impotentiality to actuality. We have tended, Agamben argues, to simply think oppositions and distinctions – law versus chaos, speech versus silence, difference or system versus an unthinkable outside – and we have failed to think about what he refers to as "threshold," "indistinction," and (more concretely) "life" before it has been abandoned and excluded as bare life. It is for this reason that Agamben is concerned both with language and with life, and this places him rather oddly in relation to other twenty-first-century theorists. After an intense focus on language in the twentieth century – such that it was often assumed that language constructs the very possibility for thinking about the world – there was a twenty-first-century reaction against the primacy granted to language, and a subsequent turn back to life (evidenced in various "turns" to affect, life, animality, embodiment, materialism, or realism (Clough and Halley 2007; Dolphijn and van der Tuin 2012)). Agamben *is* interested in life and is critical of simply accepting the system or structure of law or language, but he sees language as the locus for where this problem of life is exposed.

The very language that we require in order to express ourselves, to reach each other, and to make contact with the world is always at a distance from the singularity of living speakers and the world it supposedly names. Rather than confront this distance between the beings that we are and the speaking and writing that brings us into relation, twentieth-century theory has tended to accept and intensify the opposition by thinking of language, law, speech, or difference opposed to a life that is either abandoned or (worse) deemed to be that which is constructed through language. In this respect, for Agamben, twentieth-century thought continued a long tradition of failing to consider the fragile emergence of language. Language was either assumed to be some basic logical condition, or a system of force without reference; little thought was paid to the threshold between language as a system of relations, and the relation between language and the non-relational. What Agamben aims to achieve with the concept of potentiality (and

impotentiality) is to liberate human speech from some ideal of achieving full and accurate presence, while not simply accepting language as
an arbitrary imposed system. It is possible for humans to speak and
have language, but this potentiality is never guaranteed and must
come into being while always being possible *not* to come into being.
We therefore need to think about language's genesis and its relation to
the silent life that it always harbors as an impotentiality. Agamben
therefore reacts against a twentieth century that saw language as arbitrary and as a construction of a reality that we cannot access outside
language; language has a dimension that is not reducible to its systemic
use and this is most clearly experienced in cases of its exposed impotentiality, in moments of silence or failure when we are brought up
against the capacity of humans for not speaking, or of being abandoned
by the very language that is their milieu.

In his book on the Nazi prison camps Agamben refers to the loss of
speech that left many incapable of testifying to what they witnessed;
in such cases of language's failure to capture what *wants to be said*, the
potentiality to speak emerges. It is for this reason that testimony tells
us something about all language; what matters is not some verification
of the facts of the case, nor even so much the sense of *what* is said, but
that there is speaking. More importantly, such forms of speech expose a
difference between bare life – the human who has been reduced to mere
animal existence and deprived of speech, and a "truer and more human
life" that is evident when one lives on, after one's loss of humanity, and
survives to witness that loss:

> in human beings, life bears with it a caesura that can transform all life
> into survival and all survival into life. In a sense…survival designates
> the pure and simple continuation of bare life with respect to truer and
> more human life. In another sense, survival has a positive sense and
> refers … to the person who, in fighting against death, has survived the
> inhuman. (RA: 133)

Agamben's work is therefore curiously divided by appearing at once
to be textual, and focused on our philosophical textual heritage, and
yet at the same time to base the investigation of this tradition on a
problem that the history of thought has not properly confronted (and
that cannot be reduced or contained by language but requires language's coming into being). Agamben's claim is that we have the
textual tradition we do because of the predicament of life. In order to
live, a being must be open to the world, with the relation to the world
being genuinely potential and not determined in advance by some
script or system; at the same time, our world is always *our world*. For
Agamben, these two tendencies – between being open to the world,
and being nothing other than a singular existence in *this world* – are not

distinct but occur in a zone of indistinction or a threshold: one of the many reasons why he focuses on both life and language is that the former requires us to think about singularity, or something that simply is and cannot be "saved" by becoming other than it is, while speaking is also *not* bound by what already exists. There is a tension, then, between a free becoming expressive of life and a passivity of being that cannot be other than it is, that cannot *not be*.

One of the general ways in which we might characterize the far too broad movement of postmodernism is that there is an abandonment of any form of foundation and an acceptance that we are always within competing narratives and can never find any point outside language or culture that might give us some political or ethical lever. This might at first appear to be akin to Agamben's claim that in modernity we no longer see this world and life as justified or redeemable in terms of some prior power. (His theory of sovereignty, which we will examine later, argues that government power was once seen to be the enactment or enforcement of law, but there is increasingly no law other than power's immediate exercise.) Agamben, too, argues for a form of immanence or the absence of any foundation outside life and its potentiality; but this is subtly and significantly different from the postmodern claim that we cannot think beyond language. The idea that we are within language and culture with no access to the outside, or the idea that this world is godless and that *all* we have is a secular existence, is for Agamben a continuation of the ongoing split between sacred and secular, or being and language, with the former term being lost or set beyond our grasp. This is a form of nihilism: we begin with a goodness or reality that is beyond this world and our experience, but when we acknowledge that we cannot know or grasp that transcendent beyond we are left with a sense of loss. Rather than say, then, that "all" we have is this constituted world with no outside, no beyond, and that we are left with "only" the secular, Agamben argues that this world as it is *is God*, and that redemption lies in seeing everything as it is in its irreparable beauty. This has direct (and counter-nihilist) implications: evil is not some corruption that befalls us because our world is less than some higher good. Evil lies in the notion that our world is fallen or improper in relation to some proper being:

> Revelation does not mean revelation of the sacredness of the world, but only revelation of its irreparably profane character....Revelation consigns the world to profanation and thingness – and isn't this precisely what has happened? The possibility of salvation begins only at this point: it is the salvation of the profanity of the world, of its being-thus...The world – insofar as it is absolutely, irreparably profane – is God. (CC: 90)

We can contrast Agamben's work, as he often does, with post-structuralism or deconstruction, which argues that any supposed binary or distinction is an effect of a differential system. If this were so, then there would be something *like* language (including systems of gestures, sounds, marks, and conventions) that would create relations and oppositions. We could not think outside these systems, but we could – as post-structuralism has done in many different ways – be critical of the very notion of foundations and origins. Agamben, however, does not want to abandon what lies outside systems or relations; instead, there is always some remnant or interval between a system and its outside. Take the distinction between speech and language: we might think that our identity, the meaning we give to the world, and the sense of our experience are effects of the differential system of language. For Agamben, the problem with this approach is that it privileges the system of relations, whereas what needs to be thought is some remainder that is neither included within the system of relations nor operates as some origin, or outside. Rather than accept that everything is an effect of language or relations, we should be thinking about what is not brought into relation. So, the human who does not speak is not simply outside language, but is marked by *not speaking*, by having a potentiality to speak that is not actualized, by occupying a threshold.

This has two immediate implications: rather than think of single terms (such as human versus animal, or power and the field over which it operates) as effects of a system, we would see humans as bearing a potentiality for distinction within their own being; it would be human to be in relation to one's own impotentiality, or non-relationality. To think this way – to define "man" not as a rational or linguistic being, but as a being who is both capable and not capable of relationality – would not be a diminution of one's being. The humanity that we live and barely know is a humanity always in relation to its own *impotentiality*, and it is in moments of not speaking or not achieving something like the relation between potential and actuality that humanity can be witnessed (witnessed in *not appearing*). Second, this would entail that historical investigation would not remain at the level of the archive, seeing the present as the outcome of a series of oppositions constituted by the history of philosophy and theology; the archive would indicate something *unsaid*, or that which resists the production and articulation of relations. From this it would follow that what occurred in the death camps of Auschwitz would not be the failure of language in the case of an extreme event too horrific to be articulated; more accurately, we would say that what appears to be the normal case of humans speaking about the world always occurs in relation to what cannot be said, always occurs by setting aside that which remains. Rather than assume the impossibility of thinking outside relations, one might think of those moments when the failure to enter into relation – the silence of not speaking – fractures what we think of as the normal situation of day-to-day speech:

> In opposition to the *archive*, which designates the system of relations between the unsaid and the said, we give the name *testimony* to the system of relations between the inside and the outside of *langue*, between the sayable and the unsayable in every language – that is, between a potentiality of speech and its existence, between a possibility and an impossibility of speech. To think a potentiality in act *as potentiality*, to think enunciation on the plane of *langue* is to inscribe a caesura in possibility, a caesura that divides it into a possibility and an impossibility, into a potentiality and an impotentiality; and it is to situate a subject in this very caesura...testimony is the relation between a possibility of speech and an impossibility of speech – that is, only *as contingency*, as a capacity not to be. This contingency, this occurrence of language in a subject, is different from actual discourse's utterance or non-utterance, its speaking or not speaking, its production or non-production as a statement. It concerns the subject's capacity to have or not to have language. The subject is thus the possibility that language does not exist, does not take place – or, better, that it takes place only through its possibility of not being there, its contingency. The human being is the speaking being, the living being who has language, because the human being is capable of *not having* language, because it is capable of its own in-fancy...the relation between language and its existence, between *langue* and the archive, demands subjectivity as that which, in its very possibility of speech, bears witness to an impossibility of speech. (RA: 145–6)

In addition to language as the system of already constituted relations within which we might think and communicate, each speaking being has to take up a relation to language. Rather than see what occurs (praxis, act, archive) as something that naturally unfolds from the foundation or origin (being), and rather than have a binary that posits some divine ground (the sacred) and then the created world (the secular), the remnant seems to occupy one side of the divide while also destroying the logic of the division. We can only speak by way of language, but that same language also leaves something necessarily unsaid and unsayable: the condition for speaking is that some non-relational remainder is always left as that which is neither fully articulated nor simply abandoned. In *Remnants of Auschwitz*, Agamben focuses on the way in which the loss of speech and humanity does *not* reduce humans to the simple condition of animality, but rather exposes them as humans in their constitutive capacity *not to arrive at their (supposedly) essential humanity*. He does, quite problematically, focus on the "Muselmann" or Muslim – the name used in the camps to refer to those who were reduced to a state of inhuman lifelessness: "the *Muselmann* is an indefinite being in whom not only humanity and non-humanity, but also vegetative life and that of relation, physiology and ethics, medicine and politics, and life and death continuously pass through each other" (RA: 111). Agamben – here as elsewhere – takes up received terms (such as his concepts of "man," and his concepts of divine language) that have a difficult political valence. He never questions why those in the camps who appeared so destitute were referred to as "Muslims," and misses an opportunity to locate Nazi Germany within a broader history of colonialism (Jarvis 2014). Although one might make excuses for Agamben's silence and the political implications of the ways in which he theorizes both bare life (the destitute Jew who is now referred to as a Muslim), and the redeemed life that will no longer be subjected to the letter of the law, it is worth asking whether such political silences do not betray a deeper and unbridgeable political commitment to a proper life, or a life that is proper and authentic only in its realization that the proper does not exist, that there is no "man" other than the one who comes into being through speech. His entire project begins with a critique of the negativity that has marked the West; and yet redemption is found not by thinking of non-Western, post-colonial politics, but of a potentiality hidden in profoundly enigmatic points of the tradition. His theorization of testimony emerges from a consideration of Auschwitz – such that he finds the point of hope precisely in the culmination of nihilism – and yet it is the West's nihilism and despair that is always his final point of confrontation. His privilege of testimony is directly related to his identification of voice as a threshold, as *the threshold*, where the passage from animality to humanity takes place.

What occurs in testimony is twofold: some things cannot be said, and *what* cannot be said or spoken or articulated is the condition of the camps in which humans were no longer the speaking beings that had the fragile capacity to be. Somewhat controversially, Agamben does not see Auschwitz as some accident that can be set aside as a specific horror of the twentieth century; rather, it exposed the limits of the way humans have come into being in language. His notion of Auschwitz or "the camp" as the biopolitical paradigm has drawn much criticism, primarily because of its Eurocentric focus, and its occlusion of a broader history of violence, racism, sexism, and colonization within which Auschwitz would need to be understood (Sexton 2010; Mills 2005). Even so, the criticisms of Agamben's camp paradigm have tended to extend rather than reject his notion of biopolitics, especially with regard to the issues on which Agamben is most silent – such as race (Laforteza 2015: 126; Goldberg 2013). The significance of Agamben's conception of testimony lies in the challenge it presents to both the actual archive, and what can be recoded or actualized. Humans are speaking beings, but that capacity is accompanied by incapacity, and that which can be said is accompanied by the non-relational horror that never makes its way into the reason of language:

> This is why subjectivity appears as witness; this is why it can speak for those who cannot speak. Testimony is a potentiality that becomes actual through an impotentiality of speech; it is, moreover, an impossibility that gives itself existence through a possibility of speaking. These two movements cannot be identified either with a subject or with a consciousness; yet they cannot be divided into two incommunicable substances. Their inseparable intimacy is testimony. (RA: 146)

The remnant is not some simple phenomenon outside of language; it is not what we must assume as prior to language, nor what precedes language in any simple sense. For Agamben, then, it is necessary to redefine the subject, and the problem of the subject; rather than be concerned with the supposed "I" who is either prior to speech or an effect of speech, Agamben focuses on the threshold where speech may or may not come into being, and where *not speaking* offers a profound witnessing of the very contingency of the human, which is exposed in Auschwitz but which cannot be dismissed as a historical aberration:

> The subject...is a field of forces always already traversed by the incandescent and historically determined currents of potentiality and impotentiality, of being able not to be and not being able not to be. From this perspective, Auschwitz represents the historical point in which these processes collapse, the devastating experience in which the impossible is forced into the real. Auschwitz is the existence of the impossible, the most radical negation of contingency; it is, therefore, absolute necessity. (RA: 147–8)

Humans, as speaking animals, are not only realizations of a potential *to speak* (a potential that we witness as a refusal of silence, of not *not speaking*); speaking also discloses something singular about potentiality. Every speaking being at once enters the law or system of language, so that there is a move from language as a potential system to its actualization in speaking beings; but each speaker is always this singular speaker with *this* voice, and it is this singularity or remainder that perhaps reveals a different sense of potentiality. If we think of potentiality as nothing more than that which precedes actualization, and as properly coming into its own when fully actualized, then language is the realization of our being. But Agamben wants to say that potentiality is better thought of as *impotentiality*, so that speaking is not what must happen in order to reveal that I am a speaking being; I speak insofar as I do not remain silent. So the first thing we can say about potentiality in general is that it is not just the unfolding of what must be, but always – even when actual – maintains a relation to (also) not coming into being. Further, there is a dimension to speech and potentiality that has a deeper relation to the human, and to the problem of relations. It is by way of speech that we take up a relation to our singular being; it is through speaking that we are both brought into relation with each other, while at the same time it is speech – rather than the generality of language – that discloses each human body as singular. The singular voice with its pitch, timbre, cadence, accent, and rhythm is the threshold that enables the passage from a singular body as potential speaker to a speaking subject, but is also not exhausted in the general structure or meaning of what is said. There is something, Agamben insists, about this strange remainder or potentiality to speak (evidenced in a certain remainder and silence *in speaking*) that is akin to the structure of law, and akin to the structure of sovereignty.

2

Sovereignty, State of Exception, and Biopolitics

Agamben follows the early twentieth-century German legal theorist Carl Schmitt in defining the sovereign as he who decides on the state of exception (Schmitt 2006). In its narrowest sense, the "state of exception" is a legal-political term describing the supposedly temporary (exceptional or emergency) suspension of constituted law, with the state operating immediately and without limit. For Agamben, however, this "exceptional" circumstance both exposes what is structural and essential in any condition of sovereignty and law, *and* has implications well beyond legal discourse and modern conditions of emergency rule. In the legal "state of exception," it is when law appears to be without prior constitutional legitimation, operating as pure force, that we see into the heart of law. It is not the case that there is law that *then* needs to be executed or that occasionally deploys force in order to act; there is law because of an event of force that divides a body of law (or a sovereign power) from the domain over which it governs. This means that law must have an outside that it also ostensibly denies (the event of force by which it became law). In addition to the sovereign power and the bodies who become subjects and citizens within the law, there is also the zone of indistinction that becomes apparent precisely when constituted sovereignty suspends its actual and constituted form to become pure force. We can think of this inside/outside zone of indistinction as a remainder: when governments suspend the rule of law, are they acting outside the law (by behaving unconstitutionally) or are they preserving the law by suspending it for the sake of saving sovereign power? Consider the case of twenty-first-century counter-terrorist measures that may violate the constitution (by detaining individuals without trial) but do so, supposedly, for the sake of protecting the very conditions of legality and order. In such cases there appears to be law-lessness *and* rule by immediate or martial law. We cannot place such acts of force purely outside the law, even if they are outside the law *as constituted*. The supposedly absolutely lawless – force without limit – exists within the workings of law. The exception is therefore a border or threshold condition.

We usually understand the law in terms of a constitution, based on some conception of the good, which the sovereign then maintains. The final authority presiding over law, the sovereign is accompanied by executive forces – police and government – who institute the law. For Agamben, this distinction relies upon a long-standing theological tradition of separating the God of absolute being (who simply is), and the God who somehow acts in the world, by way of divine government or the trinity; for this reason, contemporary questions of government, sovereignty, and legitimation – including who counts as a citizen worthy of legal personhood – refer back to a theological tradition that also offers other ways of thinking about the relation between life and law. Whatever the origin, Western politics relies upon a distinction between law and force. The police, for example, do not decide upon what is legal, just as the sovereign does not actually enforce the law. In the state of exception, such a distinction breaks down and the law becomes force as such. There is just the immediate and executive action of power without any constituted or instituted body of law. It seems as though the sovereign (or government) is somehow acting outside the law, suspending the law, or exempting himself from the law. The sovereign who is at once the figure of law *is sovereign* precisely in a capacity to be outside the law, *and* it is just this power *to be outside* that constitutes sovereignty.

There can only be a sovereign or a body of law because of some event of force that created both a governing body (the king, the Constitution, the polity) and a governed body (the citizens or subjects to whom law applies). This institution of sovereignty creates a political or legal space where bodies become subjected to law, while other bodies are abandoned. In contemporary states of emergency or exception, the border between the space of law and lawlessness and between those who are citizens and those who are abandoned by law breaks down; sovereignty is no longer a constituted order enforced by executive powers, and sovereignty comes to operate by whatever means possible to maintain itself. Law acts for the sake of law, and adopts as means whatever is required to maintain the force of the state. The individuals governed are all, at any moment, possibly subject to becoming nothing more than objects of immediate executive orders (no longer protected by the constitutional limits that protect citizens). For Agamben, this contemporary tendency at once exposes the constitutive conditions of early sovereign power while also exemplifying the paradigm of modern power (which, for Agamben, is the modern death camp, where bodies become mere or "bare" life, no longer protected by law and personhood but abandoned as seemingly outside the law, and yet exposed to the suffering of the force of law).

The capacity for the sovereign power to step outside the usual limits of law, and then act immediately on bodies without trial or constitutional legitimacy, at once marks the advent of modern biopower but also expresses the ongoing Western structure of sovereignty going back to ancient law and theology: sovereign power is sovereign precisely in its capacity to suspend the very law that it supposedly maintains. Law acts directly as an end unto itself. For Agamben, states of emergency are at once the most modern and the most ancient of problems. In 2003, Agamben canceled plans to travel to the US to take up teaching invitations because he objected to the increasingly invasive security measures at immigration and border control. He subsequently explained his decision in a newspaper article entitled "No to Bio-Political Tattooing":

> All the same, it wouldn't be possible to cross certain thresholds in the control and manipulation of bodies without entering a new bio-political era, without going one step further in what Michel Foucault called the progressive animalisation of man which is established through the most sophisticated techniques...Electronic filing of finger and retina prints, subcutaneous tattooing, as well as other practices of the same type, are elements that contribute towards defining this threshold. The security reasons that are invoked to justify these measures should not impress us: they have nothing to do with it. History teaches us how practices first reserved for foreigners find themselves applied later to the rest of the citizenry...What is at stake here is nothing less than the new "normal" bio-political relationship between citizens and the state. This relation no longer has anything to do with free and active participation in the public sphere, but concerns the enrollment and the filing away of the most private and incommunicable aspect of subjectivity: I mean the body's biological life. (NP: 201)

"History teaches us how practices first reserved for foreigners find themselves applied later to the rest of the citizenry." Here, Agamben intertwines his two key ideas about the space of law and its temporality. Sovereign power opens a space of law, dividing itself from a political body of subjects who are defined through its constituted order; in so doing the sovereign "decision" or "ban" (which allows some bodies to be subjects and others not) creates an inside and an outside. There have always been those who, by decree of law, are set outside the law: transgressions can result in expulsion or exile from the body politic, while the law determines who counts as a political person. The contemporary predicament of refugees often places them within the geographical space of law – they can be, say, on Australian soil – and yet they are not Australian citizens and do not possess the rights and freedoms of Australian nationals. Conditions of exile, or what Agamben refers to (by looking back to Roman law) as *homo sacer*, have always marked the inside and outside of the law, meaning bodies can be abandoned to a zone where they are nothing more than mere life to be disposed of at will.

The claim about the inside and outside of law also has a temporal-historical component: the coming into being of law must have occurred as the emergence of a sovereign body that – by way of force – constitutes individuals as subjects to law. This emergence of law, or marking out of an inside and outside of law, is also a division within the human: a difference is constituted by way of negation where bare life (*zoe*) – mere animal existence that is impersonal – is opposed to political or deliberative existence (*bios*). Throughout his entire corpus, Agamben theorizes this intertwined historical, spatial, and existential division: the historical passage from lawless life to a life of constituted sovereign power, the spatial division between the space of the body politic and a zone outside the law, and an existential division between humans as rational speaking beings who decide their own essence, and humanity's "remainder" that is our mere animal being. That "remainder," though, is not simply outside law and the human, for it is required as an expelled limit and threshold in order for humanity to constitute itself as lawful. Agamben refers to biopolitics, or the capacity for power to act upon bodies as if they were "bare life," not so much as a historical period but rather as a constant condition that is perpetually reworked. For Agamben, this biopolitical complex that has organized Western thought needs to be questioned both because it goes back to the very emergence of political and legal history and because these impossible divisions still organize and paralyze our modes of approaching contemporary crises.

Here he is indebted to Walter Benjamin's attempt to think about a messianic event that is not some future fulfillment of this fallen world, and is instead the "happiness" of this world lived without a sense of a redemption that lies elsewhere. In an essay that has been highly important for Agamben, and twentieth-century theorists of sovereignty more generally, Benjamin defines *mythical* violence as "bloody power over mere life for its own sake"; that is, if power is mythical then it seems to be something we can do nothing about, as though it is simply something to which we are subjected; by contrast, *divine* violence is "pure power over all life for the sake of the living" (Benjamin 2006: 250). Perhaps the clearest way to think about how violence might be divine would be to think of a revolutionary force that was destructive of myth, of notions of fate or destiny, or resignation that relied on a mythic time beyond the present.

Both Schmitt and Benjamin were writing in Germany in the early twentieth century through the period of Nazism and National

Socialism (Britt 2010). It is not surprising that they both theorized the problem of authority and (for Benjamin) its seemingly "divine" appearance. If a government suspends the normal rule of law for some supposed emergency it becomes apparent that rather than there being a structure of law that pertains to all, it is always possible that the state that enforces the law becomes itself the force of law – capable of acting immediately and without any reference to anything other than itself. For Schmitt, then, the problem of sovereign legitimacy should not just be a topic of concern when the state seems to act as a law unto itself; the possibility of acting as pure force is not accidental but is the very possibility of law as such. In the day-to-day running of the state, when force seems to act to maintain an already constituted body of law, we are simply not mindful of the fact that at any point the sovereign has the power to suspend the law. Nazi Germany, then, would not be some exceptional or accidental case that we can afford to ignore; cases where the state operates without reference to anything other than itself disclose the true nature of law, not its corruption. Whereas many today use instituted law to object to supposed states of emergency – objecting to the way states are increasingly violating their own rules in order to maintain themselves autocratically – Agamben sees the current crisis and state of emergency as an opportunity to think a life without a (seemingly) transcendent constituted law. This, he argues, would prompt us to think about what it might mean to act politically. If we do not have a constitution or already instituted sense of what is right, but are exposed to a life that does not yet have law but is not already excluded as lawless or outside the law, then political action in its genuine sense would open up as a potentiality no longer bound by what is already determined as the political:

> It is this no-man's-land between public law and political fact, and between the juridical order and life, that the present study seeks to investigate. Only if the veil covering this ambiguous zone is lifted will we be able to approach an understanding of the stakes involved in the difference – or the supposed difference – between the political and the juridical, and between law and the living being. And perhaps only then will it be possible to answer the question that never ceases to reverberate in the history of Western politics: what does it mean to act politically? (SE: 13)

As long as there is a "normal" rule of law there is a distinction between the constituted law and the sovereign power that enforces the law. This distinction becomes indistinct in the state of exception: constituted law is suspended and the sovereign rules by immediate force. We have a state of pure force, reined in by nothing other than itself. Such a structure, for both Schmitt and Agamben, cannot be understood without paying some attention to the history of theology. Whereas God was once the being whose force generated law while not being himself subject to law, the modern sovereign might at first seem to be the representative of the will or good of the people, but sovereign authority is ultimately capable of suspending the rule of law for the very sake – supposedly – of saving law's authority. According to Agamben, Schmitt's articulation of the state of exception was in implicit dialogue with Walter Benjamin's critique of violence. Whereas Schmitt wanted to see violence as that which is captured by law, accepting the "fiction" that law's outside is without form and is nothing more than "bare" life already requiring sovereign power (so chaotic and violent as to require absolute sovereignty), Benjamin argued that there was another violence, and that this potential was exposed when sovereignty – in the state of emergency – is seen to have no ground other than that of its own violent and lawless positing of a lawless outside. In addition to the violence captured and externalized by the sovereign, there is a divine violence that is revolutionary and that would destroy the opposition between law and its other:

> Benjamin calls this other figure of violence "pure" (*reine Gewalt*) or "divine," and, in the human sphere, "revolutionary." What the law can never tolerate – what it feels as a threat with which it is impossible to come to terms – is the existence of a violence outside the law; and this is not because the ends of such a violence are incompatible with law, but because of "its mere existence outside the law." ... The task of Benjamin's critique is to prove the reality (*Bestand*) of such a violence: "If violence is also assured a reality outside the law, as pure immediate violence, this furnishes proof that revolutionary violence – which is the name for the highest manifestation of pure violence by man – is also possible" ... The proper characteristic of this violence is that it neither makes nor preserves law, but deposes it (*Entsetzung des Rechtes...*) and thus inaugurates a new historical epoch. (SE: 53)

On the one hand, such a destruction of law would be counter-theological, as it would destroy the notion of a sovereign power or pure law outside life; on the other hand, such a deposition of law would be messianic in a restoration of power to life as it is, not life as it is governed from outside.

We might say that God would not be truly and supremely powerful if He were compelled to be good; rather, because He is God, what He does counts as good and He can be subject to no essence other than that of His pure existence: this authoritarian dimension of theology would not exhaust the possibilities of the Christian tradition, especially its "messianic" aspect, where God would be incarnated in this life. For that reason, modern politics and ethics harbor profound problems of authority or legitimation; if we no longer appeal to God as the force that brings law, life, and the good into being, how do we think about the legitimate force of law? This is a problem both at the level of the state and the individual: is it coherent to hold the modern conception of a self as a being who is moral because she acts according to what she freely wills, or does this not harbor some unthought privileging of a force that brings itself into being? For Agamben, the state of exception exposes an aporia: we think of the law as that which requires force in order to be enforced. If this is so, then there is some good (or meaning – something we want to enforce, an end) that allows for the use of force by law. But in the state of exception the constituted body and meaning of law is suspended; what remains is force without significance. For both Schmitt and Walter Benjamin, this suspension of law for the supposedly exigent circumstance of saving lawfulness is – though exemplified by Nazi Germany – not at all exceptional. Increasingly, the state of exception is the condition of modern politics. For Benjamin, though, there is something uniquely redemptive about this exposure of the real face of law: if law has tended to conceal its force behind constituted power, the state of exception exposes law *as force*. And once that exposure occurs we might be in a state of renewal where, rather than simply accept law as constituted, we ask the profound and revolutionary question of law's coming into being, by way of force. One of the ways to think about the state of exception is to say, first, that if it is possible for such an emergency or supposedly exceptional state to occur, then this should alert us to something about the possibility of law and sovereignty as such, and how they are possible. Second, there is something historically specific about the modern state of exception, where law increasingly has no outside; the distinction between sovereign power and the force it uses to maintain itself breaks down. For Agamben, that breakdown is at once catastrophic but also opens a possible horizon for rethinking the distinction between law and force for the future; to do so requires thinking about the emergence of the relation of the stability of law and the dynamism of force from some threshold where they are not yet fully distinct:

> Sovereign violence opens a zone of indistinction between law and nature, outside and inside, violence and law. And yet the sovereign is precisely the one who maintains the possibility of deciding on the two to the very degree that he renders them indistinguishable from each other. (HS: 64)

State of Exception

For the most part, or so we would like to think, we exist as citizens under the law, with rights and recognized duties and norms. We are not "mere" life to be disposed of as some simple means toward an end.

Modern liberal political theory argues that no one can make an exception of themselves by claiming to know the good better than any other individual, and this would include those in power. The principle is most clearly articulated by Kant, and becomes crucial for modern liberal anti-foundationalism:

> Reason depends on this freedom for its very existence. For reason has no dictatorial authority; its verdict is always simply the agreement of free citizens, of whom each one must be permitted to express, without let or hindrance, his objections or even his veto. (Kant 1965: 593)

However, those who are non-citizens (such as illegal immigrants, suspected terrorists, or those deemed to be unworthy of rights and recognition) do not have the dignity and presence within the law granted to citizens, but become disposable life. Not only does *every* person become potentially devoid of rights and personhood in the state of exception, where we can all be detained, stopped, and searched, or even killed without due process, it has always been the case that supposedly normal law and citizenship produce a remainder of bare or abandoned life. At its simplest, we might say that political or civil recognition requires some means of identity, whether that be national citizenship, legal immigration status, ethnic belonging, or racial heritage (as in the worst cases of twentieth-century "ethnic cleansing" or genocide). The citizen or political subject can only be recognized as a person if some threshold is inscribed that sets inhuman life as that which has no voice or force against the law. The impersonal or bare life that is supposedly "outside" of law is its very condition, not only because citizenship must operate to separate those who are recognized from those who are not (producing an outside), but also because law can always potentially abandon any person and cast them as bare life. As recently as the late twentieth century, indigenous Australians were not granted the vote, and deaths of Aboriginal Australians in custody were not investigated with the same degree of concern accorded to white Australians. Such cases of abandonment were (and still are) common, ranging from the high incidence in the United States of African Americans being subject to stop and search to the condition of the Palestinian people being virtually stateless; one might even say that the history of liberal freedom and personhood has relied on a large number of humans being subjected to slavery and not being granted personhood. This is at once a material and economic condition, but for Agamben it is also a metaphysical condition whereby the human externalizes its own inhumanity which it then witnesses with horror and violence. There is a condition of recognition accorded to those within the polity who are never means to some end, and then the life of the unwaged, undocumented, unprotected mass of life excluded from the rights and dignity of persons. Being recognized before the law, having the political identity of a citizen, is an event of inclusion that necessarily entails exclusion – with any event of inclusion always being fragile and capable of breaking down to a state of emergency where "we" all become bare life. There can only be a sovereign state or a domain of constituted law through the institution of a body politic *and* its outside or remainder. Rather than argue for a state that is more accountable to its constitution or body of law, Agamben argues for what the state of exception exposes in its catastrophic form: a life that does not have an external body of law, a life that does not have form imposed from above.

In some ways, the notion of sovereignty – and the division between legal, recognized, and political order, and pure force – is mythic. There "must have been" some generating event or force that constituted law in the first place, where law granted itself the power over a domain of bodies. Of course, such an event never occurred as an event (unless we think about the drafting of the Constitution or the declaration of rights, but these events already require the coming into being of a polity or people with the authority or sovereignty to draft law). Law is built up over time, emerging from practices to become constituted into some distinct document, order, or system of a sovereign or state. To talk about sovereignty as a single locus of power or to refer to the "violence" by which sovereignty is imposed seems to miss everything we know about the historical complexity and evolution of power, and in particular modern power's dispersed bureaucratic nature. But Agamben insists that despite appearances the mythic and theological separation of a supreme authority from the "mere" life of the world still has a hold on our thought and practice of government and politics. The supposedly universal humanity that finds itself in modernity to be the recognized subject of law and rights depends upon a prior division between the formed polity and the barely living. It is that threshold between law and life that is exposed in cases where individuals no longer have the status of persons and can be killed without due process because they are abandoned by law. Against the claim for the continuous emergence of law from life, Agamben argues that there is a gap or caesura; even the most universal of laws – especially notions such as human rights – do not flow naturally or automatically from life, but are required *as law* because humans are always proximate to the inhuman that makes anything possible (such as the events of Nazi death camps). Law is possible because life may or may not take on a certain form, and it is precisely that gap or distance between life and law that appears in states of emergency or exception: the law appears for what it is, as force that has no natural ground in life.

Indeed, the supposedly natural law of maintaining peace and order, or the conception of government as "merely" facilitating or administering the law, relies upon an understanding of a proper mode of life that law would merely extend, as though there might be a law of life. Certainly, this is how modern law is conceived – not as something imposed from without but as what would follow, rationally, if humans were to recognize each other as rational agents all willing the common good. For Agamben, this modern democratic notion of the collective will is once again a legacy of the fracture between being and praxis: we imagine that the order of the world simply *is*, and law or government executes and administers that order. Such an assumption – of law as execution or bureaucracy, or life and its management – covers over just what end the law is preserving. For Agamben, unlike other theorists of positive biopolitics, there are no "vital norms"; there is nothing that life as such presents as lawful, and it is this exposure that politics has failed to confront (Esposito 2008: 185). Even if the emergence of law is gradual through time, it nevertheless requires a division or caesura; law is never "natural," never continuous with life because it can operate *as law* only by taking on some abstract formality that would apply or determine cases in advance and thereby erase the singularity of life. What looks today like an alarming aberration of increasing state power and a move away from democratic liberalism is, for Agamben, not an accident that can be somehow set outside the normal, the proper, or the essential. It is the unworking or inoperativity of law – its breakdown to disclose pure force – that displays law's essential relation to force and lawlessness.

It is when democracies seem to violate their norm of constituted and legitimate order that the ultimate condition of power is exposed; for even a democracy "of the people" has established who is to count as a citizen or person, thus abandoning those beyond its domain to being nothing more than "bare life" (as when democracies expel or imprison those who threaten the polity's border). It is not the case that there are ordered polities that occasionally and lamentably have to resort to force. Rather, there is a force *from which* "legitimate" order emerges. Law, order, and politics are therefore best considered from the point of view of the seeming exception, failure, or moment at which they appear *not* to be realizing their proper potential. It is when the legal system suspends law that we see the force of law.

What is excluded from open and egalitarian deliberative democracies are those modes of life that do not accord with the sovereign model of a self who makes a lawful, identifiable, and active subject of himself; one could therefore fruitfully use Agamben's work to think about how the model of the active rational subject excludes non-humans, as well as humans who are deprived of speech, or those who are in extreme states of suffering to the point of being *in*capacitated. Despite liberal democracies being premised on *not* imposing some norm or "good" on the body politic, it is the ideal of free, open, and rational self-legislation which maintains a figure of proper (sovereign, active, and self-determining) life, which must then exclude and abandon *bare life*.

Agamben, by contrast, suggests that there might be a politics that does not have already established ends, and that we might think *immanently* about what "we" do without having some pre-established sense of an end toward which means are directed: a "state of the world in which the world appears as a good that absolutely cannot be appropriated or made juridical" (SE: 64). This would be a non-sovereign mode of power: not "power over" (even if this were thought of as the power the individual has over his own life, or the power "humanity" has as rational over all forms of irrationality). This would be "a politics that corresponds to the inactivity [*inoperosita*] of man, one which is determined not simply and absolutely from the being-at-work of human rationality, but from a working that exposes and contains in itself the possibility of its own not existing, of its own inactivity" (WM: 10).

Many of the exceptions to democracy today – drone strikes, extraordinary renditions, enhanced interrogation, as well as the refusal of some rights to some humans (such as voting or gun ownership) – occur because of the unquestioned commitment to man as a basic, free, self-defining and rational political agent. It is as though the end of order and reason remains stable and can be achieved by whatever means or operations necessary. In recent US debates about gun restrictions, advocates for reform argued that persons with criminal records or those with a history of mental illness should not be given the right to own a gun. Whatever one thinks about gun reform, the idea of excluding criminals and the mentally ill from what is otherwise deemed to be a right demonstrates that the supposed universality of rights is nevertheless limited to some norm of the properly human and that this property of "humanity" increasingly becomes aligned with a will that is sovereign insofar as it takes command of itself and constitutes law through itself.

For Agamben, what appears to be new about biopolitics, or the use of "life" to render politics into a managerial expertise, brings to the fore the fact that there has *always* been a supposed pre-political substance of life. His use of the terms "biopolitics" and "biopower" at once follows and revises their original articulation by Michel Foucault, who first used the terms as definitive of a modern and *post*-sovereign form of power.

Foucault and Biopolitics

Foucault insisted that "biopower" or the focus of politics on the management of the human population at the level of bodily life, rather than in terms of the creation of relations through speech and action, was a specifically modern development. The classic first word (but certainly not the last) is in the first volume of *History of Sexuality*:

> If one can apply the term *bio-history* to the pressures through which the movements of life and the processes of history interfere with one another, one would have to speak of *bio-power* to designate what brought life and its mechanisms into the realm of explicit calculations and made knowledge-power an agent of transformation of human life. It is not that life has been totally integrated into techniques that govern and administer it; it constantly escapes them. Outside the Western world, famine exists, on a greater scale than ever; and the biological risks confronting the species are perhaps greater, and certainly more serious, than before the birth of microbiology. But what might be called a society's "threshold of modernity" has been reached when the life of the species is wagered on its own political strategies. For millennia, man remained what he was for Aristotle: a living animal with the additional capacity for a political existence; modern man is an animal whose politics places his existence as a living being in question. (Foucault 1978: 143)

For Foucault, history was radically discontinuous, and could only be understood if the sovereign model of power (as power *over* life and death) were to be displaced by a notion that was "capillary," or that might operate at a "micro" level, where the self-surveillance of modern discourses of therapy, sexuality, and rights would need to be understood in a manner very different from repressive or "top-down" models. Not only did Foucault see modern biopolitics as a break with sovereign models, but he also saw ancient forms of power as anything but biopolitical: for Aristotle, "life" was something left outside political consideration. Man happens to be living, but what makes him political is his capacity for decision and self-formation. Biopower is modern because it operates by knowing, analyzing, and managing an underlying substance of life. This substance or ground of life can only emerge through the technologies and discourses of modern science as well as the new "human" or "social" sciences; modern biopower for Foucault is productive rather than negative. It operates not by excluding or abandoning "life" but by producing life through various practices of knowledge and discipline. Modern power is no longer sovereign – with the paradigm being the king's exercise of execution and torture – but biopolitical. The production of life, health, wellness, disease-control, and population-management are positive ways in which power generates relations among bodies, as well as generating a self whose living being or "life" becomes a substance to be constantly monitored:

> it had to have methods of power capable of optimizing forces, aptitudes, and life in general without at the same time making them more difficult to govern. If the development of the great instruments of the state, as

institutions of power, ensured the maintenance of production relations, the rudiments of anatomo- and bio-politics, created in the eighteenth century as *techniques* of power present at every level of the social body and utilized by diverse institutions (the family, and the army, schools and the police, individual medicine and the administration of collective bodies), operated in the sphere of economic processes, their develop-ment, and the forces working to sustain them... The adjustment of the accumulation of men to that of capital, the joining of the growth of human groups to the expansion of productive forces and the differential allocation of profit, were made possible in part by the exercise of bio-power in its many forms and modes of application. The investment of the body, its valorization, and the distributive management of its forces were at the same time indispensable. (Foucault 1978: 141)

The clearest articulation of Agamben's attitudes toward Foucault can be found in the introduction to his *Homo Sacer*. Here, Agamben describes Foucault's analysis of the biopolitical processes that define modernity, quoting Foucault's famous declaration that for "millen-nia ... man remained what he was for Aristotle: a living animal with the additional capacity for political existence; modern man is an animal whose politics calls his existence as a living being into question" (quoted in HS: 3). At this point, Agamben affirms the importance of Foucault's discovery: "the entry of *zoe* into the sphere of the *polis* – the politicization of bare life as such – constitutes the decisive event of modernity and signals a radical transformation of the political-philosophical categories of classical thought" (4). It would seem, then, that Agamben has no qualms with Foucault's analysis and is uninter-ested in contesting the claims made in *The History of Sexuality*.

But, if this is the case, how exactly is Agamben intervening in this project? In very general terms, Agamben conceives of his own book as a completion of the work Foucault began on biopolitics. Lamenting that "Foucault's death kept him from showing how he would have devel-oped the concept and study of biopolitics," Agamben then proceeds to map out where Foucault would have gone had he remained alive long enough to do so. At first he remains puzzled that Foucault never ref-erenced Hannah Arendt's strikingly similar work nor that Arendt ever thought to connect her work in *The Human Condition* with "the pene-trating analyses she had previously devoted to totalitarian power" (4). In short, the failure (if we would call it that) of each thinker is their inability to bring together the various strands of their thought. For him, the crucial term is "intersection," whereby supposedly disparate ideas are revealed to have some intimate connection with one another. Perhaps even more importantly, Agamben sees this intersection of dif-ferent processes not as a contingent historical circumstance but, rather, a point of origin that has been lost or made obscure over the course of time. As such, we can conceive of Agamben's work as a kind of recovery project that seeks to unmask some fundamental truth that still functions in today's world.

After outlining how Foucault dedicated himself to examining two distinct processes, namely "the study of political techniques...with which the State assumes and integrates the care of the natural life of individuals into its very center" and "the techniques of self by which processes of subjectivation bring the individual to bind himself to his own identity and consciousness" as well as "external power," Agamben writes that "the point at which these two faces of power converge remains strangely unclear in Foucault's work, so much so that it has been claimed that Foucault would have consistently refused to elaborate a unitary theory of power" (HS: 5). As he sees it, the tissue that connects these points together exists, but it remains so obscure or unthought that it has led many to believe that a synthesis of the two is not even possible. In other words, for Agamben, Foucault is *not* a theorist who rejected the notion of a unitary form of power, he simply failed to see how the various strands of his thought were related.

Agamben then positions himself as the one who will complete the important analysis inaugurated by Foucault, asserting that the present inquiry concerns precisely the hidden point of intersection between the juridico-institutional and the biopolitical models of power. What this work has had to record among its likely conclusions is precisely that the two analyses cannot be separated, and that the inclusion of bare life in the political realm constitutes the original – if concealed – nucleus of sovereign power. *It can even be said that the production of a biopolitical body is the original activity of sovereign power*. In this sense, biopolitics is at least as old as the sovereign exception (HS: 6).

In other words, politics has always been biopolitics. Even a cursory rereading of the preceding passage illustrates Agamben's emphasis on the term "original," which appears twice in this brief span. Indeed, Agamben's investigation is rooted in a return to the past, which he believes holds the answer to the dilemmas that plague the modern world. Studying history constitutes a form of self-discovery whereby we unmask the processes that have always been at work over the entire course of Western civilization. Although never explicitly stated, it is not hard to imagine that Agamben conceives of Foucault's late work – in which he examined Greek and Roman sexual practices – as gesturing in this very direction. From Agamben's perspective, if Foucault had only been granted a little more time, he almost certainly would have seen the underlying connections between the Greek world and modern times, thereby synthesizing the work done over the course of his career into a coherent whole.

For Agamben, then, biopower does not occur as a displacement of sovereignty but rather as the intensification and extension of the sovereign paradigm. Biopower operates not so much (as in the old sovereign model) by setting bare life outside the space of law, where the polity is formed from recognized political subjects opposed to those bodies beyond the law whose being is deemed to be that of mere biological existence. Instead, this difference between *bios* and *zoe* that had once constituted the border of the polity becomes internal to every individual. The sovereign division that creates an inside and outside, by dividing and opposing constituted bodies of the polity from bare life, increasingly operates to produce every body as bare life, subject to the expulsive power of the law. For Agamben, sovereignty is not one political paradigm among others, but is a logic or mode of relation – the establishment of a border between inside and outside – that goes well beyond law and the polity. In fact, sovereignty is not an example of a political mode: there is politics – or a group of humans relating to each other in common – because there is sovereignty, or the coming into being of a relation of force that divides the proper from the improper, the inside from the outside.

Indeed, we might note a reversal of priorities in Foucault and Agamben that goes well beyond a dispute over just when biopower begins historically. For Foucault, the problem of method that follows from beginning political questions in terms of the sovereign model is that we begin with a model of subjection, or power over, and then ask how such power might be legitimated or eliminated; we see power as negative, as that which limits a body or impedes that body's natural force and right. If this were so, then we would constantly seek to liberate a body *from power*, and would also regard discourses that aim to liberate one's sexuality, or one's individual difference, as opposed to power. We imagine that there is something like a being or life that is then repressed by an external power, and in doing so (according to Foucault) we fail to recognize the ways in which liberation discourses – such as sexual freedom, or consciousness raising – produce self-managing bodies. We assume a body's proper potential and then ask about the ways in which power legitimately or illegitimately diminishes that potential. Against the sovereign or "power-over" model, where power represses or negates, Foucault regards power as positive. If there is a sovereign relation – such as a "power over" or a relation of master to slave – this is because there has already been a distribution of force, and because the terms in any relation are outcomes of a degree of power. In the beginning there is something like a relation among forces or power *from which* bodies emerge; the self or subject does not precede practices and relations, but is produced through the relations a body bears to itself and to others. Politics is not a question of individuals coming together to form a state; for the individual or self is already the outcome of practices and relations. It follows that a political field occurs as a distribution of force, as a field of relations. If something like sovereignty emerges, where it appears that there is "a" power – a central locus of power that governs or subdues bodies – then this is the *effect* of a series of forces and relations. Sovereign models, for Foucault, distort the operations of force to which a more acute analysis ought to be attendant. As long as we think of power as "power over," or as the violent force that impedes or reduces life's potential, we fail to consider the properly multiple nature of power in *all* of its manifestations. Even sovereign power, or the power of the king over life and death, was productive – and to prove this point Foucault describes public tortures and executions that created the relations of spectacle and terror upon which such power was based (Foucault 1977).

Accordingly, when Foucault examines the problem of truth, he does not see power as distorting truth, for there can only be truth by way of power. Scientific truths, for example, are the outcome of bodies asking certain questions, of individuals being invested with institutional and discursive power, and with technological relations that extend a body's force. If we want to understand looking, speaking, desiring, and knowing, then we need to look beyond constituted terms or bodies to consider the entire field and distribution of forces. This is why, after arguing for modern power as biopolitical, Foucault looks back to ancient and classical forms of ethics in which selves were formed through techniques of discipline and sexual practice that were neither repressive (where sex is some brute force to be liberated) nor private (where sexuality is what an individual simply has). Rather than sexuality being the substantial truth of the self, the self is the result of a series of disciplines, modulations, variations, and technologies (or ongoing stable practices). The sovereign model is one relation among many, and certainly not *the* difference from which all other differences need to be examined.

Whereas the sovereign model prompts us to ask questions about how we might overcome or liberate ourselves from power (because power is deemed to be external), Foucault seeks to multiply power and look at power as creative. If he is critical of biopolitical models, this is because *like the sovereign model* the biopolitical model assumes some already given term – such as life – and then grounds political action and decision on the grounds of life's maximization. Just as earlier transcendent models assumed the authority of God, the king, or the good, so biopower assumes the norm of life, which becomes increasingly *normalizing*, allowing ethical-political decisions to be treated as so many cases of management that seem to follow on from facts and expertise. In both cases (of sovereignty and biopolitics), Foucault's genealogy traces the emergence of the single or grounding term from a plural field: there is "life" in modernity because of a series of technological, discursive, epistemic, and institutional mutations that allow for new questions and disciplines of study, new ways of looking, moving, thinking, and feeling. In pre-modern polities, there is "a" sovereign because of practices and institutions, such as torture, excessive displays of consumption, the organization of public spaces, and a concomitant structuring of the visual field. Just as theories of sovereignty had assumed or presupposed what needs to be explained ("the" sovereign), so theories of bio-ethics or rights assume the living individual and life.

Like Agamben, Foucault also looked back to ancient Greece to find a contrast with the present, but this was not because ancient Greece might offer insight into the general constitution of a structure of sovereignty that remains in play today without being fully understood. Rather, something about the way bodies exist in relation, and the ways in which bodies managed themselves through practices and technologies of the self, opened up the thought – for Foucault – of an ethics: in the beginning is a practice and relation of the self to itself by way of a series of discourses and problems. It is from the relations and practices of bodies and pleasures that an ethical and political field emerges. If there eventually comes to be the figure of "a" sovereign who is the locus and origin of power, or "a" substrate of "life" that provides the ground for political decisions and procedures, this is only because such terms emerge from relations among bodies and practices. "Life" is an effect of force, not its ground. Biopower, for Foucault, is insidious not because it is the intensification of an original forgetting or occlusion of the genesis of the possibility of politics as such, but because it relies on a term – "life" – that closes down the process of posing problems.

Foucault's criticism of an "ethics of knowledge," where decisions would be referred to some external and verifiable criteria without an investigation into the positive production of truth, is quite distinct from Agamben's emphasis on rethinking sovereignty. If Foucault insists on an inquiry into relations and forces before the unfolding of distinct terms and bodies, and before the production of a relation between inside and outside, Agamben focuses on *non*-relation, and this in turn requires that he take a step beyond Foucault's inquiry into the ways in which relations produce a field of distinct points. For Agamben, it must be possible to inquire into the *genesis* of relations, or that "zone of indifference" from which forces and distinctions emerge. Like Foucault, he does not want to grant this origin of relations a single or founding term, but he nevertheless – unlike Foucault – wants to maintain the question of the emergence of relations even if that question takes us to a threshold rather than a ground.

Indeed, this is one of Agamben's key disputes with the work of Michel Foucault: for Foucault, the primary task of the present is to think radical discontinuity. What if a single term such as "law" or "power" were operating in a completely different structure from the ways in which it did in the pre-modern or classical periods? What if we had certain figures or images of power, such as "the law" or "the king" or even "authority," while power operated in a manner that could not be figured by a single body or term? What if it were not the meaning of simple terms that changed but entire relations between thought and its very orientation to what it deemed to be its world or "outside"? For Foucault, the present requires something like a dia-grammatic approach. How does a collection of practices, discourses, institutions, desires, and technologies create distinctions and lines of force and operation? Rather than a genealogy of tracing terms and possibilities back to the past from which they emerged, Foucault insisted on an archaeology: yes, the field of the present is composed from fragments of a past, but those fragments have been redistributed and rearranged and no longer have the same sense or operation (Frost 2010: 549). The same objects seem to remain but they are utterly differ-ent in force. We still have churches and royal families, but they do not form the nexus of a network of power; there have always been human organisms but they have not always been the primary object of atten-tion for governmental practices and interventions that focus on "life."

By contrast, Agamben wants not only to unify the question of power in general, across the Western tradition into the question of sovereignty as such; he also wants to locate sovereignty and power within a broader structure of relations and potentiality that characterizes language, and the human being's relation to the life that appears to be set outside human linguistic being. For Agamben, humans have been defined by a division and a potentiality, between their mere life and their formed articulate life. The question of sovereignty *is* a political question, but it goes to the heart of the split between the human species and political "man." Sovereignty is not simply the king or even the state but has come to represent, for Agamben, the "ban" on bare life – or all the ways in which the vulnerable impotentiality of our being is expelled from what we take to be proper. The capacity to speak at once distances the human being from any simple life of merely living, and yet it is also the case that when humans do *not* speak they recognize that a mere life of animal existence is precisely the ground from which all speech may (or may not) emerge; the threshold of potentiality is disclosed, *not* as a ground that inevitably comes into linguistic being, but as a life that may or may not speak and – when speaking – always bears a relation-ship (a difficult relationship) to its own silent and non-speaking life.

When law *as actual* breaks down, we see the potentiality (or the very possibility of law as such) precisely in the exercise of force without law; law is without force, and force operates immediately – but this catas-trophe is also a potentiality for a mode of life not subjected to law. Here Agamben follows Benjamin, for whom the increasing incidence of states of exception might lead to a genuinely divine violence, or the revolutionary destruction of constituted powers. And Agamben is also indebted to Heidegger, for whom we are only opened to the potential-ity of existence when our everyday world breaks down. As Heidegger argued in *Being and Time*, for the most part our lives are caught up in a horizon of already given possibilities and projects; however, if that lifeworld breaks down, we are exposed to a world *not* presented as self-evidently ours, as not-yet composed into a meaningful horizon. For Heidegger, this is when we are faced with our *ownmost* potentiality (Heidegger 1996: 170). And even though Agamben questions the concepts of self and ownness, he intensifies the radical break of potentiality; his new political future will allow for potentiality to be released from law, enabling each singular being to relate to another without an overarching norm. In the usual state of affairs and in the usual run of politics, there is a coincidence between the law – or what is deemed to be right and just – and force; the constituted power is given as the body that enforces the law; force is deemed to be the necessary action required by an already given legality. Force operates to preserve what is already deemed to be good and lawful, and serves to maintain a constituted relation of sovereign power. In the state of exception this *relation* between law and force is suspended; law suspends its constituted and actualized form and operates as force.

If, to take a contemporary example, the very features that make up the sense of the law – such as the commitment to human rights, or the US Constitution, or legal precedent – are suspended, then law becomes nothing other than force. In the case of post-9/11 states of emergency, the law has been suspended (supposedly) for the sake of some final preservation of law; terrorism, we are told, poses such a threat to democracy, freedom, and life that it is worth suspending some rights and limits (such as the right to a trial or the presumption of innocence). Ends and means start to blur; for the end appears increasingly to be nothing more than the enforcement of law, rather than law having an end outside itself (such as well-being or happiness). The law suspends itself in order to enforce itself. The sovereign no longer appears as the figure who acts in order to enforce a law that has its own legitimacy; the sovereign becomes nothing other than force. If we have some idea that law must occasionally deploy violence in order to maintain itself, and that certain events such as capital punishment, war, or imprisonment are required only when the law is threatened by violence from without, then this is because we have some notion of the law that is irreducible to force and violence. We can appeal to the constitution, or conceptions of human rights, or international law to criticize certain acts of force, and we can imagine that in an ideal world there might be something like law or lawfulness without force.

We assume a distinction between the law and the force that law requires in order to maintain itself; in the state of exception that distinction breaks down. Agamben describes this, in *State of Exception*, as "the separation of force of law from the law" (38). But while this initially seems to be exceptional, this separation is the very condition for the daily functioning of law. Every time the law is enforced or applied, something outside pure law must come into play: "In the decision on the state of exception, the norm is suspended or even annulled; but what is at issue in this suspension is, once again, the creation of a situation that makes the application of the norm possible" (SE: 36). Agamben asserts that:

> Sovereign violence opens a zone of indistinction between law and nature, outside and inside, violence and law. And yet the sovereign is precisely the one who maintains the possibility of deciding on the two to the very degree that he renders them indistinguishable from each other. (HS: 41)

In order to make this more specific we might consider the post-9/11 exceptions made to the checks and protocols of democracy and rights (and an increasing *indistinction* concerning political space – the law can now strike or intervene in areas once deemed to be private or beyond the reach of the nation-state; private calls can be monitored, personal devices (phones, "smart" watches) can act as ongoing tracking and monitoring technologies, and what counts as the legitimate space of law is no longer discernible). Those suspected of being terrorists can be detained without trial or due process, and – as revealed in the 2013 coverage of US drone strikes – it was admitted that it would be possible for suspected terrorists (including US citizens) to be targeted and executed without trial. The year 2013 also saw the exposure of the US government's "Prism" operation: a clandestine mass electronic surveillance data-mining program operated by the United States National Security Agency (NSA) since 2007. Without any constitutional support, force was exercised across a space usually deemed to be outside the law (private emails, phone records, and so on). Every act created both a law and a space of law by means of force without any end other than that of maintaining itself; the word "security" comes to refer less and less to the securing *of* anything, and more and more to a process of securing as such. Such an operation of force, in and of itself, without end is nightmarishly nihilistic, for there is a complete loss of the borders and meaning of the polity, and at the same time also signals a possible future where we might genuinely think about force as such, without assuming that there is an end or law toward which life and force ought to be tending.

When law is suspended, what is exposed is the original condition of law as force, an original indistinction. Frequently, the response to contemporary suspensions of law or states of emergency has been an insistence on human rights, rights that would be non-negotiable and would place some sort of limit on the force that a sovereign might exert in order to save what is claimed to be the very possibility of law. Against the idea that limited violations of rights are required in extreme cases of terrorist threats, the human rights activist argues that the dignity of human life is such that there can be no legal or just exceptions. The human rights activist also often returns to original acts of language – the Declaration of Human Rights, the Geneva Conventions, the US Constitution, or even the terms of democracy such as "right" or "justice," or "human." (What is *not* questioned is the coming into being of those linguistic acts, and the coming into being of language as such – a potentiality for speaking that can never be grounded or guaranteed on any right of humanity precisely because it is from such linguistic events that humans and rights emerge.)

In the state of exception it is, supposedly, because life and law are threatened that law must suspend itself in certain exceptional cases. The suspected terrorist is supposedly such an exceptional threat to the very possibility of law and its capacity to guard its citizens that he may be killed or imprisoned without trial (either by way of executive orders, or by drone attacks, or by imprisonment in detention centers). That is to say: it is by way of an unquestioning sacredness of life that law is suspended, but such suspension also abandons bare life – the lives of those outside the law. After the July 2005 bombings of central London, amid a heightened state of security alert throughout the city, a Brazilian national residing in London (Jean Charles de Menezes) was shot dead by London Metropolitan Police as a suspected terrorist, even though there was no evidence linking de Menezes to the bombings. Such a case, though utterly tragic, is possibly understandable as a panicked response to terrorist threats; but, even so, it is perhaps worth looking at the ways in which defense, security, and threat can start to render the law in its stated form volatile as it increasingly operates as force for the sake of preserving force. The twenty-first century has seen a series of incidents where individuals (who are not recognized by the law) are killed with an immediacy that exposes their lives as abandoned, as bare life. Although there were many political complexities surrounding the 2012 shooting in Florida of the 17-year-old African American Trayvon Martin by another civilian, George Zimmerman, the defense relied upon Zimmerman acting in part as a "neighborhood watch" vigilante, but also as a supposedly threatened individual. The state of Florida's "stand your ground" laws, in this respect, are exemplary of the ways in which sovereign power is no longer set outside the polity as some constituted separate body but starts to operate more and more as the execution of force over bare life. Whatever one thinks of the verdict in the Trayvon Martin case, the very possibility that an individual might be killed without trial (and with impunity) because of a perceived threat allows human life to become subject to the immediate execution of force because of a supposed emergency.

Biopolitics is, for Agamben, at once a modern phenomenon, where the life that was previously set outside the polity becomes the very substance upon which sovereign power takes hold; at the same time, we can only understand this direct seizing of life by way of the ancient Greek distinction between the formed life of *bios* and the mere life of *zoe*, for it is *that* distinction that generates "life" as lawless, and "bare." Here is where Agamben's problem of sovereignty connects with the broader notion of biopolitics, and the figure of *homo sacer*. The notion of human rights posits something like a sacredness of life, or an inviolability of the human, and this – for Agamben – presents two problems.[1] The first is the problem of life and its supposed sacredness; life can only become sacred because something like "life" as *zoe* has been distinguished from *bios*. Further, the very structure of the sacred constitutes an opposition whereby there is also that which lies outside consecrated value, the profane.[2] When *life* becomes sacred the bareness of abandoned life becomes all the more intense: one might think of all the ways in which the twentieth and twenty-first centuries rendered much life disposable – the traffic in organs, the testing of products on animals, the subjection of populations to conditions of slavery or near-slavery – and all for the unquestioned sacredness of "the individual," whose life is sacred. Does this not explain why those who advocate for the "right to life" on the basis of life's sacredness are also frequently defenders of the death penalty, precisely because those who have transgressed life's sacredness are now perceived as nothing more than life to be destroyed? Originally, the sacred had nothing to do with life, with the polity being defined against the bare life that was profane; but as politics becomes biopolitics life itself is rendered either sacred – in the dignified rights of "man" – or bare, nothing more than what is there to be used. What is originally formed through abandonment and exclusion eventually becomes the ground of all politics in the modern era.

The Aristotelian distinction was between our bodily life, our mere existence as nutritive and perceptive souls, which we share with animals and which has its specific potentiality (*zoe*), and our politically formed life – the capacity we have to be political beings, to speak, to reason, and to set ends for ourselves (*bios*). As we have seen, the problem of "life" for Foucault is that in modernity the background condition for our political being – our biological being – has now become coincident with our political being, and this constitutes biopolitics. For Agamben, the problem is the distinction between life and politics as such, and so there is a single sovereign paradigm from Greece to the present that is also proto-biopolitical and that can only be overcome by rethinking the structure of sovereignty and its constitution of bare life. Both the executive order that tortures, kills, or imprisons because of an immediate threat to life, and the human rights campaigner who appeals to the inviolable sanctity of human life assert the sacredness of life, but can do so only because profane or bare life has been utterly abandoned.

Agamben, like Foucault, argues that the notion that power or law is always "power over," and therefore prohibitive and repressive, presupposes a certain conception of life. For Foucault, this was a specifically modern problem: if we think of law, morality, and norms as repressive and as limitations of something like "life," then we constitute a prior and hidden life as something that is there, lying in wait, capable of freeing us from imposed constraints. That liberating notion of life, operative in the "repressive hypothesis," becomes, for Foucault, increasingly normalizing. We appeal to life more and more as some political, sexual, or ethical substrate that (if liberated) will guide our politics and ethics; we argue that homosexuality is "normal" because it is grounded in biological or neural reality; we argue for rights on the basis of one common sacred life (that may even include animals or plants); we account for all sorts of human practices – from altruism to gossip – by referring back to some grounding imperative of life. We argue against supposedly imposed and constructed laws by appealing to a repressed and natural life, and in doing so we regard power as negative and juridical (top-down power opposed to life). Foucault's response was to imagine ethics not in terms of the normal versus that which is opposed to life, but as formed through practices and powers that were multiple and positive. We would need to distinguish between "life" in its supposedly natural, silent, and innocent form that was produced through modes of knowledge and practice (such as the human and social sciences), and some other "life" that has no being outside the relations of practice and arts or technologies of the self.

By contrast, while being similarly critical of a juridical model, Agamben does not see the sovereign model of power (top-down power opposed to life) as either historically specific or as contingent. Nor does he see the concept of life as modern, normalizing, and only tied to contemporary biopolitical modes of managerialism. Rather, life can be approached immanently both as that which has in Western metaphysics been stripped of all modes of self-formation, and as the potentially sweet and happy life that is no longer opposed to formation and politics. It might seem that biopolitics, or the capacity for life to become managed and manipulated by immediate bureaucratic force, is opposed to the sanctity of life, but this is not so. Life can only be declared as sacred if there is something like bare life. This is made clear in the first volume of the *homo sacer* project when Agamben discusses the case of Karen Quinlan, a young woman who was kept on life support after lapsing into a permanent vegetative state. When life is saved in this manner, because life is deemed to be sacred, we are *not* thinking of a lived, formed, and identified life. What has happened is that the original distinction between *bios* and *zoe*, between recognized political life versus bare life, is still in place, and we have merely shifted value to the life of *zoe* (biological life). Biopolitics takes place on the domain of bodily life, and reduces political disputes to this terrain. The broad contrast would be between the ancient Roman polity, who refused recognition and law to certain bodies and placed them outside the protection of citizens, thus creating the *homo sacer* who could be killed with impunity, and whose life was not worthy of sacrifice, and – by contrast – the fully biopolitical present in which bare life *is* the only human life we can imagine, itself becoming sacred.

One of the possible ways of reading biopolitics, following Foucault, is to be critical of the modern production of "life" as a foundation for knowledge: the notion of some general, knowable, but also enigmatic substrate founds ethics on knowledge and expertise, and precludes the open contestation of decisions and explicit polemics. If anything, this biopolitics of expertise and managerialism has intensified since Foucault's day as new disciplines of cognitive neuro-science, cognitive archaeology, neuro-marketing, neuro-philosophy, and even complex claims made by economic advisors and other strategists, inform "us" of what "we" need to do to preserve and manage life. Oxford University is home to a "future of humanity institute," which supports research for cognitive and moral enhancement.[3] What is *not* questioned is just how this "humanity" is produced as a positive object of knowledge that provides a basis for policy. Opposing this normalization of life, Foucault refers to a counter-memory, one that does not aim to return practice to the ground of life, but would free practice from foundations, thereby liberating the body's relations into a realm of negotiated pleasures. There would still be *norms* or technologies of the self, but not some supposedly *normal* and life-generating ground. One would attend less to the human biological being – less to the general notion of "man" as some species whose being generates imperatives for labor and language – and focus more on practical political being: on selves as generated through relations (both to their own bodies and to others).

It might at first seem that this is what Agamben is also trying to do, critical as he is of the increasingly biopolitical focus of modern politics: we are now all potentially *homo sacer* – not beings recognized through a mediated system of law and judgment, but bodies who have all become just so much manipulable life to be seized and managed. Further, if the state of emergency or state of exception allows sovereign power to free itself from constituted law and instead act directly and at whim, it does so by way of the concept of life: the rise in terrorism of various forms, for example, has been deemed to be such an immediate threat that executive action on any suspected threat to life can justify the decision to kill or intern at will, thereby suspending the once-political or communally-formed realm of law. One way to think of biopolitics, therefore, is as a loss of the political, as a loss of formed and active citizen life that has been displaced by a bureaucracy acting without pause or mediation directly on the body (rather than the body politic).

But a recent maneuver by Agamben's contemporary, Roberto Esposito, should give us pause and prompt us to recalibrate the biopolitical landscape. Drawing on Simone Weil, Esposito argues that there needs to be a reversal of the relation between rights and obligations: presently there is a priority of rights, or the sanctity of the person, and this in turn obliges us to adopt respectful and protective relations to others only insofar as they are persons like us. If the situation were reversed then we might begin with something like an initial relation or indebtedness to others, and it might be from there that rights would follow, requiring procedures and regulations to sustain that fundamental obligation. So far this does seem to accord with the Foucauldian *critical* tendency: begin with relations (or forces, technologies, and practices) and from there ask about the formations of selves – including the particular case of the self who claims rights. This would also seem to reverse liberal anti-foundationalism: in liberalism it is the absence of any law or foundation, and the absence of any normative conception of life, that requires individuals to give a law to themselves. If we are all self-legislating, then we are all granted that prima facie right of sovereign self-determination and would be obliged to allow that self-determination to all others. But the post-biopolitical critique begins with questioning this isolated body, deprived of all relations, who is then able to constitute self and world from a basis of reasoned decisions and formal rule-making: rather, the capacity to speak, legislate, labor, practice, and deliberate is bound up with a whole series of discursive conditions and forces. In the beginning is the relation, not the persons from whom relations unfold. It follows that rights, for the critic of the biopolitical order, would not be the primary political concept; it would make more sense to focus political discussion on the systems, procedures, discourses, and practices that produce some individuals as blessed with rights, while the same discourse of rights and the sanctity of the individual could also be seen to have mutated into a procedure for directly intervening in life (as in cases of the rights of the unborn child, or the executive orders to intervene in cases for the sake of saving human rights – such as the military orders directed toward regime change).

However, if we look to Simone Weil, to whom Esposito makes reference and who was also the subject of Agamben's doctoral dissertation, the criticism of human rights and its attendant concept of persons is not at all based on some notion of the primacy of the political, the relational, and the discursive. Indeed, Weil appeals directly to what might – admittedly with some distortion – be referred to as the biological. It is not the *person*, she argues, who is violated when a body is attacked; it is rather the human – their bodily being, the whole of their

being. Indeed, "person" – despite the rights discourse claim of universality – is a hierarchical and elevating notion. I have rights insofar as I
am a person, but some humans are not persons – or, some humans
appear to not be worthy of personhood. The supposed universality of
rights and personhood elevates humans above their mere biology,
granting them a dignity that at once seems required by their rights but
also guarantees their rights. Insofar as I reason, speak, or demand recognition, I am a person. What this universalizing humanism of persons
does is at once elevate the human species above mere biology at the
same time as it places biology outside the domain of rights and persons.
It is perhaps no wonder then that it is in the name of rights – of the
sacredness and inviolability of persons – that the life of human bodies
has become eminently disposable. One could cite the ways in which
the war on terror's frenzied protection of human rights and dignity has
required immediate internment, executive execution, and direct action
on bodies; but one could think more broadly of the ways in which the
elevation of persons has led to an unquestioning imperative to save
humanity without questioning what grants the man of rights-based
personhood such a prima facie right to exist.

One response to the increasingly autocratic nature of contemporary
protections of both humans and their rights would be to appeal to the
proper humanity that has been betrayed by the discourses of rights and
law that should supposedly guard against the injustices of the present.
But here is where Weil's criticism of human rights and the attendant
concept of personhood make a seemingly counter-intuitive intervention that anticipates some of the complexities of the current theorization of biopolitics. One might think that there would be an opposition
between the human person of rights and the humans who have been
reduced to nothing more than their biological or animal being. For
Weil, it is because ethics in rights discourse depends on the person that
it is at once hierarchical, exclusive, and blind to problems of justice. For
Weil, it is only at the level of the *impersonal* that genuine justice and the
good can be approached. Weil inscribes a whole series of distinctions
in order to criticize rights and personhood, including a distinction
between authors such as Plato (who have some intuition of the impersonal good) and Aristotle, concerned with excellences of talent and
character. The important point for the purposes of making sense of
biopolitics and its strange relation to the rights of the person is to note
a curious relation to human life: from a Foucauldian perspective, the
problem of biopolitics lies in its reliance on life as a justification for
political decisions, and in so doing biopolitics enables discourses of
knowledge, expertise, management, security, and techno-science to
govern populations; rather than an explicit discourse of norms, there
is an increasingly normalizing attention to the species. Esposito, following Weil, argues for an "affirmative biopolitics" that would not rely

on attaching dignity only to persons, but rather involves thinking of an impersonal or even "third-person" life that is not yet the "I" of sovereign speech (Esposito 2012). Agamben is also critical of the biopolitical order that begins by distinguishing political persons from bare life, and then operates increasingly on a depersonalized life, but he takes neither Foucault's nor Esposito's path; he neither wants to think selves as the outcome of practices and relations (Foucault) nor simply reverse values and privilege bare life. Rather, by drawing attention to the *bios/zoe* distinction, Agamben focuses on thresholds and indistinction: this is neither the life of the self nor an impersonal life, but *singular* life, a life that each time is poised between being recognized and remaining silent and unto itself.

3

Homo Sacer, *Sacred Life, and Bare Life*

What is life such that it can become political, formed, and lawful, but also allow itself to be abandoned by law, to appear as nothing more than bare life? Agamben makes the crucial point that ethics and law must be attendant to a life that does not arrive at what is deemed to be its proper potentiality, as though it simply unfolded toward an end that was already actualized. Life – especially in its human and linguistic-social-political form – is defined not by proper potentiality (or Heidegger's *ownmost potentiality*), but by impotentiality. Rather than humans recognizing their freedom, sovereign will, and self-determination, and making life their own, Agamben's ethics focuses on a life that is intimately ours but also distanced from all those modes of action, determination, and command that bring life into identifiable form. Humans can reason, speak, and determine themselves; they can form their lives in accord with a conception of the good. But this potentiality is essentially intertwined with and defined by impotentiality: if language, reason, and political formations simply unfolded in the manner of a determined model or blueprint, then these would not truly be powers or potentials. One possesses a power only if its exercise carries with it a certain *not-doing*. Not only does this revise how we think about our defining capacities and humanity – such that there is an intrinsic negativity in all doing, or a relation to silence in all speech – it also allows us to reconsider the ways in which this threshold between potentiality and impotentiality that is definitive of the human has been divided amongst humans. What is actually a threshold of indifference – or every human's harboring of an impotentiality – has been excluded and set outside. This point is both political and philosophical: politically, should we only grant ethical consideration to life that forms itself, that reasons and fashions itself into some orderly and reflective mode, or might we think ethically about the silent mute life that cannot articulate and express itself? Even more importantly, rather than a sovereign divide between a pure active force that determines itself without remainder, and then an abandoned life that is consigned to a passivity without force of its own, Agamben focuses on the threshold and indistinction of these two tendencies.

What has been deemed to be separate – being and act, active and passive, potentiality and impotentiality – and what has been excluded are ultimately co-determining. This is evidenced throughout the *homo sacer* project, where Agamben argues that political processes of abandoning and excluding "bare life," or a life without self-determining law, are ways of dividing and separating an internal and impossible division. What has been divided by way of philosophy, political theory, and rituals of sacrifice ultimately consists of neither a false difference imposed on unity, nor two distinct terms that have become confused, but a threshold, zone of indistinction, or indifference that humans labor to render coherent. The task of Agamben's project is to expose indistinction and to provide a new philosophy and politics that are less about the relation between being and action, or human and animal, or the polity and its abandoned outside, than exploring whether the threshold might be thought non-relationally. That is, rather than see the political sphere as having emerged from life (a relation of law/system to origin), and rather than see culture or language as the originating force that generates distinct terms, Agamben focuses on the threshold, zone, or border that is neither unified nor differentiated, such as the experience of the speaking human being who is proximate to but never reducible to their own living, animal being. Rather than see the two terms of potentiality and impotentiality as a relation between doing and not-doing, we might see the two as intertwined and indistinguishable. In any genuine action, the relation to not-doing is sustained. This is why Agamben increasingly focuses on inoperativity and suspension:

> To render inoperative the machine that governs our conception of man will therefore mean no longer to seek new – more effective or more authentic – articulations, but rather to show the central emptiness, the hiatus that – within man – separates man and animal, and to risk ourselves in this emptiness: the suspension of the suspension, Shabbat of both man and animal. (O: 92)

Sovereignty and work (both physical and metaphysical) suspend the immanent order to create a separation that subordinates this singular life to some conception of what it properly *is*; to suspend this suspension – to abstain from the ongoing labor of negating this world in favor of a transcendent end would be an immanent Sabbath. Agamben is critical of the paradigm of work and will in both a political and metaphysical sense. Politically, and this is especially so in some forms of Marxism, being a self requires work, labor, and self-activation, whereas Agamben will seek less to include the abandoned in productive life and instead question the notion of selfhood based on action and production. Metaphysically, rather than valorizing being that is complete and requires nothing to bring itself to completion, and then opposing this to action or force that is unimpeded and unconstrained, Agamben works toward theorizing what is neither being nor non-being but that occupies a threshold. Rather than being that simply *is* and then acts, one can think of life that comes into being but always remains intimately involved with not coming into being. Nowhere is this more evident than in the linguistic condition, where we become who we are through speaking, and yet are always never fully expressed or realized by the language that both gives us form but also generates a remainder irreducible to the linguistic system. Whereas modernity has increasingly reduced and abandoned life as a bare existence subject to the force and act of the sovereign, Agamben uses the *homo sacer* project to analyze conditions – ranging from refugees and bodies on life support to ancient legal systems – that expose what he refers to as inclusion/exclusion:

> the refugee is perhaps the only thinkable figure for the people of our time and the only category in which one may see today – at least until the process of dissolution of the nation-state and of its sovereignty has achieved full completion – the forms and limits of a coming political community. It is even possible that, if we want to be equal to the absolutely new tasks ahead, we will have to abandon decidedly, without reservation, the fundamental concepts through which we have so far represented the subjects of the political (Man, the Citizen and its rights, but also the sovereign people, the worker, and so forth) and build our political philosophy anew starting from the one and only figure of the refugee. (MWE: 16)

For it is only by the division between formed, political, active, and recognized life on the one hand and abandoned bare life on the other that anything like the sovereign condition is possible. If law rules over life it is because law exempts itself from life, instituting a division between a life without law – bare life – and a law that may always (*as law*) suspend any of the norms or limits it relies upon to function.

To make sense of this, we might ask whether it would be possible not to have any abandoned or bare life, whether all life could be recognized and included in the self-forming polity. In some respects this is both what Agamben seeks to theorize *and* what he sees as the nightmare of modernity. We have, today, all become potentially *homo sacer*, and this is because the state has *always* had the power to suspend the limits and rule of law and act as immediate force; the division that cast individuals outside the polity as not protected by law has fallen away but in doing so it has exposed the fact that law is truly sovereign because it can suspend itself. The sovereign is sovereign because he is not subject to law. Even if there were no actual *homo sacer* – no refugees, no prisoners on death row, no immigrants in detention centers – there has always been the power of the sovereign to suspend the law that supposedly limits and legitimates his power. By the same token, *another* way of thinking about a life that is not divided between formed life and bare life is Agamben's messianic future in which taking on the recognized form of the citizens of the polity is not a condition of community; one could simply exist, not as this formed and self-constituting sovereign individual, but as simply *this*, mere life as sufficient for ethical comportment with a relation to others that is nothing more than that of being *without* any proper relation. The first stage of the *homo sacer* project is largely diagnostic and seeks to make sense of the present by way of legal and theological archival work, thereby exposing the condition of the present as indebted to an impossible division of life between *bios* and *zoe*. The later volumes of *Homo Sacer* are more positive and find alternative ways of living and of theorizing being that are not hampered by the division between being and act.

Politically, Agamben takes a different path from the liberal project of including forms of life within personhood, and instead asks whether we might not form an ethics based on a life of fragile potentiality-impotentiality that not only does not necessarily attain the dignity of speech and reason, but also always harbors silent and unformed life as the ongoing internal otherness against which it defines itself as regulated. Philosophically, Agamben articulates a counter-ontology, one that does not begin from being and actuality (or what is) and being's proper or improper ways of acting. Instead, he begins from life – which is not a being but a threshold of indistinction, a potentiality for taking on form, where there is no clear border between the life that gives itself order, and a form that is given only as emerging from an ongoing life. It is not that there are beings who then act, and act in the way they do because of the beings that they are. Rather, actions, ways of being, or forms of life unfold from a zone of indistinction; there is no being that is absolutely separate from a doing or taking on of form, but there is also – in any action or forming – something that remains and that is not entirely active. This is clear in language, where we can speak and act only because of a prior system of signs, but where every speaking is also different from the system it activates, and has an expressiveness or "saying" that is singular and outside the system of differences – even if only given *as outside* by way of the system. Concretely, we might contrast something like the pure force of the sovereign – as a pure decision that brings itself into being and has no form or order other than that which it gives itself – with life as at once never fully coincident with action, but also never graspable as some distinct being prior to action. Nor does life possess a proper form that governs the way it unfolds, and yet life nevertheless *is* only in its taking on of a form. Life never simply *is* (*as being*) but comes into being through its way of being lived, and it is in the living of a life that form emerges. The forms or order that life takes on emerge from life, even if life is nothing without the form it takes on, and even if there is always a remainder or *not doing* that is sustained in every doing or bringing into being. Being and non-being, active and passive, life and law would, ideally, not be clearly demarcated entities but lived – as they are – as tendencies that are never fully distinguishable. It is the paradigm of sovereignty as pure act that reigns over a life that is deemed to be without form that institutes a violent divide, between the form of the polity and the abandoned formlessness of bare life.

Agamben's *homo sacer* project begins with a figure from Roman legal theory – a body who could be killed without punishment and could not be sacrificed. As this project develops, Agamben's work takes on a more positive critical role, searching for alternate modes of thinking of life – not by including and recognizing all life (not by grafting person-hood, self-determination, and sovereign individuality to all life), but by searching for traditions that are outside the paradigm of sover-eignty, and outside the politics of inclusion and recognition (and this because inclusion and belonging rely on logics of the proper, and on what something *is*, whereas Agamben emphasizes what something may open itself to be, in a potentiality that is equally impotentiality). Monastic forms of life, for example, were at one and the same time quite different from the self-determining sovereign individual; the sub-mission to order in the monasteries was not the simple adoption of a list of rules: rather, one would form one's life in the way that was analogous to the life of Christ:

> the monastery is perhaps the first place in which life itself – and not only the ascetic techniques that form and regulate it – was presented as an art. This analogy must not be understood, however, in the sense of an aestheticization of existence, but rather in the sense that Michel Foucault seemed to have in mind in his last writings, namely a definition of life itself in relation to a never-ending practice. (HP: 33)

What was adopted was not so much an identity but a manner, or way of living. One would live one's life in this world *as if* the being of this world already harbored another divine potentiality. This is espe-cially so in the Franciscan Order, where the rejection of any ownership of the things of this world – any property – both allowed for everything to be held in common use, but also allowed a distance from the things of this world. To live life in this way, both as a being of this world but always with a sense of distance that would create an immanent "else-where," would be radically messianic; this would be an ethics oriented to "a movement of immanence, or, if one prefers, a zone of absolute indiscernibility between this world and the future world" (TR: 25). Such a condition would be neither passive submission nor active self-fashioning, but a threshold of becoming who one is by taking on a form that was neither a pure form beyond the world *nor* simply this mere life. This is quite different from a modern conception of doing one's duty, where one is nothing more than the work one completes, for it has a far greater relation to a certain passivity or de-creation, or *not* being. Christianity is, then, important for Agamben because as a tradi-tion it oscillates between the sovereign paradigm – a God who is pure act, or sovereign, and has no law other than his supreme force, and who is a being that requires no other being or action in order to be – and another notion of a life that at once takes on a form or is incarnated in this world but always maintains a relation to a certain not doing, or not being reducible to this world.

The figure of Christ exists in Agamben's account as a way of think-ing divine economy, or the relation between a God who simply is (fully and completely without need of action) and a certain living in the world. If *homo sacer* is the stripping of holiness or sacredness or the proper from a life that becomes bare life, opposed to a force that is sovereign, then one might find another possibility within a counter-theological tradition concerned less with a distant God who has left the world to be governed by force, but instead regards the divine as an inflection or manner of living – not a set of rules. There would then be two models of government: a sovereign power that is set apart from the world as pure and indomitable force, and this because life is deemed to be bare life; and then a power that was not radically opposed to mere life, and that emerged from life's potentiality as impotentiality. At its simplest, one might think of a power that was defined as much by not exercising force as it was by power as force. The indistinction of the present, where – as Agamben argues – we might all be *homo sacer*, all potentially bare life exposed to immediate force, is close to another scenario where there is no longer a distinction between the order of the polity and life, and where life can be lived as mere life, as "this" sin-gular existence, without needing sanctification. This more emancipa-tory conception of indistinction – that is not the nightmare scenario of all the world as *homo sacer* – emerges in Agamben's work on St. Paul, who wrote of living in this world – marrying, working, obeying – and yet always with a sense of one's doing these things as if also not doing them. It also emerges in his conception of free or common use, as though one could live and play in this world but as if the world were not one's own, and certainly not one's property. Alternatively, in the conception of duty, one might think of the self who does what she ought to do, and realizes that the taking on of a role gives life form, even if there is also a distance – that is never a clear line – between what one does and who one is. This would be quite different from the detachment that defines modern work, especially where one claims one is "only doing one's job," as if there were a self distinct from a labor that were taken on as an act that was other than one's being.

One way to think of the modern individual is as a self who has the right to sell his or her own labor, which is an extension of a more general tradition of the proper and property. It is as though the world and all life has a proper end, and this becomes increasingly so as everything becomes a mode of property (owned and distributed *because* it is identified – and we can think here of intellectual property and even the ownership of images, technologies, DNA sequences, and so on). Against this notion that one has rule over what is one's own, including one's labor and one's person, Agamben turns the *homo sacer* project to the Franciscan tradition in which the monasteries rejected property, thinking of a world that was there for common use (and this notion of common use is tied to another strand of thinking profanity – not a secularism opposed to the sacred, but a world outside sacred logics):

> what remained untouched was perhaps the most precious legacy of Franciscanism, to which the West must return ever anew to contend with it as its undeferrable task: how to think a form-of-life, a human life entirely removed from the grasp of the law and a use of bodies and of the world that would never be substantiated into an appropriation. That is to say again: to think life as that which is never given as property but only as common use ... Such a task will demand the elaboration of a theory of use – of which Western philosophy lacks even the most elementary principle – and, moving forward from that, a critique of the operative and governmental ontology that continues, under various disguises, to determine the destiny of the human species. (HP: xiii)

Here, we might begin to make sense of why Agamben combines legal theory with theology and a broader question of life. The legal concepts of constituted systems, and the distinction the law must make as an institution between the law and its execution, need to be seen as emerging from a broader tradition in which law is problematic. That is, law should not be regarded, as it is today, as a system that is opposed to a lawless and silent life; nor should life be regarded as either properly ordered (possessing a natural law) or as something purely outside the law. Might we imagine a life that was *common* without being "ours," or as something that we live rather than something that we own or manage? The purpose of Agamben's historical genealogy, which is to describe an increasing abandonment of life by the law, to the point where modern sovereignty can reduce all life to an animalistic, blind and abject target for immediate force, is to highlight a historical and always persistent indistinction. Law is never pure, formal, or definitively sovereign; law becomes law, and opposed to violence and lawlessness, by an event of violence, whereby law exempts itself from the life over which it dominates. Law is not the pure ideal that must occasionally deploy violence to sustain itself, for law must always work by way of force to exclude the chaotic unformed life that is its origin (producing it *as chaotic*). In the sovereign paradigm, life exists as that which defines law by being outside the law.

Against this abandonment of bare life, Agamben poses the question of life that would not be that which law seized, nor that which could only be recognized if it took on the dignity and reason of law. The *homo sacer* project finds life at its most abandoned, and in its radically ethical potential, in a similar moment of lawless life: as bare life, stripped of any right to the law, *homo sacer* typifies the extreme violence of a law that can suspend its limit at any moment. As mere life, considered not as deprived of law but as no longer defined as that which law excludes, the possibility of life beyond the law offers a new future. Life might be thought of as mere life with a potentiality for taking on form, which could neither be seen as pure form (such as the sovereign self-constituting individual) nor as absolutely bare life. It is precisely when life appears as singular, silent, and impersonal that one might begin to think of a law that would not be that of imposed force, and that would not divide the sacred from the abandoned.

The *Sacer* of *Homo Sacer*

If the way the sacred has functioned has been to subordinate the fragile becoming of the world to some external and stable good toward which it ought to tend, then this has implications far beyond the religious sphere. It is for this reason that Agamben focuses on the function of *homo sacer* in ancient Roman law, where *sacer* is at once outside the law (in not being suitable for sacrifice, and in being able to be killed without penalty) and yet also crucial to the law's creation of its own limit. *Sacer* here is outside, not in the sense of being divinely transcendent, but in the sense of being at the threshold of the law – what the law expels from itself. It is the sacred, and its ambivalence in the figure of *homo sacer*, that reveals something about potentiality. If we think of this life as properly oriented to some external divine good, then life in itself (as mere life) is also merely secular, redeemable only by something beyond itself; life is thought of as a potential that has its being in a proper good (an actuality). It follows that a life that does not orient itself to the law, but exists as mere life, would be abandoned by the law, cast out as bare life. And yet life is the very medium through which law posits itself and operates. The fact that life today has been deemed sacred, or *sacer*, occurs only because life becomes that which is managed, saved, or operated upon by the good of the law (a law which is other than the fragile potentiality of life).

Agamben's work is neither oriented toward returning the sense of sacredness back to some original conception of the transcendent divine, nor of rendering what is secular and ordinary sacred. To claim that every life is sacred, or to argue for the sacredness of human person-hood, precludes us from thinking about life in its singularity; rather than behaving ethically toward others because we recognize the sacred-ness of "life," Agamben asks whether there might not be forms of ethics and politics that were oriented to *this* mere life, in its singularity. His is not a project of rendering the body and humanity divine. Rather, the bigger ethical-political problem involves asking if we could live without the sacred and sanctification, without a border between the proper and the improper or the pure and the defiled. In this respect, Agamben's work differs markedly from Georges Bataille, who granted an impor-tance to the uniquely human capacity to create a border between the sacred and the profane, or to organize life through a prohibition and a limit (which might then be transgressed or destroyed). For Bataille, whom Agamben refers to frequently on questions of the sacred and the proper, there would be a revolutionary mastery and liberation that fol-lowed from a violation of the very limits by which human life had ordered and mastered itself. Or, to state it in terms of Bataille's theory of transgression and evil, there might be an absolute mastery or sover-eignty that would follow from freeing oneself from all claims of order and limited sovereignty, no longer relying on "power over," but achiev-ing pure force.

For Agamben, the problem with such an account of the sacred and transgression is twofold: it traces the structure of political life back to something psychological (the self and its desires), rather than investi-gating the distinction rigorously and by way of terminological struc-tures of power and politics. Second, it begins with ambivalence, such as a desire for mastery and its transgression, rather than accounting for the distinction between sacred and profane that transgression dis-turbs. Agamben argues that early twentieth-century thought inherited a "scientific mythologeme" that precluded numerous writers – Marcel Mauss, Claude Lévi-Strauss, Émile Durkheim, Georges Bataille, and Sigmund Freud – from genuinely accounting for the logic of the sacred (which, for Agamben, requires genuine legal-political analysis and not speculation on psychological origins). Rather than explain the sacred by referring back to some claim about human psychology, Agamben sees what counts as human as enabled by the inclusive–exclusive logics of the sacred that continually divide proper from improper. For Agamben, genuine theology concerns the revealed word, or how the world comes to be through language – how relation and distinction emerge. Beginning from a genealogy of Roman law, the *homo sacer* project increasingly focuses on the thresholds of indistinction through which political personhood is constituted (KG: 188). If the subject of the polity emerges from the borders and exclusions of the sacred, then it would be mistaken to begin analysis from the human self, explaining religion by way of some personal experience of ambivalence. The assumption that "the sacred" is nothing more than feeling is on a par with the general reduction of properly political questions to the operation of nothing more than "life":

> What is at work here is the psychologization of religious experience (the "disgust" and "horror" by which the cultured European bourgeoisie betrays its own unease before the religious fact)…Here, in a concept of the sacred that completely coincides with the concept of the obscure and the impenetrable, a theology that had lost all experience of the revealed word celebrated its union with a philosophy that had abandoned all sobriety in the face of feeling. That the religious belongs entirely to the sphere of psychological emotion, that it essentially has to do with shivers and goose bumps – this is the triviality that the neologism "numinous" had to dress up as science … An assumed ambivalence of the generic religious category of the sacred cannot explain the juridico-political phenomenon to which the most ancient meaning of the term *sacer* refers. On the contrary, only an attentive and unprejudiced delimitation of the respective fields of the political and the religious will make it possible to understand the history of their intersection and complex relations. It is important, in any case, that the originary juridico-political dimension that presents itself in *homo sacer* not be covered over by a scientific mythologeme that not only explains nothing but is itself in need of explanation. (HS: 78–80)

Agamben argues against Bataille's celebration of transgression, whereby liberation would follow from a violation of the limits of sovereignty and the sacred. Strategies of transgression maintain the structure of sovereignty, keeping the border with the sacred and the profane, and then celebrating the elevated mastery of violating the very limits that maintain human normativity. The self sacrifices its ongoing identity in order to achieve a force. What is required is an overcoming of sacred and sacrificial logics. This would be achieved, in part, by retrieving an "experience of the revealed word." Rather than accepting the split and tension (between purity and defilement) of the word *sacer*, and rather than referring back to some "feeling," one should consider the indistinction that it covers over. Why does *sacer* function to signal *both* life that is abandoned and lost to the law, *and* sacredness that elevates a holiness or divinity or power above mere life? Perhaps this is because life *as such* has a double tendency or tension, to be mere life *and* to form some relationship to itself in terms of what is not yet actualized but remains potential.

For Agamben, a genuinely futural thought would not intensify transgression but would confront the possibility of a life that did not have a boundary of propriety that would invite transgression, not an acceptance of law's distance, but a closing of the door that indicated a divine distance. This requires rethinking the relation between modern political structures, which have supposedly abandoned the sacred in order to operate immanently (without the need for some external good), and traditional cultures, which have a supposedly mythic or mystical attachment to some divine transcendence. One might think of this in terms of Kantian modernity: Kant argued that we cannot know the good, for concepts such as the good are infinite and can be *thought* but not experienced; the structure that follows from this acceptance of not knowing transcendence is negative. We know that there must be law, but not what that law might be. Accordingly, thinkers like Jacques Derrida write about a "justice to come," for no actual worldly justice could exhaust the infinite demand of justice. By contrast, Agamben asks us to abandon the structure of abandonment: let us *not* think of this world as radically distant from justice and the law, but commit to the task of immanence where life is not the life that realizes a possible form, but "a" life with no form other than that which it brings into being. The relation between immanence and transcendence – and the problematic nature of this relation – is for Agamben an "aporia" that can only be dealt with if we confront the structure of sacredness that still determines contemporary borders of the polity, and the bare life that is still abandoned in the same manner that characterized the ancient figure of *homo sacer*. For this reason, Agamben's *homo sacer* project is at once a historical genealogy, but it is also less concerned with a specific actual history and more with how and why the division of the sacred emerges, and why the indistinction from which it is generated becomes an ongoing labor for politics and ethics.

The sacred covers over a threshold that is only experienced after the event of its distinction; moving toward a secular present keeps this opposition in place. Agamben's project is therefore not a secularism that denies the sacred, but a genealogy that will uncover a profane world that is not defined in opposition to the sacred:

> This is why those who try to make the world and life sacred again are just as impious as those who despair about its profanation. This is why Protestant theology, which clearly separates the profane world from the divine, is both wrong and right: right because the world has been consigned irrevocably by revelation (by language) to the profane sphere; wrong because it will be saved precisely insofar as it is profane. (CC: 90)

Agamben's new politics is less oriented toward a refusal of transcendence than it is in deriving transcendence from immanence; in this respect, his new messianism lies not in denying the divine but in seeing this life as sufficient without sanctification or legitimation granted from elsewhere. This new immanent messianism requires an account of the sacred's emergence and ambivalence, rather than beginning with the sacred as an explanatory mechanism.

For Agamben, to argue that this original conception of the sacred emerges from a religious past that subsequently becomes rationalized in law fails to confront the genesis of the sacred as such, and also assumes a historical distinction between religion and law that he seeks to challenge. The reason why theology remains pertinent is precisely because today's secularism is defined in opposition to the sacred, whereas Agamben wants to find an alternate path of the profane. Indeed, the assumption of an original religious or spiritual value from which law might derive is one of Agamben's frequently targeted presuppositions. We cannot look back to something like the constitution of the sacred as an origin, for the sacred is split from within, and it is the sacred that requires explanation rather than offering itself as some means to clarify what follows. Agamben increasingly insists that all distinctions refer back to a threshold, and this threshold itself is disclosed in the passage from non-relational to relational that is enabled by a certain type of language, a language that addresses power, or that does not speak but pledges to speak of a power of truth that is not its own. In the beginning, prior to law and religion, is the sacrament of language:

> the magico-religious sphere does not logically preexist the oath, but it is the oath, as originary performative experience of the word, that can explain religion (and law, which is closely connected with it)....
>
> The oath can function as a sacrament of power insofar as it is first of all the *sacrament of language*. This original *sacratio* that takes place in the oath takes the technical form of the curse, of the *politike ara* that accompanies the proclamation of the law. Law is, in this sense, constitutively linked to the curse, and only a politics that has broken this original connection with the curse will be able one day to make possible another use of speech and the law. (SL: 66)

If the law is possible because of language's power to *curse*, to set something apart by way of violent positing, then "another use" would require language to be poised on a threshold rather than instituting a border. In Roman law the figure of *homo sacer* (who could be killed but not sacrificed) indicates an aporia or structural incoherence in legal and political thought. By casting certain bodies outside the polity, marking them as insufficiently worthy to be offered as sacrifice, Roman law secured the sacred not so much as a divine realm beyond human life but more as a way of dividing humanity into a bare abandoned life, which was then opposed to a properly political-legal life. The *homo sacer* was not therefore completely inhuman but operated to distinguish, from within the human species, the proper from the improper – bare life from political life. On the one hand, there would be the citizen, recognized by way of determining predicates (*bios*), and, on the other hand, an impersonal life (*zoe*) cast out beyond the law. As a comparison between Roman law and the present, we might consider the terrorist who is deprived of due process in the detention camp, or the refugee in an immigration center awaiting possible inclusion in a polity that may or may not save her bodily being on the basis of human rights; these individuals are "bare life," not included in the constituted freedoms and protections of the polity, and yet existing at the borders of the polity as its limit.

Similarly, the patient in the hospital on life support is also at the immediate mercy of political intervention, often with panels of specialists deciding whether the body still possesses the sacred quality of "life." What is not considered is the singularity of "a" life, but some abstract sacred quality of "life," that the polity preserves as sacred or abandons. Agamben's point is to stress that the border between biological being and included political being is *not clear* and that the wars over the sacredness and inviolability of life appeal to a precarious distinction that frequently breaks down, and that the complexity of the distinction appears as such precisely when it breaks down, or does not operate. That is, when any body (as happens in contemporary biopolitics) can be reduced to bare life, then both the border between the human and inhuman, and the very concept of the human as such, is exposed in its *impotentiality*; if a body and all that makes it human can equally be deprived of speech and personhood, then what counts as properly human needs also to be considered alongside all that has been abandoned and excluded as improper.

Today, when certain individuals are deemed to be expendable without trial or without due process – as in cases of executive orders following terrorist threats – we see life split from within: life is at once so immediately sacred as to warrant any means for its preservation, while at the same time life becomes that which might be expelled or reduced to so much bare and manageable matter. In the death camps of Nazi Germany, humans were divided from the population and the polity precisely on the spurious basis of the purity of life: Nazi discourse appealed to the health and integrity of the species, and exterminated those whose bodily being threatened "man" – not only Jews, but homosexuals and other bodies deemed to be expendable and disposable for the sake of saving everything that made human life sacred. The appeal to the German *Volk* as that which must be preserved at all costs was at once biological (based on spurious concepts of racial integrity) and sacred, relying on a mythic nationalism of German exceptionalism. One might say that all forms of racism, including Nazi anti-Semitism, are not violations of the sanctity of human life so much as they are enabled by the logic of the sacred now transferred to the domain of bodily life. This might also explain why the sacrificial term "holocaust" was used to describe genocide. The sanctity of life was maintained and presupposed and then used to expel what is deemed to be not sacred in life: without a reliance on the value of some sanctified ideal of the human being there would not be a possibility of excluding certain forms of life as less than human.

If I grant worth to life because of some ideal of personhood or humanity (or what counts as *properly* human or as proper life based on a conception of race or the species), then I also assume that life as such, bare life, has no value without the added value of some substance of humanity. I save and recognize what I deem to be human, even if what would truly be ethical would be to respond generously to suffering, even if the life I were witnessing appeared to me as not fully human, *or if the life I encountered were so afflicted as to have fallen into a less than human state of mere life.* Writing about Auschwitz, Agamben does not respond to the condition and the horror of the camps by insisting on the inviolable dignity and rights of the human being, nor on the sacredness of life. Instead it is the capacity of the human *not* to bear all the predicates that have defined humans in their actuality – speech, reason, ethics, dignity – that discloses both the impotentiality of what we have taken to be essentially human, and the need for a new ethics that does not rely on the sacredness of humanity but can be ethical in the absence of the sacred. It is when the human is reduced to an animal, while also being perceived as lacking or being deprived of humanity, that the very ethics of the proper is thrown into profound question (Eaglestone 2002).

We have only known life as already divided into a properly formed humanity versus an abandoned animality; this opposition has been used to divide humans from each other, but also divides every human within herself. One becomes a person by being set against one's own animality; one's political and human being is achieved through recognition, identity, and personhood – certainly not through impersonal life, and yet, as the institutions and conceptions of personhood suffer attrition, all we are left with is the remainder that is the negation of political life. The distinction between *bios* (or a properly human and active life) and *zoe* (or a life that simply "is" and does not determine itself) structures every individual, every polity, and sets certain bodies and beings outside the polity, even if what once counted as *bios* is less and less available. If we could question that distinction by confronting the "zone of indistinction" or remainder that emerges increasingly in late modernity, when political life becomes increasingly biopolitical and impersonal, we might no longer have some notion of a pre-political "bare" life as such that would be the basis of the sanctity of life.

How do we think about, to take just one example, humans who are on life support? They are at once human, but are left without speech, reason, self-determination, action, or affect; their existence is neither reducible to mere animality, and yet all the tokens that we apply to human persons are missing. Should these individuals be abandoned, set outside politics? Increasingly, such bodies become the site for profound political struggles, evidencing that what has come to matter more and more politically is not *how* one lives (as though life and being human were a capacity that may or may not realize itself) but life itself, such that life is now divided between violable or non-violable, life and non-life. It is for this reason that new disciplines of bio-ethics have been formed, while hospitals and researchers are subject to ethics guidelines; politics takes place within and across the threshold of life and its institutions, while ethics is increasingly concerned less with relations among persons and more and more with bodily life. It is now the body itself that becomes the battleground for political wrangling, as has become increasingly evident in a series of political skirmishes in the United States including the supposed "war on women" of 2013 (where Democrats and Republicans disputed access to reproductive and birth control medical technologies). The body politic is no longer the state that sets *homo sacer* outside its range of law and recognition, excluding bare life from what counts as citizenship; rather, the body is immediately political and potentially *homo sacer* in its being available for direct management. A whole series of abandoned lives – ranging from prisoners on death row to bodies in persistent vegetative states – become objects of political dispute, with the terrain of battle being fully biopolitical. In 2014, the United States encountered a series of problems with the death penalty. Because pharmaceutical companies objected to the use of their products in lethal injections, various states had to seek alternative mixes of substances to perform lethal injections; subsequent outrage regarding botched and lengthy executions focused primarily on the bodily responses of the prisoner. The pros and cons of the death penalty were fought less at the level of justice and what counts as a good life or good polity (or the ways in which life is brought into being and relation), and more over the physical body of the condemned and its responses to injected substances, as well as the most efficient or compassionate ways to take a body from life to death.[1] Debates over the right to life, euthanasia, the limits of compassion in executing prisoners and the broader questions of what counts as life both evidence the extent to which the life of politics is bare life (a life cast outside the law that becomes law's substance) and demonstrate that the border between *bios* and *zoe* exists today precisely in the abandonment of *bios* or the formed life that emerges from mere life.

Agamben therefore directs the entire *homo sacer* project to examining this threshold, remainder, or zone of indistinction between mere life and the formed political life that comes into being through time. Even though he writes mournfully of us all being *homo sacer* in a world that is increasingly lived with an immediacy without sense, he does not seek to restore life's meaning or form but rather to find an ethics that does not require a transcendent and proper system of relations. Such a new politics would regard life as neither that over which law rules immediately and without question, nor as that which bears a law or propriety as its natural end:

> The messianic life is the impossibility that life might coincide with a predetermined form, the revoking of every *bios* in order to open it to the *zoe tou Iesou*. And the inoperativity that takes place here is not mere inertia or rest; on the contrary, it is the messianic operation par excellence. (KG: 249)

4

New Ethics, New Politics

Agamben often makes the claim for a "new politics," while other related phrases such as "coming community," "inoperativity," and even the very notion of "a" sovereign paradigm, suggest that his work seeks to mark a radical break with the broad tradition of Western thought. His work is primarily futural, not only because it locates the present within a long and sustained history of sovereignty that it seeks to surpass, and not only because of rhetorical gestures such as claiming a "new" politics or "coming" community, but also because he simply refuses to engage with what a critical reader might deem to be *the* pressing concerns of the present. Agamben is not only silent on questions of race, sexuality, ethnicity, climate change, and the highly specific form of neoliberal capitalism, but many of his central gestures appear regressive. He returns to a problematic opposition between "man" and animal. He reinscribes tired tropes of femininity – such as the figure of the nymph who is between biology and spirit, and who in turn is likened to "the Jew" – and he accepts uncritical categories such as "the Jew," "the" *Musselman,* and even "poetry." Although a number of astute thinkers have turned to Agamben to theorize topics such as race, sexuality[1] (if not gender), human rights (for all Agamben's diagnostic critique of the term), and colonialism, his entire corpus sustains a predominantly uncritical use of the term "man" (Edkins 2000). Worse still, Agamben refers to figures of the feminine (such as the nymph, or the female forms of advertising) as though one of the ways of thinking beyond "man" might be to take up a received conception of the un-self-conscious feminine. Writing after Walter Benjamin, he declares:

> For a long time now, advertising, pornography, and television have habituated us to those mutant beings who linger ceaselessly between individual and class and vanish utterly into a series precisely in their

most characteristic idiosyncrasies. That young woman who smiles at us while drinking a beer, that other who rolls her hips so mischievously while running on the beach, they belong to a people whose members, like the angels of medieval theology (each of whom individually constitutes a species), elude the distinction between the original and the replica; and the fascination they exert on us is due in large part to that capacity (properly "angelic") to make themselves typical through that very thing which appears to belong to them exclusively, to replicate and to confuse themselves with a new, unique example, each time without remainder. The exclusive character becomes the principle of serial reproduction: such is the definition of the type (which, at once, reveals its proximity to the commodity). In fact, familiarity with this process is immemorial: it is at the basis of the most ancient expedients from which woman draws her power of seduction, namely make-up and fashion. Both circumscribe the ineffable uniqueness of the individual body in order to transform its singular traits into a serial principle. (EC: 20)

Despite the uptake, expansion, and criticism of Agamben's work through questions of race and gender, his focus has – if anything – retreated from the edgy political question of states of emergency, camps, and political community, to questions of duty, and the management of the world that would have an immanent sense of the divine. So, rather than condemn Agamben for being arcane and blind to the important issues of his time, and rather than smuggle him back into heaven by extending his work to the questions of race and sexuality that he ignores, one might argue that his conception of the relation between life and politics necessarily precludes him from questions of race, sex, gender, and ecology. If it is the case that humans as speaking animals are distanced from a life that they have always violently excluded in order to recognize themselves as human, then moving toward more diverse forms of recognition and identity would only intensify the failure to consider the indifferent threshold between life and its expressions. Many have criticized Agamben's use of the figure of Bartleby as a political exemplar, as though passivism and not doing would be forms of retreat (Power 2010), and would endorse the humanist alibi of markers such as sex and gender ultimately being illusions that cover over an ultimately general "life" that "we" all share. The only way to read Agamben's work that does not align him with a conservative Catholic nostalgia that would regain a paradise that is only known by way of being lost, and that would be other than all worldly forms of good that must be set aside or sacrificed, would be to read Agamben on his own terms. This would require setting aside or rendering inoperative the current political markers that enable politics – the politics of agonistics amongst competing selves and forces – and would take seriously a suspension of all the ways in which life has only entered politics in terms of already formed critical terms.

Might there not be a new ethics that does not subject life's potentiality to some external value of the proper person (or the sovereign individual, or a "we" constituted as a recognizing and self-constituting community) but that is also not based on the management or sacredness of the bare life that was defined (against *bios*) as pre-political? To make sense of this question within Agamben's corpus, we must see the way he negotiates the thinkers to whom he is (critically) indebted: Heidegger, Benjamin, Arendt, Foucault, and Simone Weil. From Heidegger and Heidegger's reading of Aristotle, Agamben takes up the concept of potentiality: rather than think of humans as unfolding through time to actualize their proper form, potentiality is something that exceeds actuality. For Heidegger, the task of thinking is to seize potentiality and accept one's "ownmost" or authentic future: if we are *not* given any proper form other than that which we bring into existence, then we define ourselves in our own relation to the world. For Agamben, by contrast, the potentiality that exceeds any actuality always remains as impotentiality, and rather than self-definition he focuses on a way of relating to others that accepts their life as such, without demanding that life seize hold of itself and give itself form. The forming of life is not so much an achievement of the sovereign subject as it is an openness to what does not yet have proper form. From both Judaic and Christian traditions, Agamben creates a curious amalgam of ethics that has been criticized both for being overly passive or acquiescent in its tragic acceptance that revolution occurs only in the moment of extreme catastrophe (Whyte 2013), and for being unthinkingly Christian and Eurocentric in writing almost as if the Holocaust or Shoah was a necessary sacrifice in order to fulfill metaphysics (Librett 2007), and for accepting the figure of the Muselmann or Muslim as the exemplary figure of dehumanization, thereby erasing the broader history of colonialism. Such criticisms indicate a difficult tension in Agamben's work, which is partly to do with his genealogy that is at once Heideggerian in its focus on potentiality and actively retrieving the task of thinking, and Judaic in its almost tragic acceptance of enigmatic alterity, *and* Christian in its Franciscan attention to living in this world without a sense of owning this world, plus being indebted to St. Paul's notion of living in this world while also attendant to a messianic dimension that is not of this world.

From Benjamin, he maintains the revolutionary task of suspending the state of exception, or arriving at a world where the door of law is closed once and for all, and yet he also sustains a sense of life as that which will be redeemed only if one abandons the drive for a life that needs something other than itself in order to be redeemed. One of the more curious and less visible debts in Agamben's work is also to the work of Simone Weil (Ricciardi 2009). Weil, highly critical of the concept of person (which relied on recognition of certain predicates, and attributed human dignity only to those who attained a certain normative ideal), argued for a radically impersonal ethics directed at feeling compassion for the bodily suffering of other humans; her ethics of "de-creation" opposes the sovereign subject who is nothing other than his own will, and instead focuses on the openness to grace.

While Agamben does seem to grant ethical worth to the experience of others in their fragile singularity, he is also critical of basing ethics simply on the bare life that is *opposed* to personhood or the political subject. Rather than endorse the human life that is abandoned when we only recognize the dignity of persons, he pays attention to those thresholds between personhood (the self who can speak and say "I") and the life that is felt or lived as a silent remainder. One way of reading the multiple valences and tensions in Agamben's work is to diagnose his writing as oddly composed of disparate voices – from Pauline and Franciscan Christianity to Judaic mysticism. Another, and more fruitful approach, would be to see the tensions in Agamben's work as having to do with the difficult task he sets himself of forming an ethics that is neither grounded on some pre-political life *nor* on some proper form that is not of this world. By focusing on the threshold from which political life emerges, he aims to avoid following Hannah Arendt's path of lamenting the ways in which contemporary politics now foregrounds the material and laboring life that was once deemed to be pre-political, and yet he does not uncritically accept this life as a positive ground for an affirmative biopolitics. Language is one of the ways one might think about this threshold, for it is language that is at once the milieu of political, communicative being, at the same time as it can – in certain cases – expose a life and potentiality that is not that of the recognized and active political subject.

In his earlier work Agamben had focused on poetry and its relation to philosophy to interrogate a fundamental scission that is exposed when one asks about the object of poetry:

> Access to what is problematic in these questions is barred by the forgetfulness of a scission that derives from the origin of our culture and that is usually accepted as the most natural thing – that goes, so to speak, without saying – when in fact it is the only thing worth interrogating. The scission in question is that between poetry and philosophy, between the poetic word and the word of thought. This split is so fundamental to our cultural tradition that Plato could already declare it "an ancient enmity." According to a conception that is only implicitly contained in the Platonic critique of poetry, but that has in modern times acquired a hegemonic character, the scission of the word is construed to mean that poetry possesses its object without knowing it while philosophy knows its object without possessing it. In the West, the word is thus divided between a word that is unaware, as if fallen from the sky, and enjoys the object of knowledge by representing it in beautiful form, and a word that

has all seriousness and consciousness for itself but does not enjoy its object because it does not know how to represent it.

The split between poetry and philosophy testifies to the impossibility, for Western culture, of fully possessing the object of knowledge (for the problem of knowledge is a problem of possession, and every problem of possession is a problem of enjoyment, that is, of language). (S: xvi–xvii)

Whereas the focus in *Stanzas* (published in Italian in 1977) is on poetry cases of language, Agamben later in *Remnants of Auschwitz* turns to testimony, for it is precisely here – when a person desperately tries to speak their irreducible suffering and witnessing (or what they alone have lived in an unrepeatable present) – that the disjunction between language (or meaning, or general repeatable sense) and saying (*this* person here in their suffering) is manifest and fugitive. The title of Agamben's book on Auschwitz refers to *remnants*, or that which cannot be subsumed by the calculative rationale that dominated the camps but remains as that which suffers and which seeks to speak and be heard; the figure of the remainder also indicates an opposition between witnessing and the archive (and it is here that he is critical of movements like deconstruction that remain within the order of the letter and inscription and only see what is not inscribed as a negated outside). Agamben is insistent that what language marks out, the specific and singular events it denotes, bears an excess or remainder that is not captured in sense. Here, in the remainder or excess – either in the saying of poetry that is not the designated object, or in the life that is not caught up in recognition and speech – there lies the potentiality for a new politics. But the life that he sees as the basis for a new ethics is *not* the life that has been abandoned or set outside language and the polity.

For this reason, Agamben is critical of modes of thought that reverse the Platonic denigration of work and manual labor by valorizing productive life. In this respect his work is quite different from two of his Italian contemporaries: unlike Robert Esposito, who follows Weil in arguing for a politics that is impersonal (and that is a "positive biopolitics" that embraces the basis of life), Agamben's mere life is neither biological nor impersonal, but is experienced as a threshold. (The threshold between humans and animals, between humans and the divine, between the person and mere life, between speech and noise – all these are intra-human, which is also to say that they cannot be parsed into good and evil.) Indeed, an ethics is to be found not by including forms of excluded (laboring, bodily, impersonal) life, or favoring such forms but by occupying – in law and language – the zone of indistinction where life is neither silent and passive, nor fully captured in language and action. Refugees, prisoners on death row, bodies on life support, sufferers of trauma who cannot articulate what they have witnessed: such liminal and problematic states are to be resolved more by exposing thought and experience to conditions where the human touches upon what seems most intimate and most unbearable, than by recognizing us all as human or by celebrating life.

Unlike Antonio Negri, Agamben does not locate a purely productive and emancipatory power in the life from which the polity emerges, and in this respect he remains closer to Martin Heidegger for whom the power of a being *not* to arrive at its ownmost essence is constitutive rather than accidental. Rather than regard life as something that properly unfolds to arrive at what it essentially is (as though there were simply life or being that went through time), Agamben sees existence through time and the impotentiality as "essential." What is essential is the lack of any essence. Humans are not so much *beings* that come to use language; rather, it is by way of speaking that they exist as always distanced from their own life, which they must nevertheless continue to suffer or witness. For reasons that are similar, but not identical, to those of Heidegger, Agamben questions the entire history of Western thought and its privileging of being. For Heidegger, "Being" is not something that simply "is" and that happens to go through time or come into appearance; being *is* its unfolding through time, *and* is as much given in *non-appearing* as appearing. For something to appear or be revealed, it must emerge from hiddenness, and to accept this is to accept that being and non-being or not-appearing are not opposites but "equiprimordial." For Heidegger, "Being" cannot be grasped or held in any single term, for it is the very "essence," of what is to come into existence, and in this respect being and non-being are not opposites but are intimately enfolded into each other. The task for Heidegger, notoriously, became one of returning thinking to the "nearness" of Being – away from the distancing technologies and systems that had reduced the relation to Being's disclosure to one of calculative rationality. As more of Heidegger's notebooks are published, the anti-Semitism of his philosophy appears to be more and more structural rather than accidental. Heidegger associated Jewish culture with a certain distance from authentic dwelling, a contamination of thinking by an element that is not proximate to the house of Being. In some respects Agamben's task of returning thought to its practical calling does seem to echo a demand for a certain nearness and an overcoming of a Western tradition that has forgotten its proper site of dwelling and emergence, and it is precisely for this reason that Agamben is critical of deconstruction and its insistent refusal of all forms of proximity. However, Agamben does not simply reiterate claims for an overcoming of tradition that would retrieve authentic dwelling.

Agamben also writes of finding some way of thinking other than an opposition of being and non-being; and he also writes of thinking of potentiality and impotentiality non-oppositionally, precisely because if there were nothing other than power then everything would already be fulfilled and as it is. But this is not so, and everything that lives or has a power becomes the power that it is by sustaining a power of not-doing. But whereas the language of being and potentiality are metaphysical and ontological terms, Agamben locates the non-oppositional or non-relational in life, and more often than not in *human life*. On the one hand, there seems to be an exceptional status granted to humans who, in speaking, aim to secure a stability and sense to the singular and fleeting; and yet, on the other hand, Agamben defines this exception as a failure, and a violence that we need to confront rather than explain away. It is perhaps more accurate to say that Agamben does not regard humans as exceptional so much as animals who speak in order to deny their animality and therefore suffer an ongoing linguistic state of exception. The failure to divide the properly human from the inhuman is constitutive or revelatory of what the human "is," which is not to say that there is some human essence that is indefinable, but that the labor of defining, speaking, or naming – in its failure – "is" human.

For this reason, Agamben will not be able simply to find "life" as some positive outside to ideals of the human person:

> Every attempt to rethink the political space of the West must begin with the clear awareness that we no longer know anything of the classical distinction between zoe and bios, between private life and political existence, between man as a simple living being at home in the house and man's political existence in the city. This is why the restoration of classical political categories proposed by Leo Strauss and, in a different sense, by Hannah Arendt can have only a critical sense. There is no return from the camps to classical politics. (HS: 187–8)

Agamben is indebted to Hannah Arendt (Adler 2014) and her history of charting the human polity's lamentable division of laboring life from the supposedly properly cognitive work of the philosopher, and yet – far more than Arendt or any other thinker before him – Agamben is less concerned with destroying or deconstructing oppositions and more with experiencing these differences in their indistinction. Whereas deconstruction accepts something like an event of differentiation (writing, trace, gramma) that we only know after the event of its having been, Agamben seizes upon experiences that allow the experience of difference and threshold. In this respect, if his corpus is defined critically against sovereignty and associated logics of exclusion and division (ranging from the moral distinctions between proper and improper to metaphysical distinctions between potentiality and impotentiality), it is equally defined by attention to experiences of the threshold, or to singularity.

This insistence on the simple existence of life that is not defined by a language or essence that would determine what it ought to be is a way of reversing the theology of essence and existence. God – at least according to Aquinas – is pure existence and cannot be limited or determined by any essence. God is not defined or determined by any essence, form, or meaning, and in this respect one might think of God as pure force, or a capacity to be that is absolutely unconstrained by any definition (Zartaloudis 2010). He is the God of negative theology, for whom any predicate or determination would be a limitation. It would follow that such a God could not be experienced as such, but only thought of as *other than* the delimited and determined beings of this world. His law would not be what it is because it answers to some criterion of the good, but just be the absolute force it is. All the beings that God creates are examples *of* an essence; so that they ought to fulfill their proper potential (becoming what they ought to be): evil would be the failure of something to take on the form that is its essence or ideal. Although theology has various and contentious ways of parsing the relation between God's pure existence and the determination of essence, it is nevertheless the case that the world is what it is because it is the incarnation or example of an essence or sense, whereas God in his pure existence cannot be captured by essence. The world then is not divine because of its existence or its simple "thisness," but only as an example or instance *of* some thing. In its contemporary form this logic plays out in the negativity of language, where we can only know things *as* some instance of a prior meaning, with the pre-linguistic only given as pre-linguistic after the event of language.

By contrast, Agamben argues for an existence of all that composes the world, *not as God's fulfilling of essences* as though the good and meaning of life were elsewhere, but as existence without essence – a pure taking place. This would mean that things are not examples, instances, or incarnations of essences, but are the things that they are – thus generating a logic of the paradigm, where things display for themselves what they are as simply "thus":

> God or the good or the place does not take place, but is the taking-place of the entities, their innermost exteriority. The being-worm of the worm, the being-stone of the stone is divine. That the world is, that something can appear and have a face, that there is exteriority and non-latency as the determination and the limit of every thing: this is the good. Thus, precisely its being irreparably in the world is what transcends and exposes every worldly entity...the good is not somewhere else; it is simply the point at which they grasp the taking-place proper to them, at which they touch their own non-transcendent matter. (CC: 15)

Agamben's work suggests less that we critique the world as it is by seizing upon the promise of another world (whether that be a world of the living labor of Marxism where it is work rather than transcendent ideas that open to a better politics, or a world of justice to come), and rather suggests that suspending the abandonment of the world allows us to overcome the state of exception. Rather than see life as that which is insufficient or never fully answering to what it ought to be, one might think of the life that is *not* subsumable by essence as a messianic opening to a different time: this would not accept things as they simply are, nor promise a proper future, but would see in every now or singularity that everything we experience is encountered as a generality (yet one more person) but also never reducible to personhood. Could we think of happiness, not as Aristotle does as a well-formed life, but by way of life "as such"?

If life no longer becomes divided from itself by being set over against its proper potentiality (or what it ought to be), then we arrive at an ethics and politics before or beyond good and evil: "ethics is the sphere that recognizes neither guilt nor responsibility; it is, as Spinoza knew, the doctrine of the happy life. To assume guilt and responsibility – which can, at times, be necessary – is to leave the territory of ethics and enter that of law" (RA: 24). So rather than guilt and responsibility, which would require a law that is not life as such, we might think of an ethics without guilt. This has quite profound legal and ethical implications (depending upon how we read Agamben's claim that the law that is other than ethics is "at times" necessary). There is, as the *homo sacer* project outlines, the nightmare condition where law and life coincide, such as the current states of emergency where the law operates immediately, without any constitution or limits. Life would be simple rule following, doing one's duty, with no sense of life other than that subjected to law and form. But there is also the possibility that this life not be judged by a transcendent good or law against which life is found wanting. One of the most tortured ethical problems of the late twentieth and twenty-first centuries has been the relation between Israel and Palestine, both of whom assert a moral right to exist and do so on the basis of a time of the proper and property; where one stands on the issue is largely due to the narration of history, about whether the state of Israel restores an excluded people to their proper home, or whether the occupation of Palestine does violence to an equally valid claim to territory and ownness. The dominant policy of dealing with such conflicts is that of negotiating competing rights and claims, arriving at a two-state solution that would distribute right and ownership. Such a policy would also have to negotiate the various non-ethical or parapolitical factors that distort "peace processes" (such as the energy industries, arms industries, media interests, and so on). Often critical opinion performs a labor of history, looking back at the formation of territories, of armed conflicts, of geopolitical wranglings, and aims to render complex simple binaries that would allow terms such as "anti-Semitic," "clash of civilizations," "terrorism," or "axis of evil" to have purchase. Agamben's philosophy suggests quite a different path from that of placing things in context and negotiating competing claims; what if claims for propriety and ownness were subordinated or at least placed alongside that which remains outside propriety and belonging? Rather than inclusion and negotiation in categories of belonging, an acceptance of general non-belonging would mean, first, that no territory belongs to "a" people, precisely because the fiction of "the" people never captures the singularity of life from which such exceptions (or rendering stable and forceful) emerge. Rather than trying to find a domain of common law, negotiated peace, shared territory, recognition, or shared right, accepting an original non-belonging would open a different mode of ethics and politics. Regardless of the time and suffering of history, there is this singular present that makes a claim in its singularity.

Such an ethics beyond good and evil, and beyond guilt and responsibility, would have quite direct social-political consequences – ranging from thinking international relations less in terms of retribution and more in terms of how humans might live together in the absence of a prior conception of identity and personhood, to the day-to-day problems of social justice. It might also provide a way of thinking beyond capitalist and chronological time. At present, certain immediate conflicts – such as the war on terror and stark threats to national security – preclude focusing on problems of a different scale, such as climate change, resource depletion, and social justice. We can either focus on saving the constituted forms we have now – the nation, the finance system, personhood, Western democracy – *or* we can put such systems at risk for the sake of longer-term survival. Agamben's philosophy of "a" life that need not be exposed and abandoned as *bare* life offers a different conception of time in which the present itself is already messianic. Rather than saving nations, states, systems, "the" people, democracy, or any other sense that would stand in for the present, one might think of this life already as sufficient – redeemed by absolving itself of the need for redemption. That is, a certain time of future revelation and the proper – where life must realize an ideal that remains present and as a telos for potentiality – might be displaced by a messianic time in which what is most divine is what something *is*, in its being thus:

> what is at issue is a time that pulses and moves within chronological time, that transforms chronological time from within. On the one hand it is the time that remains, the time which we need to end time, to confront our customary image of time and to liberate ourselves from it. In the one case the time in which we believe we live separates us from what we are and transforms us into powerless spectators of our own lives. In

the other case, however, the time of the messiah is the time that we our-selves are, the dynamic time where, for the first time, we grasp time, grasp the time that is ours, grasp that we are nothing but that time. This time is not some other time located in an improbably present or future time. On the contrary, it is the only real time, the only time we will ever have. To experience this time implies an integral transformation of our-selves and of our ways of living. (CK: 12–13)

Perhaps the capitalist imperative of rewards and incentives for hard work and talent, and the increasing emphasis on self-development, might be abandoned in favor of an ethics concerned less with produc-tion and will; potentiality or power might not be seen as that which must actualize itself fully without remainder. In this respect Agamben's work differs not only from the Italian Marxism of Hardt and Negri (2000) that strives to think a new humanity that achieves its own full being by way of living labor, but also from all forms of identity politics, especially those that would affirm the active appropriation and explicit performance of one's own sexual identity. Indeed, Agamben's generic use of "man" is at once symptomatic of his failure to think through the ways in which human life as bare life has been figured as gendered, but it also indicates the specificity of his attempt to free ethics and politics from recognition and personhood. At the heart of Agamben's ethics lies the problem of his elevation of precisely those aspects of human existence that have been cast outside the properly human. One might ask whether focusing on bare, abandoned life as *the* zone where redemption might be finally possible does not fetishize some of the most abject conditions of twenty-first-century life, such as bodies on life support or refugees. But, for Agamben, it is only if we develop ethics from a threshold that is not yet fully human that we would find a way out of the politics that has founded itself on a form of pure sov-ereignty that is other than life. He is therefore directly opposed to those forms of liberal ethics that stress autonomy and will, as well as to forms of Marxism that privilege self-conscious praxis, and (implicitly) to the contemporary emphasis on performativity or the active taking up of a self. Instead, we might think of an ethics of potentiality in which life did not have a proper end. This ethics is perhaps best approached by a description Agamben offers toward the conclusion of his book on the relationship between humanity and animality, *The Open* (published in Italian as *L'aperto* in 2002).

We often think that ethics and even love depend on granting the other person their human dignity or personhood, but Agamben sug-gests the opposite. The exposure of two lovers and their relation to each other does not concern their *person* (or their identifiable predicates and qualities). Love is exposure to the simple or sweet life of the other that exists intimately with the form of life that one knows and loves. It may be that public policy, community, and what we know of as politics is based on personhood that has excluded the singular; this is especially so in the case of rights in which legislation is aimed at the dignity of persons. For Agamben, though, a more challenging ethics would follow from being able to love that potentiality or fragility which is not-yet formed into the identified person, but which is only given and known in the coming-into-form of life. Discussing a canvas by Titian, Agamben suggests that there are modes of relating to another human being beyond the elevation to something like human dignity or personhood. The life that is presented in Titian's painting of two lovers gazing at each other depicts a new mode of relation that is not "political" in the standard sense of being mediated by identity, value, and recognition: the gaze of the lovers, as captured in the painting, is ethical not because of a relation of knowledge or shared humanity, but in a mere "thisness" that is outside generality and established systems of relation. In being only its appearing, it is therefore "inapparent" [*inapparent*]:

> Sensual pleasure and love...do not prefigure only death and sin. To be sure, in their fulfillment the lovers learn something of each other that they should not have known – they have lost their mystery – and yet have not become any less impenetrable. But in their mutual disenchant-ment from their secret, they enter...a new and more blessed life, one that is neither animal nor human. It is not nature that is reached in their fulfillment, but rather...a higher stage beyond both nature and knowl-edge, beyond concealment and disconcealment. These lovers have initi-ated each other into their own lack of mystery as their most intimate secret; they mutually forgive each other and their *vanitas*. Bare or clothed, they are no longer either concealed or unconcealed – but rather, inappar-ent [*inapparenti*]...In their fulfillment, the lovers who have lost their mystery contemplate a human nature rendered perfectly inoperative – the inactivity [*inoperosità*] and *desœuvrement* of the human and of the animal as the supreme and unsavable figure of life. (O: 87)

This mode of ethics or love is one of the inapparent, the inoperative, and unworking: it suggests that what we might learn to value is an openness to the fragility and contingency of temporality as well as a generosity toward life without proper end. Such a blessedness or beati-tude overturns a foundational ontological-theological value of Western thought. Life has been imagined as *properly creative* – as becoming what it ought to be. Creation has been deemed to be creation toward some true or proper end; it is as though life is an ongoing fulfillment – through time – of some form that gives time meaning. We conceive of essence as that which remains the same, not being subject to change, and existence is movement toward or realization of that essence. Con-fronted with the utter fragility and contingency of life – and especially human life (which for Agamben is essentially inessential) – humans have tended to expel and deem as inhuman what is actually the most profound aspect of their humanity: there is no proper humanity. We see as animalistic, undignified, or improper those moments of silent and unworking human life – such as suffering, infancy, or the naked body – that are actually a potentiality that is definitive of who we are. In the case of the lovers depicted in the Titian canvas described above, we can begin to get a sense of how a certain "letting be" or exposure would define a love and ethics that would not seek to redeem humanity by subjection to any end outside itself. There would be something of an unworking offered by a love that did not attend to the formed and identified individual – the person who is defined by their projects, history, and values. Love would be the acceptance of a potentiality as such. Such a potentiality would be "unsavable" precisely because redemption relies on a potential achieving what it ought to be, finding its proper end – but if there is no proper end other than being "thus," then salvation is not an option. Pure potentiality, then, would neither be a stability nor sameness without difference – for that would be actuality in its simplest and minimal sense; nor would potentiality be a becoming that could do anything at all as abstract possibility. Rather, in Agamben's description of the lovers, we see two bodies facing each other, witnessing their lives, *not as formed and realized, but as a potentiality to be in their own singular thisness.*

Writing on the figure of Melville's Bartleby, the scrivener (or legal copyist) who happens not to be writing and prefers not to write, Agamben writes of "a complete or perfect potentiality that belongs to the scribe who is in full possession of the art of writing in the moment in which he does not write...The scribe who does not write (of whom Bartleby is the last exhausted figure) is perfect potentiality" (P: 246–7). Agamben, then, does not seek to include bare and abandoned life within the domain of the human and the political; he does not seek to grant recognition and personhood to all life. His work therefore takes a different path from forms of post-humanism or animal rights that aim to treat animals with all the dignity of humans, or that see no difference between animality and humanity. Rather than deem all life to be dignified and worthy of recognition, Agamben's counter-maneuver is to regard mere life – a life that is perfect potentiality because it need not act in order to be what it is – as the zone of a new ethics beyond humanism and recognition. One might accept a life and potentiality that did not contribute to the work of political formations and recognition, and that was inoperative: focused less on working toward bringing life to its fulfillment and more on releasing life from the bureaucracy of redemption.

Much has been made in twentieth- and twenty-first-century ethics of attending to the otherness of the other: rather than recognize others because they are "human like me" or because deep down "we are all the same," a number of ethical movements have suggested that ethics lies in *not* recognizing the other, but in granting a certain priority of others *before* we have achieved social, legal, or political relations. One might, as Agamben does, contrast ethics with notions of guilt and law (the latter requiring some determining system through which we encounter others). Perhaps the clearest exponent of the ethics of the "other" is Emmanuel Levinas, for whom ethics is "first philosophy," and for whom notions of being and truth and social recognition are all subordinate to the pure appearing of the other, who is given most clearly through the face (the face being the opening to another's world that I can never know or command) (Levinas 1969). Levinas argued that relating to the other *before* notions of sameness, recognition, or justice – a pure openness to the other without prior conceptions of what counts as human or worthy – was the only ethics. Against this notion of the otherness of the other, Derrida presented a strident critique by claiming that *any* approach to the other *as other* must already be a form of recognition and that ethics is necessarily a reduction of the pure alterity of others (Derrida 1978). Derrida's argument relied on the basic premise of post-structuralism that the experience of anything, even before language *as* something present before me, must already be caught up in some system of differences that enables the synthesis of experience into something that remains relatively stable through time. Agamben's various arguments for experiencing the other *not* as human like me are akin to the Levinasian notion that we do not have to attribute identity and recognition to others in order to be ethical, but Agamben's argument for experiencing the simple or "sweet" life that is not opposed to the polity but defined through a different (or counter) logic charts a path between Levinas and Derrida, or between the pure otherness of others and some acceptance that we always reduce others to some prior notion of sameness (Donahue 2013). For Agamben, we do indeed experience others "as such" before recognition, but this is not some mystical human personhood so much as their fragile bodily being, or that which is cast aside when humans conceive of themselves as bearers of rights and dignity.

What if before naming some repeatable identity we could attend to another human as they simply are, as this person here before they speak, reason, and attain to some dignity of personhood? This notion of ethics was suggested by Simone Weil, and it is her work that also helps us see how this ethics might extend to a new mode of politics. For Weil, the key motif of ethics is suffering: if I attend to the suffering of another it is not their person that is the object of my concern. If I see you harmed or violated, then I am not worried about whether you are a shopkeeper, a banker, a parent, or a footballer; I am certainly not worried that I am not respecting your rights *as a* sexual, political, or social being. It is the immediacy and pre-personal suffering that prompts me to attend to you. Whereas a common-sense notion of ethics might rely on fellow feeling, where I recognize you as just like me and therefore feel sympathy, Weil suggests that it is when I do not recognize you as my kind, when you perhaps appear to have lost all humanity, that genuine ethics might begin. (At the background of this notion is the Christian concept of grace: God does not forgive us because we are worthy or because we behave well. The majesty and beauty of grace lies in its being undeserved.) Liberal forms of ethics rely heavily on seeing others as in principle capable of the same rational choices as oneself; ethics is "impersonal" only insofar as one does not make an exception of oneself, but this is because we regard all others as persons, as ends in themselves and not as means. But, for Agamben, there is no "end" – such as humanity, the good, or personal dignity – that should mediate our relations to others. Indeed, Agamben writes of pure mediality, where all we are left with is life *without* any already given system of mediation, and thus are compelled in each case to find some way to proceed. As already mentioned, he does not simply endorse an ethics of impersonality, but he is indebted to Weil in not locating ethics in the recognition of the person; rather, what Agamben focuses on are those events where we witness the potentiality for personhood, such as a body that is deprived of speech or that does not have the power to become a form of life. In those events, we are neither experiencing bare life nor the sovereign individual, but the zone of indistinction.

Whereas liberalism is based on universal human recognition of personhood, and multiculturalism is based on the specificity of communities and recognition, Agamben suggests that one might abandon notions of redeeming life by way of personhood and community. We might imagine an ethics that was oriented to the inoperative, or those moments of suspension and unworking where life was not maximized to its full active potential and was released from the claims for recognition. Agamben's work is not only opposed, then, to notions of seeing ethics as only possible within meaningful traditions or only possible by way of identity or some ideal of a justice beyond measure; it occurs as a radical departure from redemption and inclusion. It is increasingly the case that our ethics and politics of rights are based on inclusion, and this occurs both in highly politicized moments – where, say, the terrorist or criminal is stripped of rights and life because of the decisions or capacities that define him – and also in moments of cultural politics where selves demand recognition based on identifiable predicates, such as sexuality, ethnicity, or affiliation: I become a political being only through being identified "as a" lesbian, Palestinian, Zionist, parent, vegetarian, worker, or intellectual. We seem not to be able to love the remaining aspects of our being. Weil argues that ethics occurs not when I grant others their personal dignity – when I include all others in my ideal of humanity because deep down "they" are all like us. Rather, if I were to act with generosity to another person who bore none of the qualities that I deemed to be properly human – if I could extend care to a being lacking all seeming personal dignity – then I would be behaving with all the grace that we have traditionally granted only to divinity. Such an idea, despite its strong debt to Christian ethics' conception of grace as a gift that is unwarranted and divine in its generosity because the being to whom it is extended is not subjected to some test of dignity, worth, or personhood, is – for Agamben – truly radical. What he adds to Weil, and where he differs from Esposito who champions impersonality, is that he sees human personhood and animality, or the body who speaks and the "I" who is the subject, as an irreducible threshold.

It is only by breaking with operative conceptions of a life that has worth purely insofar as it realizes its proper form that ethics finally arrives. Here, Agamben's work offers a new way of thinking about ethics and politics that is neither focused on the systems and traditions through which we make sense of the world (communitarianism) nor the primacy of the individual who enables these systems to be repeated. His ongoing criticism of the state of exception has as its positive dimension a claim that we think beyond constitutive systems and self-defining individuals; in addition, or beyond, sovereign self-declaration is the life that exceeds and remains in excess of any exemplarity, a life that is simply "this." Liberal forms of politics are based upon a will that gives the law to itself – a sovereign will, that is nothing more than the self's own act of creation – while traditional or communitarian forms see the polity as the collective realization of an ongoing shared sense of the good. By contrast, Agamben aims to form a concept of community without relying on the theological notion of a mode of becoming that actualizes itself, or brings itself into full and proper being. His conception of community and ethics *does* draw on theology, but it is a minor strand that is not concerned with redemption as a casting off of weakness, passivity, and impotentiality or non-being. Indeed, what has traditionally been defined as evil – potentiality that does not direct itself toward the good – is redefined by Agamben as blessedness.

What if this world we exist in here and now were not a shadow of a higher and proper world? What if the human body were not divine because it was made in God's image, but could be viewed as divine in being thus? The body might be regarded as divine in its appearing but not because it is an appearance *of* humanity that is the sign of some higher creator. This recasting of life as neither divided between good and evil, nor as liberated from the divine by being simply secular or materialist, relies on a blessedness beyond the distinction between good and evil. This blessedness of indistinction, or the ethics of the threshold, is at once an ideal and a method in Agamben's work.

Methodologically, as deconstruction and phenomenology had constantly argued, most histories and philosophies begin with a distinction between what something essentially is and then what it may accidentally or improperly become or fail to be. Phenomenology – especially in the work of Heidegger – argues that if something *may* happen or if something is possible, then this tells us what something is essentially (McQuillan 2005). For Heidegger, this meant that if there has been a tendency *not* to think about existence and to subordinate existence to being, then this should alert us to something about the relation between thinking and being: it is only possible to have a world of beings because being comes into appearance, but for that very reason we tend to think of being as actuality, and not as something that both comes into presence but also withholds itself from presence. For Heidegger, we have tended to think of being, time, and becoming as the unfolding of something that is present, as though life went through time to arrive at some essence or form that is already present; we think of time as the medium through which movement takes place. Against this, Heidegger theorized a much stronger sense of time and potentiality, where time and becoming are not subordinated to some already present and actual being. It was for this reason that Heidegger was critical of humanism, because it suggests that there is some being or ideal toward which human reason and life ought to develop. Heidegger therefore referred to *Dasein* (or "there-being") rather than "man" to suggest that human existence *is* its temporal relation to a world, and not the unfolding of an essence. Heidegger's phenomenology was highly critical of any form of humanism that suggested that "man" was a simple being in the world that might be known, studied, and managed, and against this argued that *Dasein* was a relational becoming (Heidegger 1996).

When Agamben argues for *impotentiality*, or potentiality being genuine only if it does not automatically reach some destined end, he is indebted to Heidegger's rethinking of time and being. However, as Derrida's deconstruction had argued, despite Heidegger's efforts to liberate "man" from any end, and to find pure and open potentiality, the notion of being defined by pure existence and potentiality reinstalls humanism as much as it overturns rigid notions of man (Derrida 1969). "Man" is now defined against animality and mere being by having the freedom to decide upon his own end. This is so much the case that "man" becomes increasingly defined as nothing more than his own existence or willed and active bringing into being. Man *is existence*, whose essence is to give himself his own essence through existence. Agamben's position on potentiality and impotentiality appears to be close to this privilege of existence, but with one key difference: our "existence" is not an act of self-creation such that we might think of ourselves as beings who are nothing more than their pure self-willed existence. Existence includes the un-willed, and impotentiality is less like the divine freedom not to do what one has the power to do and more like the power to suffer or be exposed to what is not within one's will. What if all that we would like to set aside as accidental or inessential, such as those aspects of life not capable of being willed, were ultimately what is most essential? What if being human were not distinct or opposed to animality, but took place as a constant relation to our own animality as that which is most intimate and also the most distant? That would be to say that what is inessential is essential; what has been deemed as accidental or improper is what truly is. Humans have tended to regard certain actual qualities – speech, reason, political participation – as essential and definitive, but historically the moments of most profound insight have been when these potentials have not been realized. We might think of the civil rights movement as being revolutionary *not* because "we" realized that all humans shared a certain sameness and rational dignity, but rather because a more radical politics would lie in refusal of necessary inclusion and identity. Ethics might be truly possible not when all others are included in one ongoing conversation of reason, but when those who do not or cannot speak generate a community that does not require belonging in terms of anything other than simply existing. Something like "life" before essential determining qualities, *and* before the decisive self-constitution of reason, might allow for a sense of a singular "this." There would be a distinct contrast, then, between a community in which "everyone has a voice" and one where voice was not a requirement of existence. In this respect Agamben's ethics underplays the importance that has been attributed to humans as speaking beings or rational animals, while at the same time there is a profound recognition of the potentiality for human silence and suffering that only has sense in relation to what it is *not to speak.*

There is a difference between – say – an animal that does not speak, and a human being whose potential to speak has been thwarted or unrealized (as in the case of the death-camp prisoners described by Agamben who have been reduced to silence). This difference, though, is not between two beings and does not take the form of a relation: it is a difference within the human and takes the form of relation and non-relation, or a threshold. The human differs from the animal not by some essential quality, such as speech, reason, or ethics, but by being exposed to the inessential: humans have no essence other than that which unfolds through their fragile and exposed existence. This existence is not some god-like capacity to be nothing other than one's own willed act; existence is exposure and is always a threshold condition *between* being and acting. This recognition or confrontation with the threshold has specific and general methodological implications. Generally, Agamben interrogates a series of definitive distinctions or binaries and argues for the way they emerge from a zone of indistinction, but this is not a claim about language; or, at least, it is not the familiar claim that the differences through which we think are generated from a system of relations. Agamben's insistence on the threshold prior to linguistic distinction is *not* equivalent to the post-structuralist claim that we only know distinct terms by way of a system of differences and relations. Rather, for Agamben, there are certain distinctions that structure our history, our sense of humanity, and our politics. Rather than refer this back to a system of differences or language, he objects to what he sees as deconstruction's failure to look at the ways in which linguistic ambiguity emerges because of a quality of life as potentiality that we humans have not been able to confront. We tend to expel what appears as accidental and inessential, and define certain supposedly lawful and proper instances as essential, and this includes our failure to pay due heed to that which is not articulated by language.

The difference that structures Western thought – between being and act (which can also be thought of as what the world *is*, and then the languages, institutions, and structural relations through which it is mastered) – cannot be sustained, and constantly breaks down to expose indistinction, and it is this threshold of indistinction that should prompt us to confront life as *not* clearly separated between being and act, but as impotentiality, as something that may or may not emerge into difference, distinction, and identity. Language and law at once sustain and deny this difference: both claim that the world *is* exactly as it is said, and that there is no difference or remainder outside language and law. Against this affirmation of the simple being of the world captured in law and language, Agamben seeks to focus on those moments of nonbeing or indistinction, where the world is other than the clear demarcations of law and sense. Such moments can be human – as in the Franciscan monk's ongoing task of bringing the good life into being through the very practice of living – but they can also be systemic, as when language no longer seems to offer any sense of reality exposing only itself in its saying and its distance from the said. In such moments of emptiness or absence of "a" good, one finds the good in nothing more than the living or life. Agamben's commitment to the threshold yields a methodology and project of constantly referring structuring oppositions back to something that does not present itself as a unity (not some life common to humans and animals, not some unified being prior to action).

At one illuminating point, Agamben describes this difference as a garment; this suggests, at first, that something covers over an origin, but for Agamben the garment or cover – the appearance – does not cover over something that lies behind division. We might say that there is an appearing, and it is from an appearance or division that we assume some prior unity, when in fact what appears is a threshold of indistinction. In a more specific sense, this then relates to a broader claim about power and life: there is not an authority, God, or power who creates life and who should then be the object of prayer and praise. Rather, in the beginning is something like an acclamation, or an event of saying or glorification *from which* one then assumes that there must have been some prior power who was the object of praise. This connects Agamben's recent work on glory, through the projects on the sacred, back to the earliest work on poetry. Rather than think of life in terms of perfect and complete being that then acts or speaks and might be the object of language, we can think of an acclamation or event of speech, or something like an "appearing" that prompts an act of "saying." It is from that original saying, speaking, or acclamation that a division occurs between what is glorified (power) and the structures or "economy" of glorification:

> The theology of glory constitutes, in this sense, the secret point of contact through which theology and politics continuously communicate and exchange parts with one another...Theology and politics are, in this sense, what results from the exchange and from the movement of something like an absolute garment that, as such, has decisive juridical-political implications. Like many of the concepts we have encountered in our investigation, this garment of glory is a signature [*segnatura*] that marks bodies and substances politically and theologically, and orientates and displaces them according to an economy that we are only now beginning to glimpse...What is the relation that so intimately links power to glory? If power is essentially force and efficacious action, why does it need to receive ritual acclamations and hymns of praise, to wear cumbersome crowns and tiaras, to submit itself to an inaccessible ceremony and an immutable protocol – in a word, why does something that is essentially operativity and *oikonomia* need to become solemnly immobilized in glory? (KG: 194–5)

Agamben's archaeology of glory appears first, then, as a specific and highly arcane history of theology, but has profound implications for the twenty-first century. He offers a distinct theory of power, whereby something like a sovereign or supreme power is created by acts and events of glorification. It is from sovereign force that law institutes itself as the power to wield force over and against a lawless outside. This has a positive side in the sense of the "empty throne," such that we do not worship because the king is glorious, but it is glorification that creates the king's power. Agamben ties this archaeology quite specifically to twentieth-century fascist politics, and the society of the spectacle. We can mourn that there is no content to power and law other than its appearing *as* power or *as* law. By the same token, this might also yield a messianic difference of the "now," realizing that the present already harbors its own capacity to recognize that law has no significance, and therefore no force. Rather than aim to recover a genuine law that is not mere force, one might look to a history of theology and messianism that theorized a coming into being of the divine that is given only in its becoming.

It is by way of events of glorification that power comes to be separated from the world it rules, and this has its source in an original problem of theology and the relation between God's complete being and then His appearance in, and governance of, the world. For Agamben, tracing the genealogy of glory allows us to think of power less as something held by a separate being and more as something that has taken hold by way of a history of divisions, distinctions, and "signatures." So, rather than beginning with being and then proceeding to action, there is an "original" threshold that becomes distinguished (but also always remains indistinguishable) through events of language; such events are not impositions of a system of structure but are closer to signatures – events that both refer beyond themselves but are also unique in their inscriptive singularity. These linguistic events have a "sacred" or mythic quality, akin to the form of an oath; they create something to be honored and feared at one and the same time – constituting the original ambivalence of the sacred. Agamben has written at length both on the oath and the signature, and in doing so suggested a new path for thinking about the relation between language and life. Rather than see language as an imposed system of differences, we might think of localized or singular events of saying – something like motifs – that are not names (for they do not label pre-existing entities), but are closer to performative exclamations, as though language was something like a response that creates a relation. Our history then becomes a series of linguistic fragments that create thresholds and distinctions that are also decisive politically and spiritually:

> It is clear that the *arche* toward which an archaeology seeks to regress cannot be understood in any way as a given that can be situated either in a chronology (even in a broad character like "prehistoric") or even beyond it, in an atemporal metahistorical structure (for example, as Dumezil ironically suggests, in the neuronal system of a hominid). It is, rather, a force working in history, exactly as the Indo-European language expresses first of all a system of connections among historically accessible languages; just as the child in psychoanalysis expresses a force that continues to act in the psychic life of the adult; and just as the "big bang," which is supposed to have given rise to the universe, is something that never stops transmitting its background radiation to us. Yet unlike the "big bang" which astrophysicists claim to be able to date, even if only in terms of millions of years, the *arche* is not a given, a substance, or an event but a field of historical currents stretched between anthropogenesis and the present, ultrahistory and history. And as such – that is, insofar as, like anthropogenesis, it is something that is necessarily presupposed as having happened but that cannot be hypostatized into an event in

chronology – it can eventually render historical phenomena intelligible. (SL: 10–11)

In the beginning, then, is something like a division or split from some prior threshold that can only be known in its indistinction, and never experienced as some fully graspable presence. We cannot explain our legal and political concepts by referring back to religion, for religion itself is a site of incoherence and indistinction that generates gaps that are constantly reworked but never bridged. At the heart of the problem is the human animal's relation to speech, for it is language that creates the distance from the world that enables law, power, glory, prayer, poetry, and the very division in the human itself between man and animal:

> My hypothesis is that the enigmatic institution, both juridical and reli-
> gious, that we designate with the term *oath* can only be made intelligible
> if it is situated within a perspective in which it calls into question the
> very nature of man as a speaking being and a political animal... Ultrahis-
> tory, like anthropogenesis, is not in fact an event that can be considered
> completed once and for all; it is always under way, because *Homo sapiens*
> never stops becoming man, has perhaps not yet finished entering lan-
> guage and swearing to his nature as a speaking being. (SL: 10–11)

Law and religion share, for Agamben, this oppositional and rigid expulsion of inhuman from human, and both are different ways of dealing with the problem of the relation between being and act, and both come down to an event in which the human "must have" (in some past that cannot be accessed) *addressed a power other than itself*. Agamben begins by quoting Aristotle for whom "the oath is the most ancient thing, no less ancient than the gods ... as if the origins of the cosmos and of the thought that understands it implied the oath in some way" (SL: 19). Agamben refers back to ancient Greek sources that are themselves referring back to a mythic past in which the oath, or an exclamation, establishes some divine power *that is not yet good or evil and not yet legal or religious*. One might say that in the beginning is an address or a sound that is experienced as the speech of someone to another power; animal sound is split from human hymn, and in so doing the human becomes what "he" is by an event of language that is not *about* anything but *to* some force other than mere life. Agamben then comments that we cannot simply say that the notion of power derives from religion, but that religious power itself emerges from a certain event or understanding of language as having a spiritual or glorifying power:

> The entire problem of the distinction between the juridical and the reli-
> gious, in particular as regards the oath, is thus poorly put. Not only do
> we have no reason for postulating a prejuridical phase in which the oath
> belonged solely to the religious sphere, but perhaps our entire habitual

way of representing to ourselves the chronological and conceptual relationship between law and religion must be revised. Perhaps the oath
presents to us a phenomenon that is not, in itself, either (solely) juridical
or (solely) religious but that, precisely for this reason, can permit us to
rethink from the beginning what law and religion is…The oath, defined
by the correspondence between words and actions, here performs an
absolutely central function. This happens not only on the theological
level, in that it defines God and his *logos*, but also on the anthropological
level, since it relates human language to the paradigm of divine language. (SL: 19–21)

Oaths, like other aspects of the sacred studied by Agamben, indicate
thresholds where life divides a proper interior from an improper
outside, but also where language is effective or constitutive – and this
then goes back to notions of sovereignty which have the force to institute division without themselves being comprehensible within the
terrain they organize.

Agamben, then, wants to posit some force beyond the divisions
within which we think and operate but that is not itself a self-conscious
or willed division or decision. At the same time, confronting the threshold forces us to take up ownership for the divisions within which we
think and move:

> It is perhaps time to call into question the prestige that language has
> enjoyed and continues to enjoy in our culture, as a tool of incomparable
> potency, efficacy and beauty. And yet, considered in itself, it is no more
> beautiful than birdsong, no more efficacious than the signals insects
> exchange, no more powerful than the roar with which the lion asserts
> his domination. The decisive element that confers on language its pecu-
> liar virtue is not in the tool itself but in the place it leaves to the speaker,
> in the fact that it prepares within itself a hollowed-out form that the
> speaker must always assume in order to speak – that is to say, in the
> ethical relation that is established between speaker and language. *The
> human being is that living being that, in order to speak, must say "I," must
> "take the word," assume it and make it his own.* (SL: 71)

The standard historical distinction between religion and law fails to
confront the theological and ongoing mythic kernel of law: we still
expel as evil and inhuman that which lies outside some supposed
universal and rational law. What we do not confront is the threshold
that generates division, power, force, and the subject: "the magico-
religious sphere does not logically preexist the oath, but it is the oath,
as originary performative experience of the word, that can explain
religion (and law, which is closely connected with it)" (SL: 65). As
Agamben explains:

> With a tenacious prejudice connected to their profession, scientists have
> always considered anthropogenesis to be a problem of an exclusively

cognitive order, as if the becoming human of man were solely a question of intelligence and brain size and not also one of *ethos*, as if intelligence and language did not also and above all pose problems of an ethical and political order, as if *Homo sapiens* was not also, and of course precisely for that reason, a *Homo iustus*. (SL: 68)

Agamben suggests that a new ethics would emerge from abandoning abandonment: if we did not cast out or abandon that which seems to lie outside the law and the human, then life as such might be blessed, rather than achieving redemption via some higher world. This would require attributing more significance to both "the becoming human of man" – rather than assuming that the human is given as a rational order in advance – and also attending to the ways in which that becoming is exposed and achieved by way of language, which is always closer to poetry (or making) rather than simply communicating or representing: uniquely among living things, man is not limited to acquiring language as one capacity among others that he is given, but has made of it his specific potentiality; *he has, that is to say, put his very nature in language* (SL: 68).

Rather than begin with a privilege accorded to a mode of creation and becoming that is the fulfillment of some proper form, we would be able to embrace potentiality as such, the potential for coming into relation. And, for Agamben, this relation is that between language and life, *not* a language that simply copies, represents, or differentiates life, but language that takes the form of an oath or promise, so that when humans speak they testify or bear witness and can be held to account. It is because of this promissory or testimonial aspect of language – or the fact that language always begins with something like an implicit "I swear" – that language creates a self and a world, *and a gap that can never be fully closed*. If humans can speak and testify to the world, this is because language never follows automatically or rationally from life but is always necessarily something that is distanced from that which it hopes to preserve:

> In order for something like an oath to be able to take place, it is necessary, in fact, to be able above all to distinguish, and to articulate together in some way, life and language, actions and words – and this is precisely what the animal, for which language is still an integral part of its vital practice, cannot do. The first promise, the first, and so to speak, transcendental – *sacratio* is produced by means of this division, in which man, opposing his language to his actions can put himself at stake in language, can promise himself to the *logos*. (SL: 69)

Let us imagine that we accept Agamben's genealogy of sovereignty as articulated here: rather than say that there is a world, and that some beings in that world seize power over other beings, and that politics would then be whether such power was legitimate (which would then require adjudicating or redistributing power, or questioning *who holds power*), Agamben sees power as occurring through an event of speech that opens a threshold. This is importantly different and opposed to power as performative. It is not as though it is by way of speaking that a distribution of power occurs. For Agamben, the first event of speech generates something like a promise, but of a certain type. This is not a promise *to do*, but a promise to hold what is said to be true. If, then, the first speech is prompted by the world – a hymn or expression *that there is a world* – the holding of one to the force of that hymn opens a field of time and language. The power here is not that of one who speaks and holds authority, for that is precisely the sovereign model that Agamben seeks to contest; in order for *that* sovereign performance of one who holds the law to be possible, there must have been a speaking that generated the one who promises to hold true to what he declares. In the beginning is a testimony that promises to hold on to its truth, but – because it has taken place by way of language – may always allow that swearing to truth to become something like a technical operation or "law." A new politics would therefore refuse power as constituted, and refuse *that there is law, and that law might be held*. Such a politics would be beyond good and evil precisely because every instituted threshold or declaration of "the" good would be haunted by its coming into being, and its distance from, and openness to, the truth that it aims to hold near.

5

Politics Beyond Good and Evil

The theological problem of evil lies (partly at least, it is often argued) in the historical relation between myth and law. At a mythic level it makes sense to think of a world beginning with opposed forces of good and evil, but once one starts to think of an absolute, perfect, and rational God who is the supreme creator of the world, then evil cannot be seen as something that God creates; nor could there be some other force opposed to God. Instead, evil is lack or privation – a failure of a created being to arrive at its good and proper form. It is for this reason that potentiality and impotentiality are such important concepts, allowing God to be all powerful, with all He creates being understood as perfect as long as it arrives at the proper end that is in accord with the divine order of the world. But it is also for this reason that the world in which we live is deemed to be good only in relation to an end toward which it ought to tend. As Agamben constantly reiterates, Western thought is left with an aporia, fracture, gap, or impasse – oriented as it is to completion and perfection while nevertheless not wanting to see life and the polity as completely abandoned. The answer is to render evil as something that occurs only when the proper operation of the world goes awry.

Going back to the early Christian theologians, such as Augustine, evil was not regarded as a positive counter-principle to God, but was merely lack or failure to achieve a being's proper or divine potential. The notion of evil as privation or lack rationalizes a mythic opposition, such that we no longer have to deal with evil as a distinct and destructive force opposed to creation. For Agamben, such a rationalization attributes a certain evil to impotentiality, and this in turn means that law, philosophy, politics, and ethics merely leave the mythic past unexamined rather than confronting the ways in which our entire framework of thinking has not examined its real condition of emergence. More specifically, it does no good to account for history as some definitive transition from myth, to religion to law, for all of these possibilities emerge from a common threshold of indistinction. That "threshold" can be thought of as non-relational, prior to the distinction between the self who can say "I" and testify to the world, and the silence of the world as it simply is. One of Agamben's many original claims is that rather than see language – like law – as a system of differences and relations, one should consider the non-relational or the threshold as always haunting and remaining *as impotentiality*. When I speak, in each case there is some general sense (what is said) and also *this event of saying*. We have, however, tended to expel or externalize the non-relational – placing it outside the human polity. We have externalized impotentiality, as the improper and non-relational, rather than experiencing it as the always present capacity not to act that remains in any act, or as that which remains unsaid in every saying.

While Agamben suggests that a new ethics would be enabled by attending to the other person not as an expression of human dignity and personhood, but in the fragile border of potentiality and impotentiality, he also makes a claim for a new politics in the form of a "coming community." There seems to be a tension between the singularity of each being, not yet defined or realized as *human*, and the ethical demand for some form of community that would not be defined by liberal notions of the autonomy of persons. It is fairly clear that Agamben would be opposed to forms of political liberalism that rely on the self-determining individual, who has no good or norm other than that which he decides for himself. Such a mode of politics intensifies the privilege accorded to act, will, and self-positing law, and never questions how that political space of deliberation and freedom comes into being (and also does not ask who is abandoned by such a norm of reason and self-constitution). By the same token, communitarian models of politics whereby individuals have the personhood they do because of shared norms and ongoing practices of cultural deliberation are, for Agamben, also part of a Western tradition of sovereignty in which a distinction operates between the polity and its outside, with no genuine thought being directed toward the coming into being of that political space, and whether there might be a new mode of politics that does not operate with a dichotomous model that places certain bodies outside the law. Agamben's "coming community" would not be based on individuals recognizing each other as persons, either by way of the liberal concept of the rational subject or the communitarian norm of collective formation; if there were no already established norm and no already instituted mode of political relation – no conception of proper or normative personhood, and no ideal of recognition based on the common – then the "coming community" would have an ongoing task of creating fragile relations, rather than relying on relations and identities deemed to be proper or essential.

Agamben frequently suggests that the very concept of relation as such needs to be rethought. It is not the case that there are beings who have a relation of lack toward the good that they ought to realize. Rather, there is potentiality that is not yet relational, but that has the capacity to orient itself beyond itself. This means that neither beings nor relations are primary: the world is not composed of distinct essences or beings that enter into relation; nor is it composed of some relational field or system that generates beings. There would not be actual beings who then possess potentials, for there would be potentials from which something might be actualized. Theologically, we would not begin from a complete, divine, and transcendent God, and then ask how such a God may relate (or not) to creation and the world, but would instead pose the question of how this immanent world – this life – can create a relation to what is not present, and to what is only potential.

This line of argument may seem abstract to the point of being merely scholarly and – worse – so metaphysical as to be incapable of being proven one way or the other. However, the implications for political theory and ethics are profound. If the world were composed of beings that subsequently enter into relation, then relations would be dependent upon the essence or proper being of individuals: this is why liberal theory has a polity defined by allowing a maximum degree of deliberation, reflection, fairness, and equal opportunity. The nature of the whole – and whether a polity is just – is dependent on the extent to which it maximizes the freedom and rational choice of the individual. If, by contrast, individuals or beings emerge from relations, then the burden of theory and politics is to explain the nature of the force that produces relations: if we are Marxists, relations are explained from labor and production, whereas psychoanalysis begins with desire, while evolutionary theory deploys various notions of mutation and selection. Again, some normative conception of life operates in order to evaluate the whole, and this is certainly so in the cases that Agamben targets when he discusses biopolitics: it is in contemporary biopolitics that all decisions become nothing more than means to the end of sustaining an abstract substance of "life." If, however, there are neither foundational beings nor some productive relational ground (such as the supposed biological life that precedes formed political life), then rather than explain relations from individuals, or individuals from relations, we might investigate the potentiality for relations. This is at the heart of Agamben's conception of what a coming community might be.

In many respects Agamben's notion of "whatever being" overturns the Western tradition of ontology and theology, both of which appear to begin from the assumption of a being with a proper essence that then goes through time or existence in order to become what it fully is. Rather than have an essence – what something is – that may or may not be brought into existence, Agamben begins with existence: not something *as* something with an identity or proper form, but a singular "isness," or "whatever," that might then through time and becoming enter into relation or take on an identity or form, through existing. Here is where an arcane ontological and theological problem, for Agamben, enables the thought of a new ethics and politics. Traditionally, we imagine the good, the divine, and identity as having a form or sameness that is then brought into existence. There is the possibility of there being any number of actual humans, with each individual human being standing as an instance of a kind, and with each instance being what it is by virtue of its identifiable predicates or qualities; we have genders, or modes of being human. But another way of thinking would be rather than see a species that comes into existence each time in a different mode, to see each existence as exactly what it is. Agamben writes a great deal on the notion of the "example" following from the Greek *para-deigma*: as "that which is shown alongside" (CC: 10). We can imagine timeless essences or forms that are then expressed in particulars. The example, however, complicates this hierarchy and temporality, because it is the example, or the thing itself, that then generates what it is an example *of*, or what it presents. The example is both a single "this," but in pointing to it *as an example*, we are also saying it is not simply or just this, but stands for something other than itself: "Neither particular nor universal, the example is a singular object that presents itself as such, that *shows* its singularity" (CC: 10). An example complicates the relation between essence and existence, because it is at once an existent, but it is an existent that indicates a potential to be more than itself. Considered in relation to life, and especially human life, we might imagine a community not as the coming into being of some sense of collective identity, nor as the fulfillment of what individuals ought to be, nor as what individuals essentially are. Rather, in their existence, each being and each community is at once a "this," not an essence that has come into existing, but something that in existing presents a "this."

God, traditionally, is pure existence and is not subject to being an instance of any kind, nor of having a specifiable identity. God's essence is his existence, nothing more. For Agamben, that way of thinking about God as pure existence not limited or marked out by being of a certain kind is a better way of thinking about all existence. The key difference is that because, traditionally, God is the only pure existence and is not the expression of any essence, his pure existence is at a distance from the created world of determined or specified forms. However, if we think of all being as just being the existence that it is – a "thisness" that is not the expression of a prior being or form – then existence becomes multiple. Before this flower is a rose or tulip or example of fauna, which would mean it would be an actualization of a potential kind, it is simply a "this," and what makes it what it is *is* just its existence. Before I am "me," before I am "human," before I am "female," there is existence, and while there are other humans, and other females who are also marked out by the same predicates, my existence here and now is singular, and is given in its singularity not as this identifiable and ongoing identity, but as a "thisness." If the world is occupied by large numbers of humans (or any other type or instance of being), what makes this human the human that it is? Is it the predicates (being tall, fair-skinned, and possessing certain virtues), or is it nothing more than its existing in its here and now? Agamben considers two possibilities: there is a general kind (humanity) that is individuated by the material instances (in which case it is my specific incarnation in matter that makes me me); or, there is a thisness ("haecceity"), which is not an example or actualization of something, but just an existence that is the form in its utmost being. In the latter case the existence is not the form plus its coming into being, so much as the utmost being of the existing thing:

> Whatever is the matheme of singularity, without which it is impossible to conceive either being or the individuation of singularity. How the Scholastic posed the problem of the *principium individuationis* is well known. Against Saint Thomas who sought the place of individuation in matter, Duns Scotus conceived individuation as an addition to nature or common form (for example, humanity) – an addition not of another form or essence or property, but of an *ultima realitas*, an "utmostness" of the form itself. Singularity adds nothing to the common form, if not a "haecceity" (as Étienne Gilson says: here we do not have individuation in virtue of the form, but individuation of the form). But for this reason, according to Duns Scotus, common form or nature must be indifferent to singularity, must in itself be neither particular nor universal, nor multiple, but such that it "does not scorn being posed with whatever singular unity... The limit of Duns Scotus is that he seems to conceive common nature as an anterior reality, which has the property of being indifferent to whatever singularity, and to which singularity adds only *haecceity*. Accordingly, he leaves unthought precisely that *quodlibet* that is inseparable from singularity and, without recognizing it, makes indifference the real root of individuation." (CC: 17)

The History of Being

The heavy burden of Agamben's work lies in the working assumption that politics and life are in a state of crisis today precisely because of deep metaphysical presuppositions that compose the ways in which we experience our very being (and for Agamben there is very much a "we" and it is deeply mired in Western metaphysics and theology). Now is the time where "we" must confront a metaphysical crisis that is at once both intimate (to do with life) and distant (to do with the history of concepts). The present, Agamben claims, is not simply one more moment in the history of the human animal as a being who has civilized himself by way of language, law, and art. The present is a moment in which all these supposedly constitutive features of human existence – speaking, governing, creating – have fallen into near mis-use:

> language not only constitutes itself as an autonomous sphere, but also no longer reveals anything at all – or, better yet, it reveals the nothingness of all things. In language there is nothing of God, of the world, of the revealed: but, in this extreme nullifying unveiling, language (the linguistic nature of human beings) remains once again hidden and separated. Language thus acquires for the last time, the unspoken power to claim a historical age and a state for itself: the age of the spectacle, or the state of fully realized nihilism. (MWE: 84–5)

It is precisely because we are now not realizing the potential that has marked us out as human that we can start to rethink the relationship between potentiality and humanity, and what it means *not* to have any end or essence that we are destined to fulfill. Traditionally, humans are defined by their open and free relation to realizing their *proper* potential; if other forms of life are governed by the demands of surviving, humans possess reason as their end and are thus essentially self-determining. In Aristotle, for example, human reason is a capacity to intuit and bring into being (either by thinking or making) what our reason decides upon as our own end: humans – understanding themselves as rational – give a form to their lives as a whole. From Aristotle to Kant, despite differences of emphasis, humans have been defined as ends in themselves, oriented to nothing other than the fulfillment of their rational potential. In theology, because God creates the world with each being having a proper potentiality toward which its becoming is oriented, the failure to actualize that potential is deemed to be evil. Humans who do not freely choose and orient themselves toward the good become mired in their determining being; they are deemed to be less than human, inhuman, or mere life. Even without theology and philosophy, we can see the way, today, that notions of identity and personhood serve to delimit the human from the inhuman, with stateless persons or those without self-forming reason constantly being abandoned by the law. Such conceptions of proper human potentiality divide good (forming) human life from inhuman (zoological/animal and determined) life.

If, however, we live in a present that does not allow for the actualization of our rational and freely creative potential, then maybe we can rethink potentiality and humanity. It is the loss of the actualization of what has always been deemed to be properly human that marks the distinction of the present but that also allows – finally – for a new mode of potentiality that is not determined in advance by being the means toward "our" proper end. Indeed, the very notion of the proper – or of what is authentically ours – is challenged by Agamben's project of potentiality whereby we do not own or master our own becoming, and it is for this reason that we might then take up a different relation to the "life" that we have always cast outside of ourselves as inhuman. Rather than project or externalize impotentiality on to an external other, or regard it as an extrinsic evil, Agamben insists on the intimacy of impotentiality with the very freedom required for good and evil:

> The potential welcomes non-Being, and this welcoming of non-Being *is* potentiality, fundamental passivity. It is passive potentiality, but not a passive potentiality that undergoes something other than itself; rather, it undergoes and suffers its own non-Being...Every human power is *adynamia*, impotentiality; every human potentiality is in relation to its own privation. This is the origin (and the abyss) of human power, which is so violent and limitless with respect to other living beings. *Other living beings are capable only of their specific potentiality; they can only do this or that. But human beings are the animals who are capable of their own impotentiality. The greatness of human potentiality is measured by the abyss of human impotentiality*...To be free is not simply to have the power to do this or that thing, nor is it simply to have the power to refuse to do this or that thing. To be free is, in the sense we have seen, *to be capable of one's own impotentiality*, to be in relation to one's own privation. This is why freedom is freedom for both good and evil. (P: 182–3)

Here is where Agamben's attempt to think an ethics and politics beyond the blame/guilt of the law and the good/evil of morality connects with aesthetics. This is not an aesthetics of artists as subjects who will their individual artworks into being. Opposed to the notion of art as the work of a subject, and opposed to the notion of the subject as good insofar as he wills himself into being, Agamben defines freedom as the capacity to disclose something like coming-into-appearing as such: not the subject exerting their pure will, but a certain open encounter with language or matter. Freedom occurs by way of surrender, openness, and suffering. To suffer would not be a negative or punishing event, but would be a form of undergoing that is not one's own: to suffer change. Viewing another human as suffering would be attending to their exposed and fragile potentiality. For Agamben, the need to think about the human relation to the world, *not* as something already determined but as something that comes into being from a certain suffering of the world, or from being exposed, has implications for ethics and aesthetics. We have, he insists, lost the richer and fuller sense of human "doing" that was once articulated in ancient Greek thought: we now think of a force or will that exerts and actualizes itself, instead of thinking of different forms of doing that are tied to vulnerable exposure. Rather than see all doing or action as forms of work, operation, or effectivity, Agamben seeks to draw thinking back to a more complex and divided origin. As in the *bios/zoe* distinction, he sees an initial expulsion of mere life (the life of work) in favor of creative and forming life, and then sees modernity as having lost the division while assuming only a conception of life as bare, surviving life. Art eventually becomes nothing more than the exertion of will, and loses all relation to truth, exposure, and openness:

> For while poiesis constructs the space where man finds his certitude and where he ensures the freedom and duration of his action, the presupposition of work is, on the contrary, bare biological existence, the cyclical processes of the human body, whose metabolism and whose energy depend on the basic products of labor...In the Western cultural tradition, the distinction between these three kinds of human doing – poiesis, praxis, and work – has been progressively obscured. What the Greeks conceived as poiesis is understood by the Romans as one mode of *agere*, that is, as an acting that puts-to-work, an *operari*...Christian theological thought, which conceived the supreme Being as an *actus purus*, ties to Western metaphysics the interpretation of being as actuality and act. When this process is completed in the modern era, every chance to distinguish between poiesis and praxis, pro-duction and action, is lost... work, which used to occupy the lowest rank in the hierarchy of active life, climbs to the rank of central value and common denominator of every human activity. (MWC: 70–1)

Agamben's entire corpus depends on a radical separation from the contemporary scene: on the ways we view art, on the ways we govern ourselves, on our experience of pleasure, and on our ways of seeing. In one respect, at least, Agamben is a profoundly backward-looking thinker, relying heavily on philosophy, theology, and philology. He remains one of the few thinkers left today who would refer to something like "the" Western tradition as a whole, as though there is some unified history that runs from early Christianity and ancient Greece to the present.

In this way, he remains indebted to two strands of twentieth-century German thought: Martin Heidegger's method of investigating Western thought as a whole, and Walter Benjamin's project of interrogating something like the emergence of political thinking as such. There is an ostensible tension between these two lines of thought: Heidegger's philosophy is primarily one of authenticity, whereby he frequently refers to our "ownmost potentiality." Like Agamben after him, Heidegger regards the present and its condition of unthinking as an opportunity to free thought from its inauthentic modes, an inauthenticity that arises from thought's proper potentiality. For Heidegger, we are our comportment toward the world, a world that is disclosed through the ongoing relations we take up toward various things with which we are concerned. However, it is precisely because we exist in relation to a world of things that we tend to think of ourselves as things – as beings, or as "man," who has some proper or determining essence. The only way we can retrieve our ownmost potentiality is when that definitive relation to things breaks down: the very having of a world, or existing in relation, seems to fall apart in moments of complete boredom, disengagement, or even terrifying freedom. In such moments when one loses the meaning and care for the world, one becomes aware *that there is a world*, and that one is not a thing among things but a relation of care through which things appear (Heidegger 1996).

Heidegger's task is for *Dasein* to free itself from an unthinking, everyday relation to things. For the most part we conceive of ourselves and our world as simply present before us. If we were to become aware that our world is as it appears to be because of the relations we take up toward it, then we would once again be able to think the coming into being of the world. Even though Heidegger speaks of this coming into being of the world via a language of clearing, unveiling, revealing, and disclosing (rather than mind constructing the world), his goal for philosophy, poetry, and thinking is one of retrieving a more original relation of disclosure – rather than simply accepting that the world is so much "standing reserve" available for our consumption and cognition.

This "authentic" drive in Heidegger's work has occasionally been tied to his lamentable sympathy for Nazi National Socialism, whereby the notion of taking up an active and original relation to one's world could be associated with some notion of decontamination or returning to cultural purity. Although indebted to Heidegger, Agamben does not use the concept of potentiality to reconceive humans as nothing more than their existence, or as nothing more than the free comportment and projects that they take up into a world that they ought to make their own. Heidegger had argued for a distinction between humans who are open to a world (a world that is given through projects and an orientation to an undetermined future) and animals, who are "poor in world." Heidegger's philosophy of authenticity has therefore been criticized both because it privileges an active and self-forming humanity over "lesser" forms of corrupted humanity, and because it divides the animal from the human definitively, and thereby cannot acknowledge a fundamental passivity and non-relation within the human (Derrida 1989b: 46).

The non-relational life or world-less-ness that Heidegger had confined to animals is, for Agamben, one that marks our human potentiality as also an impotentiality. And it is here that Agamben draws on Walter Benjamin's far less existential mode of thinking to consider "bare life": could we abandon notions of violent self-creation and progress and somehow grant silent life a certain blessedness? Only within a biopolitical horizon will it be possible to decide whether the categories whose opposition founded modern politics (right/left, private/public, absolutism/democracy, etc.) – and which have been steadily dissolving, to the point of entering today into a real zone of indistinction – will have to be abandoned or will, instead, eventually regain the meaning they lost in that very horizon. And only a reflection that, taking up Foucault's and Benjamin's suggestion, thematically interrogates the link between bare life and politics, a link that secretly governs the modern ideologies seemingly most distant from one another, will be able to bring the political out of its concealment and, at the same time, return thought to its practical calling (HS: 10).

Pure potentiality *could* be thought of almost as a divine becoming – the freedom to be nothing other than one's own self-unfolding existence. Alternatively potentiality can be thought of more radically as something that may or may not come into being, that may or may not actualize itself, and that would be disclosed beyond all actuality or will: such a genuine potentiality would be always (at least in part) impotentiality: a silence or suffering that would be disclosed less in moments of revelation than in loss, hidden-ness or non-being. Poised between Heidegger and Benjamin, Agamben investigates the Western tradition of ontology that privileges actualized or present being over potentiality and becoming. He also approaches the opening of this problem as primarily biopolitical, for it is the sovereign power over life, and its splitting into lawful versus abandoned life that gives philosophical questions their urgency. The political dimension of Benjamin's thought not only tempers the solitary Heideggerian emphasis on authenticity; it also alters how we understand the very nature of a philosophical problem. For Agamben, the emergence of the space of the world is originally political, to do with the *collective* speaking in common that we might again retrieve only if we return thought to its practical calling. So, like Heidegger, Agamben insists that we need to think the coming into presence of the world, and this will be achieved through thinking authentically about art and speech as world disclosive. Rather than see politics as a form of art – as the way in which we make the world – we might think of art and politics as revelations of a coming-into-being that is neither willed by a subject nor simply given as an object. The artwork is not the work of an artistic will; it emerges from the collective "solidarity and common ground":

> To look at a work of art, therefore, means to be hurled out into a more original time: it means ecstasy in the epochal opening rhythm, which

gives and holds back. Only by starting from this situation of man's relationship with the work of art is it possible to comprehend how this
relationship – if it is authentic – is also for man the highest engagement,
that is, the engagement that keeps him in the truth and grants to his
dwelling on earth its original status. In the experience of the work of art,
man stands in the truth, that is, in the origin that has revealed itself to
him in the poietic act. In this engagement, in this being-hurled-out into
the *epoche* of rhythm, artists and spectators recover their essential solidarity and their common ground ... This original structure of the work of art
is now obscured. At the extreme point of its metaphysical destiny, art,
now a nihilistic power, a "self-annihilating nothing," wanders in the
desert of *terra aesthetica* and eternally circles the split that cuts through
it. Its alienation is the fundamental alienation, since it points to the
alienation of nothing less than man's original space. (MWC: 102)

Like Heidegger, Agamben treats contemporary problems and questions as symptoms of a deeper metaphysical malaise, or a malaise that
has to do with the very existence of metaphysics: why has Western
thought been concerned with what truly is, as that which remains
present or actualized, beyond the contingencies of potential existence?
Why has it progressively seen the artwork as the will of an artist and
not as the primary disclosure of a world that is not a simple collection
of things but something that comes into appearing? Agamben's debt
to Heidegger lies precisely in this commitment to recalling the question
of being with an emphasis on the very problem of the posing of this
question: why do we ask primarily about being? For Agamben, the
impasses of the present require a renewed investigation into questions
of deep metaphysical import (such as being and the ongoing subordi-
nation of potentiality to actuality). Like Benjamin, however, Agamben
understands this inquiry into the deep past of metaphysics as intertwined with the political emergence of law and politics, and in this
respect Heidegger's privilege of *thinking* and dwelling is inflected and
somewhat displaced with a more inhuman or "divine" attention to
forces that bring relation into being and that are *not* those of "man" or
Dasein. For Agamben and Benjamin, the deeper and more necessary
question is how political relations and persons come into being. How
is it that something like a bordered polity and the very notion of law
in general (with its abandonment of bare life) comes into being? This
coming into being of the polity, in turn, requires an interrogation into
the very possibility of religion, or transcendence, and this is because
religion is a curious attempt within the contingency of time to create
some relation to eternity – to what truly is.

Combining a Heideggerian commitment to Western thought as a
whole, and a Benjaminian attention to the opening of thought via a
political/mystical space, Agamben presupposes something like the
possibility of a single tradition of "the law" as such. (Agamben speaks

of "we," "the West," and "man," and never asks about other modalities of humanity that are not bound up with the history of ontology, sovereignty, and the threshold of language.) This single tradition is a tradition of conflict and torsion, where the ongoing history of law or what counts as the good is a continual wrestling with a foundational incoherence. We have inherited an origin, for Agamben, that continues into the present, but it is always a split origin; it consists of what Agamben variously refers to as a "fracture," "aporia," "threshold," or zone of indistinction. We turn back, not to retrieve coherence, purity, and the proper, but to confront an "essential" impropriety – a force that can only be discerned *as it hides itself.* That is, there is *not* something like being, actuality, or presence that then undergoes certain changes or comes into appearance; instead, everything that is may or may not become actual and may come to present itself differently. For Agamben, to grasp the world – *here and now in its "thisness"* or singularity – requires that we neither see it as the appearance *of* some foundation nor regard it as a process of becoming that is on its way to some final fulfillment. Here, again, we see both Benjamin and Heidegger. What unites Heidegger, Benjamin, and Agamben is not only a strong sense of the fragile potentiality of the world that might have been otherwise but has turned out to be simply "thus," but also a recognition that the forgetting, dismissal, or abandonment of potentiality occurs because of the difficulty – once we have a world – of thinking that it might be just as it is for no reason other than its coming into existence, without essence, reason, or prior cause.

For both Agamben and Heidegger, this forgetting is not some lapse or accident: thought and language, in the very event of *saying,* give the world a presence that at once allows for appearing but also a disappearing, silence, or unsayability. It is the very nature of being to be ungraspable outside the various appearances it offers. And it is the very nature of language, in speaking about the world, to also be distanced from the world. There can be no experience of Being as such, only beings. For Heidegger and Agamben, the modern world of technology and spectacle has tended to reduce any capacity for questioning or thinking about the coming into being of the world, and yet they both insist that it is in the moment of the absolute loss of anything outside the simple appearing of the world – the loss of God, being, and foundations – that we might confront the event of the world's appearing, which has no foundation. Similarly, for Benjamin, we experience a political world where laws are enforced and where force is always the force of some sovereign body; what we do not experience is the force that opened up the political space of distributed forces. For Benjamin, it is precisely in the modern world where sovereignty becomes nothing more than force without legitimation or limit that we might think about the violence that brings law into being.

Here, we can tie Agamben's political and aesthetic theory to a nuanced grasp of nihilism: the modern world has lost all sense of origin and accepts a world of empty spectacle and language. Rather than insist on a foundation, Agamben will argue that the absence of grounds might allow us – finally – to accept the world in its mere appearing. We can only reach this messianic moment if we understand the ways in which our present sense of life and law represents one side of an opposition that has dominated Western theology and philosophy. We begin with a distinction between God and the world, but when we no longer believe in God or the good, we imagine this world as lacking, as godless. What is required, then, is an archaeology that explains the incoherence of the present, by charting a history of the ways in which we have continually forgotten, excluded, or abandoned life as such, a life that is not lacking in divinity precisely because there is no divinity, no transcendence other than life's being at odds with, or beside, itself.

In the beginning of Western thought, for Agamben, there is an impossible ambivalence (but this ambivalence is not psychological, but precedes the coming into being of selves or individuals): it is by way of an experience of language or distance that there is a positing of something that absolutely is (being, God, divinity) that is then set before or above a created or external world that must somehow be governed or redeemed. But it is this fracture of split that constitutes an ongoing aporia: if we think of this life as other than the proper, how can it ever be redeemed? The past harbors difficult distinctions that have never been clear or stable. It follows, for Agamben, that the entire edifice of the present – the way we speak, the way we view artworks, the way we live as humans – occurs only because we have forgotten highly charged distinctions that, in the beginning, were never clearly or properly distinguished, and did not emerge from some pristine unity.

Agamben is preoccupied with one overwhelming question, and this question cannot even be asked, let alone answered, by remaining with the terms of the present. Agamben, we might say, is a singularly *untimely* thinker: every problem posed in his corpus is placed at one remove from contemporary assumptions and current terms of debate. Despite the apparent specificity of some of his theoretical interventions, such as his book on Auschwitz, his reading of Melville's short story "Bartleby," and his comment on the medical case of Karen Quinlan, the framing of these questions is always that of a Western trajectory of thought and its paradoxical comprehension of life. Perhaps in the most unfashionable manner possible, Agamben seems to be making a claim for a broad diagnosis of the present by reading our current problems as symptoms of a grand history of the West, a history that he also posits as potentially capable of being destroyed, overcome, and redeemed.

Even so, for all his untimely distance from many of the current assumptions about the world of the present being thoroughly determined by languages, technologies, and systems that have no outside, Agamben's work is dominated by an insistent sense of *the present*. Rather than see politics as a domain of multiple problems, we might think, as Agamben does, that there is a general political problem *of the polity* or the very way in which humans think of themselves as living in common and the modes of force and power that are generated from those political relations. The abstract problem of potentiality – or the relation between what something is and what it may or may not become (which is also the problem of being and acting) – expresses itself concretely in politics as the relation between the body politic in its legal and constituted mode and the ongoing events of politics. Every event or decision that requires the law to move from generality to singular cases is not guaranteed by law in advance and is marked by an openness of potentiality that is more than the simple passage to actualization. *The* overwhelming political question for Agamben, then, is the problem of relation, including the relation between what we may be, and the ways in which we determine that being with each event of existence. The acute and singular nature of the present is, for Agamben, only thinkable if we expand our horizon to consider the Western tradition as such, and its ongoing struggle to come to terms with the very existence of a humanity increasingly estranged from its own life. We have tended to begin with distinction and relation (human and inhuman, being and act), when the real question is not the *difference* between these terms, but the emergence of difference – the genesis of a relation from the threshold of the non-relational.

Agamben is at once in line with a twenty-first-century reaction against forms of theory and philosophy that remain within the limits of language, human systems, and cognitive conditions. His work, in this respect, might be aligned with a trend toward new realisms and new materialisms (Coole and Frost 2010). At the same time, Agamben places a profound importance on the event of the emergence of language, and undertakes his inquiry into this genesis via a textual tradition of philosophy, theology, philology, and poetry. Agamben's work is therefore poised between an intense focus on language, text, and tradition, and a commitment to thinking beyond the language of the tradition. His work is profoundly historical in its insistence on the need to recompose the questions that have constituted the Western tradition, but is also radically future-oriented in the idea of breaking away from the impasses of the present to create an entirely new mode of politics and community. In this sense, the commitment to language and the past is based on a belief that without such a looking back there can be no moving forward. It is this dovetail between an attention to the ancient past and the unimagined future that also explains the link between the oldest questions of sovereignty (as *homo sacer*) and the modern problem of biopolitics. If Agamben claims that there is not as stark a difference between democratic hedonism and totalitarianism as we would like to think, this is because he sees both movements as dominated by a managing of life as an unquestioned end, or – more accurately – the management of life as a means that maintains nothing more than the end of managing life (thereby abandoning a question of how life ought to be lived). This modern biopolitics that has abandoned the broader question of the forming of life is only possible because that tradition of formed life had already abandoned mere life. The present political divisions between individualism and communitarianism, and between liberalism and socialism, or between a positive biopolitics that affirms our milieu of life and a counter-politics that focuses on a formation of practices and living, need to be set aside by thinking the threshold from which such oppositions emerge.

Many explanations of fascism and totalitarianism have tended to regard such political events as the outcome of a late capitalist and modernist breakdown of norms, traditions, and the sense of community. One response to such a process of attrition would be to find new modes of collectivity that – unlike fascism – would not be imposed summarily from the top and would not draw on regressive modes of social unity (such as racism or cultural purity). Such immanent modes of politics emphasize the creative and positive potentiality of life as labor, or of the imagination of collective humanity as expressive and relation-constituting. This is Michael Hardt and Antonio Negri's approach in *Empire*, relying as they do on the conception of the multitude as a creative, productive, and self-constituting potentiality that has no end outside that of bringing itself to fruition. Another response is to regard liberation from tradition and collective norms as a mode of enlightened progress, where individuals move toward increasing autonomy and self-determination. One would therefore oppose and conjoin communitarianism and liberalism as paradigms of sovereign self-constitution: liberalism is an anti-foundationalism that recognizes that there can be no common good outside the recognition of the absence of any essence, allowing individuals to be self-determining, while communitarianism acknowledges the existence of individuals only as enabled by constituted traditions. Often, contemporary problems are diagnosed as a conflict between these ideas: we want to be tolerant and accept the ideas and traditions of various cultures, religions, and ethnicities, but at the same time we want to respect the self-determination of individuals. The conflict between individual rights and group rights – between advocating self-determination, while remaining tolerant of traditional cultures that do not subscribe to the norm of individualism – marks a whole range of political problems (Gatens 2004).

If we assume that late capitalism and modernity are either break-downs of a once enabling traditionalism, or (alternatively) liberations from a once restrictive social code, then it makes sense to look forward to creating new political forms. In many ways this appears to be Agamben's project too, although there is an important distinction. Rather than see modernity as a unique conflict between self-determining freedom and constituted polities (or individualism and communitarianism, or rights versus cultural respect), he sees both motifs of sovereignty as exclusions of non-relational life. Both these approaches (communitarianism and liberalism) are instances of abandoning mere life insofar as they begin from a political unity (the community or the individual) and do not consider the genesis of the polity or "man," all the while presupposing some proper norm of the human (whether that be the individual person or the self-forming community). We might find this response in approaches as diverse as neo-Aristotelianism, where the self is given purpose, meaning, and definition only through a critical relation to tradition and other selves, and in contemporary liberalism where it is the absence of founding tradition that requires individuals to form a fair society, all the while mindful that they must make such a decision with an awareness of other rational decision-makers. Communitarianism assumes that selves are formed through a political process of conversation, deliberation, and reflection enabled by already constituted conditions and conventions. Liberalism assumes a regulating ideal of justice or fairness: because no single tradition is binding or universal, a just society can only be one in which any decision might in principle be made by any individual whatever. Both of these approaches – relying either on the community as political ground or the individual as political agent – assume a constituted political space.

What Agamben draws from both Schmitt and Benjamin, in opposition to liberalism and communitarianism, is an attention to a force or violence prior to the emergence of any individual or community, and a continuing attention to a violence that will then mark any political border by expelling the improper as outside its space of law. Whereas Schmitt will consider the ongoing power of sovereign violence to be necessary to maintain the space of law *against* the violence of lawlessness, Benjamin will offer Agamben a way of thinking beyond the distinction between the violence of law that keeps the violence of life at bay; what is violent is this very opposition between sovereignty and life, and what is redemptive is not so much a better law as a different conception of politics that does not rely on sovereign law. The problem with both individualism and communitarianism is that political questions begin from some presupposed political space – such as the assembling of free individuals or a constituted tradition of normativity – and they do so without questioning the violent genesis of norms and the proper, and the opening of political space which, for Agamben, is not so much political as *poetic*. That is, rather than think of an opposition between praxis (or acting and working) and *poiesis* (or a making that generates something other than oneself), Agamben thinks of an original *poiesis* that opens the political space of action. It is not that there are agents who speak and generate a polity, for it is in speaking as a form of action that a political space emerges. Questions of self and community are only possible after this "common."

This is why, for Agamben, it is less important to mark a distinction between older models of sovereignty based on a transcendent value or good, and modern immanent models in which there is no good outside that of individual procedures of deliberation. In both these cases, there is already a relation between the one who decides and the political space or body over which a decision is made. In both cases, modes of non-relation, such as individuals who do not determine themselves, are set outside the space of political legitimation. What sort of ethics and politics might be able to bear witness to the increasing condition of non-humanity: would it be possible to build a community that did not require a norm of personhood or the good and that would attend to humans in their impotentiality or fragility? What comes to the fore in the entirety of Agamben's corpus is a humanity that is always structured by a relation of exclusion, where what is set outside is the non-relational or that which simply "is" without this singularity of being fulfilling a definition or essence. There is either the community that identifies itself through its practices and cultural norms, or there is the individual as presupposed agent of an ideal decision that would in principle apply to any body whatever. For Agamben, neither approach is adequate precisely because what is required today is a questioning of the very emergence of the relation between the site of the political decision, and the political space over which the decision operates. Before there is this or that specific political decision, and before there is a process of legitimating a source of decisions – granting an individual or a community a right to speak – there is the opening up of a relation that is the very emergence of political force.

If we speak either about the community or the individual as political agents or grounds of a political decision, then we necessarily forget the force or "decision" that constitutes the individual or community as such. This is not a personal decision adopted by someone or something who bears a relation to a domain of procedures; it is a "decision" that generates the power and distance of one who decides. Agamben's work, here, resonates with, and differs subtly from, Jacques Derrida's deconstruction of the decision. For Derrida, a decision is only possible because of undecidability. That is, if there were a correct or perfectly calculable choice to be made, then the decision would not be a decision. For Derrida, like Agamben, this means that there is no political or ethical foundation that could guarantee or guide our decisions, and we must therefore have a heightened ethics of responsibility that is mindful of the groundlessness of every decision, even if that decision presents itself as the straightforward application of a law. However, that paradigm of deciding in the absence of any foundation for the decision, or of operating in absolute undecidability, repeats, according to Agamben, the sovereign ban: what needs to be attended to is not the pure force of the decision but the decision's relation to that which remains above and beyond any decisive force.

The difference in Agamben's work lies in the attention he pays to the zone of indistinction or indifference that he identifies outside and before the event of the decision. Whereas Derrida refers to an "undecidability" as an abstract condition of every decision, Agamben undertakes a political, juridical, and historical inquiry into the spaces and events where this decision emerges. We might say that, for Derrida, in the beginning is difference and relation, *from which* we presuppose that there must have been some ground, but that ground is an effect of the difference it seems to precede (Swiffen 2012). For Agamben, it is irresponsible to remain at the level of differences, relations, and the abandoned outside; what is required is the thought of the threshold before relations and difference. How does sovereignty emerge, and where might one discern undecidability as a form of life or space outside the law? When the US president suspends certain rights or procedures for the sake (supposedly) of security, it becomes evident that there is not a law that provides a ground for decisions, but that there is a decisive power from which both law *and its suspension* follow. There is always something of a decision in even the most unremarkable events of law, precisely because it is always potentially the case that any application of the law might also always be a suspension of the law. Any position that is an execution of the law is not only an actualization of a constituted system, but also an ongoing decision to keep the law in play (or not). Sovereignty, then, marks the various institutions that open up the space of a decisive force. This applies to sovereignty in the specific political-legal sense, but also to a more general structure of the passage between being and act, and speaker and speech act. We cannot simply say that speakers and speech acts are effects of language as a system of differences, for it is also possible that one *not speak*, and it is that event that cannot be included within language and difference.

The general assumption against which Agamben's work is directed is that there is a sovereignty, a good, or even a true being (a full actuality) that then acts, decides, or enters into relation. But Agamben is also opposed to simply accepting the polity as a system of differences or forces. From his perspective, rethinking the sovereign decision requires a new conception of the non-relation; it is through some event of decision that a relation emerges between the sovereign and the system of law that forms the ground of subsequent decisions, just as it is through the event of speaking that there emerges a speaker. It is by way of speaking that a space or distinction is opened up, and it is for this reason that Agamben often places a great deal of emphasis on events of poetry – not because poetry communicates some special meaning, or says something of profound significance – but because in poetry the original decisive power of language is exposed, as the pure decisive event *that there is speaking*: "A model of this operation that consists in making all human and divine works inoperative is the poem. Because poetry is precisely that linguistic operation that renders language inoperative" (KG: 251). Sovereignty, like the structure of language, is best considered not as a transcendent or legitimate body that has the power to decide, but rather as a decisive power from which a space of law and a sovereign power emerge.

Agamben's ongoing inquiry concerns a moment or space of potentiality before religion and law, before the split between a divine power that is the origin of law, and some worldly conception of law: "one should avoid the very terms 'religion' and 'law,' and try instead to imagine an *x* that we must take every care in defining, practicing a kind of archaeological *epoche* that suspends, at least provisionally, the attribution of predicates that we commonly ascribe to religion and law" (ST: 90). In this respect he is highly critical of any political theology that does not interrogate the emergence of its own concepts, just as he is equally critical of any modern political theory that simply accepts the imposition of law without asking how such a relation of power or authority is constituted. If he is interested in sovereignty it is not just that he inquires into how a power legitimates itself, but rather how there is something like power as such. In this way Agamben explores a far more profound sense of power than might be thought of under the terms of either a political or a theological context.

6

Power Beyond Recognition

Several motifs marked the post-1968 generation of French thinkers with regard to power. To this day the student riots of May 1968 and the Paris Communist Party's insistence that only a workers' revolution could lead to a renewed future mark the ways in which contemporary theorists consider power. Both Agamben and the French thinkers with whom he is in dialogue (such as Jacques Derrida, Michel Foucault, Alain Badiou, Jacques Lacan, and Gilles Deleuze) drew upon art and aesthetic creativity rather than traditional work or production to think of a break with systems and relations of power. Rather than praxis, or an activity that remains close to and enables the bodily life from which it emerges, more emphasis was placed on *poiesis*, or an activity that yielded a separate object that could not be reduced to use: art provided the possibility for thinking a life and creativity not oriented to survival, self-maintenance, or the sovereign claims of identity. Agamben, too, asks the question of the relation between work and *poiesis*, but he is at once critical of the twentieth-century conception of *poiesis* as an artist's free creativity, and instead wants to rethink a broader notion of *poiesis* as disclosure of a world:

> If the death of art is its inability to attain the concrete dimension of the work, the crisis of art in our time is, in reality, a crisis of poetry, of ποίησις. Ποίης, poetry, does not designate here an art among others, but is the very name of man's doing, of that productive action of which artistic doing is only a privileged example, and which appears, today, to be unfolding its power on a planetary scale in the operation of technology and industrial production. The question about art's destiny here comes into contact with an area in which the entire sphere of human ποίησις; pro-ductive action in its entirety, is put into question in an original way. Today this productive doing, in the form of work, determines everywhere the status of man on earth, understood from the point of view of

praxis, that is, of production of material life; and it is precisely because Marx's thought of the human condition and of human history is rooted in the alienated essence of this ποίησις and experiences the "degrading division of labor into intellectual and manual labor" that it is still relevant today. What, then, does ποίησις; poetry, mean? What does it mean that man has on earth a poetic, that is, a pro-ductive, status? (MWC: 36–7)

The French Hegelian tradition of negativity tended to grant art in its broadest sense an oppositional role that would be destructive of constituted fields of sense. Even today, feminist theorists such as Judith Butler, whose first book was on French readings of Hegel, see a radical capacity in art and performance not because of any positive content articulated by artworks and performances, but because the repetition of everyday structures of power destabilizes power. For Butler there is no point outside a system of power – no space of innocence or redemption – but there is a capacity for power to be negated or destabilized from within its own constituted field (Butler 1987, 1990). Prior to Butler's work, the thinkers of the post-1968 generation, such as Jacques Derrida, insisted on a negativity or difference that would be anarchic and unproductive, and could not be grounded upon either a subject or intent, and certainly not in any ultimate reason or purpose. There was a strong emphasis on writing, text, or systems of inscription to indicate a force of difference that possessed an anarchic power to *say nothing*, and to destroy communication. To some extent, Agamben's conceptions of inoperativity or unworking are similarly counter-Hegelian in their attempt to theorize relations that do not recover negativity or expenditure in some greater moment of productive recognition, and nowhere is this clearer than in his references to Herman Melville's "Bartleby, the Scrivener" where Bartleby's repeated response to the demand to work – "I would prefer not to" – allows for a form of being that is neither that of full realization nor recognition.

Melville's story has received a great deal of critical attention from contemporary European philosophers, but it offers itself to (at least) two contrary readings. Melville describes Bartleby who, employed as a scrivener, proceeds *not* to work; he is still identified by his work – he is Bartleby, "the Scrivener" – but nevertheless, when asked to work, expresses a preference "not to." According to Michael Hardt and Antonio Negri, Bartleby's "absolute refusal" is – in its rejection of the imposition of labor – a liberating affirmation of a universal humanity. Theirs is a more classically Marxist response to the relation between labor and revolution, such that the refusal of imposed work nevertheless yields a different form of collective creativity: "The contemporary cooperative productive capacities through which the anthropological characteristics of the multitude are continually transcribed and reformulated cannot help revealing a telos, a material affirmation of liberation" (Hardt and Negri 2000: 395). By contrast – and here Agamben is closer to Spinoza's concept of a positive and expressive power, rather than one of Hegelian negation – Bartleby's preference does not tie him to some ultimate refusal in the name of humanity, but opens up the thought of *potentiality as such* before all active and interactive negation, as if the world were composed *not* of differences between or among, but of *"powers to."* These potentialities can only be disclosed in their pure potentiality before they are actualized into relations of opposition, recognition, or mastery. As Agamben writes in relation to Melville's story, "Our ethical tradition has often sought to avoid the problem of potentiality by reducing it to the terms of will and necessity" (P: 254). Agamben asserts that "Bartleby calls into question precisely the supremacy of the will over potentiality" since he "is capable only without wanting ... his potentiality is not, therefore, unrealized; it does not remain unactualized on account of a lack of will. On the contrary, it exceeds will ... at every point" (P: 255). The emphasis on potentiality *before* relation allows us to think of a different mode of post-Marxist politics. Whereas the Marxism that remains indebted to the Hegel of negativity and difference focuses on individuals actualizing themselves through collective action and recognition, another Marxism considers power less as relational and negative, and more as a power that may *or may not* enter into relation.

As we have already seen, one of the thinkers with whom Agamben engages in *Homo Sacer*, Georges Bataille, was typical of the French thought of the twentieth century in being opposed to the Hegelian system of reducing negativity and difference to the ultimate work of human reason. For Bataille, Hegel's acknowledgment of negativity, non-identity, or forces that were destructive and not conducive to life, stability, and sameness was immediately recuperated by the Hegelian insistence that all seeming un-reason ultimately would serve reason (or, in Marxist terms, that the sufferings of capitalism would eventually generate revolution and recognition of the conditions of labor). Like Agamben after him, Bataille wanted to think about history less as a rational progress to a polity of mastery, recognition, and mutually productive negation, and more as a passage to inoperativity, whereby humanity liberated itself from its enslavement to mastery *over life*. But Agamben wonders just what such an inoperativity would mean, and he challenges the Hegelian tradition's way of thinking about what an end of history, or an end of mastery, might amount to:

> Everything depends on what is meant by "inoperativeness." It can be neither the simple absence of work nor (as in Bataille) a sovereign and useless form of negativity. The only coherent way to understand inoperativeness is to think of it as a generic mode of potentiality that is not exhausted (like individual action or collective action understood

as the sum of individual actions) in a *transitus de potential ad actium*. (HS: 61–2)

Perhaps, Bataille thought, there could be a negation that was destructive of recognition, production, reason, and coherence, and that could annihilate self-identity and stability without returning to recognition. Bataille, like those whom he influenced, was opposed to any Marxism that would see revolution and freedom as simply unfolding from the logic of history. Instead, genuine transformation would be destructive of man, recognition, and the relations of work and production. Bataille wanted to intensify negativity and difference, and did so by insisting on the destructive capacity of non-meaning and non-production, and even defined the thought of the sacred in terms of the power of destruction without redemption, without any thought of sustaining or maintaining life. True sovereignty would be liberated from the desire for "power over ..." and would be an almost divine abandonment of anything other than the intensity of the instant. For Bataille, there would be a strong link, then, between literature and evil, or a refusal of those ready-made concepts that made life easy and enjoyable – based on the self-sameness and recognition of the self. Literature would be sacrificial, not by being holy, nor by reflecting the will of some divine purpose, but in a breaking free from such all too human and comforting realities: "Poetry alone, which denies and destroys the limitations of things, can return us to this absence of limitations – in short, the world is given to us when the image we have within us is sacred, because all that is sacred is poetic and all that is poetic is sacred" (Bataille 2001: 84). For Agamben, as we have already seen, modern theories of power have been led "astray" by a "mythologeme" to do with the sacred: the idea that the sacred is an original ambivalence, in which purity and impurity are coupled and inseparable. It is this notion that, for Agamben, constitutes a profound laziness of thinking: we explain liminal figures – such as *homo sacer* – by referring back to some supposed pre-political moment of myth in which the border between the auspicious and inauspicious was not clearly distinguished. This simple dependence on a magical past then leads to a use of the concept of sacrifice and the sacred to explain too much when it is precisely what is in need of explanation. While the logic of sacrifice explains a violence one would do to life in order ultimately to save life, the phenomenon of *homo sacer* destroys the idea that the lives we sacrifice are deemed worthy or sacred; there appears to be a remainder or indifferent zone between sacrificed life and sacrificing mastery that establishes itself by externalizing itself. When we destroy abandoned life it has nothing to do with the ambivalence of the sacred or the logic of sacrifice, which for Bataille was the sovereign capacity to set up a limit and then defile or transgress the very taboos one established. For Agamben, there is a mode of life that cannot be explained – as it too often is – as some sovereign moment of negativity in which we indulge in self-destruction and annihilation for the sake of higher redemption.

For Agamben, this means that our entire theory of power needs to be thought outside the logic of sacrifice and the sacred, and what needs to be thought in its place is unsacred life, or life as such. Bataille's commitment to the mythologeme of the sacred has structured modern thought on sacrifice and has prompted Agamben's contemporary, the French philosopher Jean-Luc Nancy, to affirm a life that would be "unsacrificeable." But, for Agamben, this only leaves the logic of sacrifice and the sacred intact. What we should be doing, he claims, is not aiming to include more life in some category of the sacred in which life elevates itself to the position of sovereign supremacy. It is here that the very nature of Agamben's thought starts to make sense in terms of the present. The problem has been (he argues) an ongoing production of the sacredness of life, at the expense of an unthought and abandoned remainder. The sanctity of life today has nothing to do with sacrifice and sacredness in the sense of a border between pure and impure; on the contrary, it is a life that can be killed or disposed of because it lies outside institutions of sacredness, as mere life:

> If our analysis of *homo sacer* is correct, and the Bataillian definition of sovereignty with reference to transgression is inadequate with respect to the life in the sovereign ban that may be killed, then the concept of the "unsacrificeable" too must be seen as insufficient to grasp the violence in modern biopolitics. *Homo Sacer* is unsacrificeable, yet he may nevertheless be killed by anyone. The dimension of bare life that constitutes the immediate referent of sovereign violence is more original than the opposition of the sacrificeable and the unsacrificeable, and gestures toward an idea of sacredness that is no longer absolutely definable through the conceptual pair (which is perfectly clear in societies familiar with sacrifice) of fitness for sacrifice and immolation according to ritual forms. In modernity, the principle of the sacredness of life is thus completely emancipated from sacrificial ideology, and in our culture the meaning of the term "sacred" continues the semantic history of *homo sacer* and not that of sacrifice. (HS: 67–8)

Several important moves are undertaken by Agamben in the above paragraph, helping us to understand how his conception of power and relations contrasts with Bataille's post-Hegelian conception of life and difference.

There are two histories, according to Agamben: the history of the sacred, in which life casts a portion of itself aside for sacrifice. Life that sacrifices itself or elevates itself above its own everyday survival is sacred life, and this conception of the sacred relies on a life that can negate or destroy itself for the sake of itself. (One can think here of the ways in which saints, heroes, soldiers, patriots, believers, and martyrs give up their life for the sake of an ideal of life. To use the logic of

Hegel's conception of power, their mastery lies in their capacity to liberate themselves from the needs of everyday life; they posit an end or idea beyond life and are thereby elevated, or sanctified, by negating the merely living.) In Bataille's radicalized version of this ultra-mastery, there would be a divine liberation in any act that did not seek to maintain itself, and that could abandon all desire *for* mastery or self-maintenance, becoming desire as such, freed from any end and any self. For Agamben, though, there is a "semantic history of *homo sacer* that is not that of sacrifice" that better explains modern biopolitics. This bare life or the life of *homo sacer* precedes the opposition between sacred and profane, and is outside the sacrificial mode of self-negation that abandons a part of itself in order to sanctify or purify itself.

First, Agamben wants to posit something like life that is prior to or more original than the ambivalence of the sacred, and beyond the threshold between purity and impurity, and yet this life is not given as a unity but has always been divided and classified, and then posited as a prior and elusive ground. Quite specifically, this means that the only way in which power and violence can be understood is *not* via some notion of a sacred or sovereign life that possesses the power to sacrifice or negate itself; that event of sacrificial force is an effect, not a ground, and comes into being by way of exclusion/inclusion or a never-fully-differentiated border. More generally and abstractly, this means that rather than begin with sovereign *self-relation*, or a humanity that abandons an aspect of itself in order to elevate itself, there would be something outside, before, and beyond this relation. Second, Agamben makes a claim regarding modernity, which is that what now appears as bare life, or a life that was once deemed to be outside political relations of mastery, is now the life that is deemed to be sacred, and that forms the end of biopolitics – reduced to that which must be managed and saved as an unquestioned end. What is *not* able to be thought is a life before the oppositional structure of the sacred, a life that is neither human/political nor animal/biological. Finally, if there is another space of life – outside the self-negation of life that is responsible for sacrificial logics – then this means we need a new conception of power and relations. We would suggest that Agamben here turns to a positive or pure conception of potentiality that is Spinozist insofar as it aims to think a life that *may or may not* generate relations of recognition, but that has a capacity to differ that is not that of destructive negation, or – more accurately – has a capacity *not to be* that is definitive.

Immanence, Potentiality, and Beatitude

Spinoza's conception of God was not that of some ultimate substance outside existence, but was existence itself – with one substance expressing itself in different modes, *none of which was the foundation for the other*. (That is, body and mind were not distinct substances, nor was mind a negation of the body, or housed in the body; they were two aspects of the same substance.) This tradition of immanent philosophy generates a different thought of power distinct from that of sovereignty, where rather than power over (*potestas*) one begins from power to (*potentia*), and rather than the division between political life and the animal life that it expels, one might be able to think of a life not abandoned or placed outside the sacred.

> The fact is that for Spinoza all living beings without distinction express God's attributes in a certain determinate manner. But this absolute onto-logical proximity, not only between men and animals but also between all individuals of every species, is confirmed by their divergence on the plane of ethics. Precisely because they are all modes of a single substance, they can gather together or not gather together according to the diversity of their natures.
>
> The great right of man over animals does not, therefore, express a hierarchical or ontological supremacy; instead it corresponds to the general diversity of living beings. If, for the sake of hypothesis, there were a man whose existence was increased by the spider or the fly, or who could develop friendships with them, this man according to Spinoza would do well to take the greatest care to protect these creatures' lives. (EP: 105)

Mere life (not life that is rendered bare by being stripped of sovereign or sacrificial power) is just this presupposed but never external life. When a body hovers on the border between life and death or is captured by a life-support machine we are, according to Agamben, at once in a lamentable political milieu, which can now take hold of this life; but at the same time this abandoned life promises a different political future. Could there be a polity that was not established by way of the sovereign negation and mastery of life? That very question ties the increasing loss of the distinction between *bios* and *zoe*, or formed life and biological life, to both despair and utopia. As long as we live with a notion of the distinction between formed life and biological life, then the shift to sanctifying the latter only allows sovereign power to exist in a more extreme form: now all life is mere biology, and there is no political space of self-formation, only the domination of biological existence. If we thought beyond that sovereign relation of negativity – outside the oppositions of the sacred – life would not be saved by being sacred but would be regarded just for the life that it is.

Consider the current pro-life and pro-choice debates that set the mother's right to choose against the fetus's right to life: in both cases bare life is deemed to be all powerful. Either (for the pro-choice advocates) my life as a human individual grants me the right to choose, or (for the pro-life campaigners) the living fetus – by virtue of life – is sacred and inviolable. This life that is sacred and that grounds all decision is, however, also outside the decision: there is a sovereign split between the arbiter of rights and the bare life that is saved or abandoned. The language of rights and choice refers to a disembodied and purely formal individual, who legislates over a life that is nothing more than a "bare" substrate for the self. To say that "I" have a right to choose what I do with my body splits the self between a decisive or legislative power and its living being. Agamben's philosophy is concerned with confronting this split or threshold, not so much to favor one side over the other or create a higher unity, but to think the fracture as such. Agamben's suggestion throughout his corpus is that there might be a retrieval of life that is neither the formed life of sovereign self-positing, nor the mere biological existence that increasingly becomes politicized. Could we value life without granting it some sort of sacredness of rights and personhood? Could there be a silent, fragile life that opened a domain of ethical and political questions? In the case of women's reproductive politics, perhaps rather than thinking of competing bodies with rights – rights of women's bodies versus the rights of the unborn child – we could ask about the forming of a life, such that both mother and child are not entities that pre-exist the question of what it is to live? What political forms would attend to the fragility of life, especially life that does not claim rights and personhood? How does a political space open that produces living bodies as competing substances – the rights of the mother versus the rights of the fetus? Rather than the basic biological life of the person – rather than the human life that is now the basis for biopolitical population management and measurement – we might begin to think of life as such, as that from which the community might be generated.

Agamben suggests that there is a potentiality or force that is outside that of the self-relating or self-negating logic of sovereignty. In very specific modern terms, we can see this life only in its abandonment. There is a silent, suffering, non-relational, and pre-political life – a life that has not placed itself in relation to itself – that is now the object of political power. However – thought positively – this same life might allow for the thought of a polity generated from life rather than over life, but this life would always be suspended or poised between the political/relational and the absolutely singular. Consider this in terms of today's most common discourses of the sanctity of life, debates regarding the termination of pregnancies, euthanasia, and the death penalty. Currently the bio-ethics discourses that address these issues focus on personhood – at what point persons emerge from fetuses, at what point there is no longer a person, or at what point a person loses his right to personhood. But could we have an ethics of life that did not divide bare life from sovereign personhood? Rather than debating whether the body on life support is a person, could we not think about compassion and love for suffering life – a love that might wish to release the body from pain? And rather than see the struggling single mother's right to choose as a power competing with a fetus's right to be born, we might think of a life before these divisions into living bio-logical bodies: what sort of polity attends to the silent suffering of life, and considers a life before personal struggles? If life were impersonal, and not placed outside the supposedly sovereign and deciding self of rights, then instead of seeing the right of the mother versus the right of the fetus, one might think compassionately of singular potentialities: what might become of a woman who is either compelled by shame or indignation to continue or terminate a pregnancy, and how might she be able to nurture (or not) a life that she has only in some very broad sense "chosen" to bring into being? Such questions would generate a quite different conception of community: not a world of masters in which each individual becomes maximally self-determining, recogniz-ing themselves as an agent in relation to other self-determining agents. Instead, the community would be immanent, in which the coming into being of each singularity would be the fragile expression of a form of life. Referring to a practice (rather than principle) of care that he draws from Foucault, Agamben responds in an interview on subjectivity that:

> There is, therefore, an aporia: a care of self that should lead to a letting go of self. One way the question could be posed is: what would a practice of self be that would not be a process of subjectivation but, to the con-trary, would end up only at a letting go, a practice of self that finds its identity only in a letting go of self? It is necessary to "stay," as it were, in this double movement of desubjectivation and subjectivation, between identity and nonidentity. This terrain would have to be identified, because this would be the terrain of a new biopolitics. (I: 117)

Agamben's thought, here, is marked by something like a "positive negativity" – a suspension, or *not* working, that is not defined against or in destructive opposition to power, but is a capacity not to be enabled or enacted. In the Spinozist-Marxist tradition, rather than the Hegelian-Marxist tradition, less emphasis is placed on the negation of external power or arriving at collective self-consciousness of the excluded, and more emphasis on an expressive coming into being that is singular. Indeed, Agamben's contemporary, Roberto Esposito (2012), has argued that this exposure to an outside of language, and an "affirmative bio-politics" is what marks contemporary Italian thought. A life just is its singular and contingent exposure to what is not itself. At first this might seem to go against a Spinozist ideal of immanence, where there is just one substance that is nothing other than all its singular modes of appearing, and where freedom and political liberty would lie in making the systems and powers of the world one's own. This, indeed, is how Agamben's contemporaries Hardt and Negri define their Spinozist Marxist project: the new forms of immaterial labor that characterize the twenty-first century liberate workers from being dispersed across the globe in factories and subjected to external technologies of production. New communicative systems have enabled the possibility of a new self-forming humanity. Sovereign power has now been rendered immanent, and humanity has become self-forming and self-governing in common. But Agamben has quite a different conception of Spinozist immanence that is not about the sovereign split between "power to …" and "power over" becoming humanity's own. Whereas Marxism generally regards the world as that which is negated or labored upon in order for humanity to become conscious of itself, and whereas Hardt and Negri see the process of global immaterial labor as one in which humanity produces itself through itself (by communally affecting itself in a mode of positive expression and creation), Agamben's Spinozism is far more passive and far less focused on the self becoming its own sovereign. Rather, there is a surrender to *not* owning oneself, and an openness to one immanent life that is not subject to the sovereign mode of recognizing a properly human political being at the expense of an abandoned bare life. The genuine power of accepting immanence would entail a mode of politics that was not the relation of power over, even if that were the power of humanity over itself. If we accept the claim of immanence – that there is just one life and that neither redemption nor divinity can be sought (or mourned) in a site beyond life – then this leads to a radical acceptance of exteriority. If there were some good or God toward which the potentiality of life ought to become, then every being would have a proper end to which it ought to develop. On such a transcendent (or equivocal) understanding, each being would have its own identity that could become alienated in the exposure to life and contingency; a proper community would either have its own enabling identity (in the form of a tradition) or would allow each individual to come to their own self-forming identity.

For Agamben, by contrast, immanence and univocity – or the acceptance that there is only one life without any good, God, end, identity, or form that would grant it meaning from without – entail that any self or being becomes what it is only through exposure to what is not itself (an exposure that is suffered or given affectively, rather than occurring by way of negation). Rather than a self that recognizes itself and becomes proper to itself by relating to others and otherness, Agamben argues that selves are exterior to themselves – their very being is not their own. Humans in particular, through speech, take up a distance to their own being that they can never appropriate. The very speech that gives them their distance from the world is at once the most intimate potentiality of humans, and yet this language through which we become is never transparent to us, and can always abandon us. We can either mourn this exposure and yearn for a more integrated and proper life, in which case the life of this world would always be deemed to be fallen and improper, *or* we can conceive of a new mode of life in which life itself would not be that which would need to be redeemed by the divine, for there would be no other divinity than the fragility and exposure of life.

This is the key point in Agamben's notion of coming community, where political being is not dependent on being recognized by (or through) a tradition. For Agamben, my mere "thisness" before all predication should be worthy of attention. This is the very opposite of identity politics (where, say, I take on an ethnic, sexual, or gendered identity for the sake of political strategy), and is also quite different from communitarianism where I become who I am by taking on and negotiating a tradition. Agamben's community that is nothing more than an attunement to singularity would also be very different from – say – Judith Butler's post-Hegelian notion of performance, where I become who I am by performing some role, even if performance is both repetition and destabilization of given norms (Butler 1990). We might therefore contrast two modes of unworking or inoperativity: the first would be a negation or refusal of identity in a form of sovereign self-annihilation where I refuse all forms of sameness and recognition. This is the way in which writers such as Bataille responded to Hegel and the sovereignty of the master; there would be no greater mastery than the refusal of all norms of identity, where the self would express its supreme liberation by way of transgressing and annihilating (or sacrificing) every form of stability. The second mode of inoperativity, which Agamben aims to articulate, would be a more positive and yet passive attentiveness to a potentiality that does not necessarily come into actuality. Impotentiality is not the failure of potentiality, and should not be placed outside the achievement of mastery and sovereignty as that which needs to be expelled from the good life; rather, impotentiality, or something's not coming into being, is also its power to come into being or take on form. Rather than regard potentiality as that which fulfills itself by becoming what it ought to be, and rather than express a supreme potentiality that can refuse all forms of determination and actively refuse or destroy any stable form, Agamben writes about new modes of community and relation where potentiality does not bring itself forth into self-present distinction.

The concept of inoperativity or unworking, as Agamben notes, can be thought in a manner different from Bataille's sovereign mode in which one desists from self-production and self-maintenance and engages in distanced and elevated laughter and transgression. Agamben's conception of unworking strives to be profane and immanent:

rather than an abandonment, transgression, or sacrifice that would liberate the self from life in its determined or *mere* (non-self-forming) mode, Agamben suggests a new community and politics where a blessed simplicity attaches to being in its simply being "thus." There is no end or telos toward which life and language are working. Whereas Bataille thought one could destroy teleology and mastery through sacrifice and transgression (or an overcoming of identity), Agamben seeks to find a mode of un-working outside models of redemption, transgression, and overcoming (all of which remain sovereign in their establishment of a negating relation to a life deemed to be non-relational). It is this refusal of distancing and redemption that explains why Agamben frequently cites two ideas that are tied to inoperativity. First, a new ethics might be opened by beginning from *that which cannot be saved*; the unredeemable has no higher end or godliness which would bring it to a state of blessedness. Second, the new world will not be some grand transformation of this world, but this world just as it is, with a difference of inflection. There is thus a difference between counter-Hegelian conceptions of inoperativity, such as Bataille's, and Agamben's more Spinozist notion. The former privileges a form of mastery over work, over identity, and over mere life in a defiant act of refusal; the latter asserts that if there is one immanent life then there need be no active differentiating of the self, or the polity or the good *from life*, and that life itself in its singular "thisness" is enough to generate something like a belonging that has no general or transcendent norm toward which it is oriented. This is so even if Agamben's later work focuses less on the singularities that compose a community and more on lives that generate ongoing formation. If the concept of the coming community is enabled by freeing singularity and potentiality from some proper end, Agamben's focus on a life as the achievement of manner, habit, style, or form shifts emphasis increasingly toward a threshold that is both between and beyond life and form:

> Perhaps the only way to understand this free use of the self, a way that does not, however, treat existence as a property, is to think of it as a habitus, an ethos. Being engendered from one's own manner of being is, in effect, the very definition of habit (this is why the Greeks spoke of a second nature): *That manner is ethical that does not befall us and does not found us but engenders us.* And this being engendered from one's own manner is the only happiness possible for humans. (CC: 28–9)

Art

This is a subtle distinction, and can perhaps be understood through two ways of thinking about art and about labor. In the French Hegelian tradition, destructive negativity takes the already constituted systems of meaning and communication and frees them from any production of sense and communication. Working against notions of established community and recognition, art is celebrated as a force of refusal and pure difference: not subjected to any ideal other than its own force, pure art is not the making *of* anything. The avant-garde artwork would neither present nor disclose anything other than its own empty form; art nullifies or destroys the practices and conventions of constituted definitions (including what counts as art). An example would be Marcel Duchamp's *Fountain*, in which the act of placing a urinal in a gallery is not a gesture of meaning or reference – not the presentation or disclosure of the world – so much as a self-reflexive gesture that draws attention to itself. Art becomes an act of the artist separating himself, constituting himself as nothing more than pure act, and an act that negates what is currently accepted as art. Art is presented solely as a counter-convention, and not as a means for disclosing anything other than itself. One can imagine a page of writing, text, or script that did not say anything, *presenting text as text*. It was this ideal of the work as having no end or sense outside itself that marked deconstruction's emphasis on literature as a "right to say anything": the word is detached from the context of bodies and communication in order to float freely as text – thus tying literature (for Derrida at least) to democracy (Derrida 1992: 36–7). By contrast, even though at first glance there might seem to be a similarity, Agamben constantly turns to works of art – literature and the visual arts – not for this purely formal destruction of already constituted systems, but because of a disclosure of a potentiality (or "power to...") that can be considered before there are constituted or established systems against which art might direct its powers of difference and negativity. Agamben draws a marked contrast between art considered as an expression of *will* and art as that which discloses a world. Writing critically about Nietzsche, Agamben claims the following:

> Art presents itself to Nietzsche's meditation as the fundamental trait of the will to power, in which the essence of man and the essence of eternal becoming are identical to each other. Nietzsche calls *art* this standing of man within his metaphysical destiny. *Art* is the name he gives to the essential trait of the will to power: the will that recognizes itself everywhere in the world and feels every event as the fundamental trait of its character is what is expressed, for Nietzsche, in the value *art*. (MWC: 92)

Heidegger had already argued that Nietzsche's concept of the will was the culmination of Western metaphysics, a metaphysics that seeks to find a privileged Being that accounts for all other beings. Nietzsche's "will to power," according to Heidegger, is a pure force that underlies the world as it comes into appearance. Against this, Heidegger wanted to insist that Being is not some actual substance that underlies all things, but *is only as it appears*; being is its fragile, exposed, and never fully exhausted appearing. For this reason, Heidegger saw art *not* as an expression of will but as an opening or revelation of a world. Agamben contrasts Heidegger's revelatory notion of the work of art as origin with Nietzsche's conflation of art and will. Agamben seems to agree with, and follow, Heidegger's notion that to think of art "aesthetically" as an object of enjoyment to be viewed by an audience who admires the artist's "work" is to preclude a genuine relation to the world:

> When the work of art is…offered for aesthetic enjoyment and its formal aspect is appreciated and analyzed, this still remains far from attaining the essential structure of the work, that is, the origin that gives itself in the work of art and remains reserved in it. Aesthetics, then, is unable to think of art according to its proper statute, and so long as man is prisoner of an aesthetic perspective, the essence of art remains closed to him…In the work of art man risks losing not simply a piece of cultural wealth, however precious, and not even the privileged expression of his creative energy: it is the very space of his world, in which and only in which he can find himself as man and as being capable of action and knowledge. (MWC: 102)

Heidegger had argued that we have a comportment to nature that is dominated by our increasingly overwhelming conception of *techne*: we imagine that the growth and becoming of nature is a movement toward some actuality (in the manner in which a builder creates a thing according to a plan and function). Heidegger had also argued that we tend to think of humans in the same way: as though there is a reason or "logic" that is the essence of humanity, and one which we ought to strive to realize (Heidegger 1988). For Heidegger, there was a fairly stark contrast between a Western metaphysical tradition that was "logical" or that had reduced the disclosive event of saying (*logos*) to some rigid system of representations that simply double the world, and a poetic dwelling where we would be close to the language through which the world comes into its unique appearing. Agamben, too, makes a contrast between a philosophical tradition where language is a means to know the world (a negation of the world, but a negation or gap that does not acknowledge, reducing all to its sovereign closure), and a poetic understanding where language is at a distance from a world it can never *quite say*, but comes to an awareness of the positive power of that distance, of that *not saying* of the world (Dickinson 2012).

It should not surprise us that, as in every conception of the event of language that places in a Voice its originary taking place and its negative foundation, language remains even here metaphysically divided into two distinct planes: first *die Sage*, the originary and silent speech of Being, which, inasmuch as it coincides with the very taking place of language and with the disclosure of the world, shows itself (*zeight sich*), but remains unspeakable for human words; and, second, human discourse, the "word of mortals," which can only respond to the silent Voice of Being (LD: 61).

What both philosophy and poetry share – and what is lost in modern societies of spectacle – is a sense of the distance between the event of saying and what is; poetry is an event of saying that can never quite take hold of or master itself. One of the constant themes in Agamben's work is that language cannot say itself; it is always split between the singular event of its saying, or the bodily sonorous voice speaking, and then the system through which it names what it says – which is general and can only grasp the singular through reducing difference and singularity. This is given most acutely in "shifters": when I use the word "I" it is the same word that you use, but it has a different force on each occasion. Nothing about the system of language (its present actuality, its being) can ever contain the singularity of language (its event or actualization in the act of saying). Agamben's more recent work on the theological problem of Western thought – its impossible problem of being and acting, or of God who absolutely *is*, and the world that is his creation and through which he acts – extends and problematizes his early work on language. Agamben makes explicit the relation between theology and grammar; for both discourses, the singularity of the event is distanced and irreducible from the origin (whether that origin be God, language, or Being). Both have the same sovereign structure whereby a relation must have been opened by an event of speech, and yet we only experience that force within an already constituted system. As Agamben explains in *Language and Death*, it would only be when language breaks down or fails to mean and signify that we would experience language as language:

> The sphere of the utterance thus includes that which, in every speech act, refers exclusively to its taking place, to its instance, independently and prior to what is said and meant in it. Pronouns and other indicators of the utterance, before they designate real objects, *indicate precisely that language takes place*. In this way, still prior to the world of meanings, they permit the reference to the very *event of language*. (LD: 25)

He expands on this idea years later in *The Kingdom and the Glory*. One might say, then, that the sovereign exception or state of exception is when there is force that acts without law, or has no law other than itself: we become aware of force *as force*, as the force that brings law into being, rather than being law's means of operation. And we might say, theologically, as Agamben has also done, that before we glorify this or

that god or sacrifice *to* this or that power, there is an event of glorification or sacrifice that opens the distinction of the sacred and the divine
(KG: 200).

Sovereignty and Divinity, or Power and God, are connected for
Agamben by way of the logic of grammar; before we speak about this
or that, before we have this or that law, and before we sacrifice this or
that being, there is some event that marks out a relation, that enables
life to be split between what is and what acts. It is this coming into
being of relation by way of force – a force of uttering law or prayer, or
a performative force that in saying or acting brings about the relation
that established the terms of power – that creates sovereignty and
divinity. For Agamben, politics and theology are profoundly connected
to grammar, not because theology and divinity can be reduced to language, but because language itself is only possible if something or
someone speaks, and it is in speaking that one becomes a subject, a
political being. Before one says this or that about something, there is
speaking as such. And it is this dimension of *utterance* (that is not concerned with content but the saying or speaking as such) that opens a
domain that says nothing but provides the conditions in which something might be said. In its fallen mode this becomes the modern biopolitical state where there is no law other than a system that acts always
to save itself – all measures are security measures ensuring the force of
law or *that there is law*, rather than some end or life to which law would
be subservient. In its messianic form, this force without law would be
something like Agamben's form of life, where *what I become and who I
am* unfolds from a mode of living that takes on form:

> A form of life would thus be the collection of constitutive rules that
> define it. But can one say in this sense that the monk, like the pawn in
> chess, is defined by the sum of prescriptions according to which he lives?
> Could one not say with greater truth exactly the opposite, that it is the
> monk's form of life that creates his rules? Perhaps both theses are true,
> on the condition that we specify that rules and life enter here into a zone
> of indifference...(HP: 71)

In a similar manner, we would not think of language as a straightforward labeling of a world that was already differentiated, but as an
event of disclosure that is never without remainder, both leaving the
specific self who speaks and what is spoken about irreducible to each
linguistic event. So rather than looking at *what* language says, or
remaining within the system of constituted terms, it is imperative that
we think the genesis of the very potentiality of language *that there is
speaking*, before anything specified or determined is said. Again referring to the relation to text and law in the monasteries, Agamben writes:
"The text of the rule is thus not only a text in which the distinction

between writing and reading tends to become blurred, but also one in which writing and life, being and living become properly indiscernible in the form of a total liturgicization of life and a vivification of liturgy that is just as entire" (HP: 82). Only when we focus less on this or that law, or this or that utterance, and instead on the force of saying – that there is speaking – can we experience the power of that which enables any constituted language to function. Language might, then, be best examined when it *says nothing, or when it cannot speak.*

It is this being or silence of language that Agamben finds disclosed in poetry. Just as any event of witnessing or testimony must always belie the singularity of that about which it speaks, so all speaking and all language is about something other than the event or coming into being of language. While any instance of language is to some degree a rendering general and communicable of a unique and singular sense, poetry and testimony are distinct in their rendering inoperative of the very communicative and functional dimensions of language. It is in poetry that language appears as language, and foregrounds the event of language, or *that there can be language* – not a saying of this or that, but something like a "saying" as such. For Agamben, the inoperativity of art is not the negation or destruction of order and identity, but an impotentiality or a not-saying or not-doing that is disclosed in what poetry and testimony disclose as unsayable. Art is beyond good and evil: in its un-working or not saying, or in its potentiality for transmission and sense that still harbors and displays what cannot be transmitted, art displays a simple "thisness" or singularity that is the very opposite of sovereign self-mastery.

This conception of an inoperativity is closer to a positive sense of impotentiality – or a not-doing that is neither destructive nor productive but is essential to any capacity – and also has a political dimension. Agamben insists frequently on politics not as negation but as retrieving an impotentiality: before we are caught up in powers and relations, there is a power of not doing. Such a thought means that rather than conceive of politics solely as a relation among competing powers, one might think of politics as a more radical potentiality to enter into relation. This would generate a being-with that was not specified in advance by belonging as this or that identity, but simply as a power *to be, as being-with.* This might sound impossibly abstract but it has very direct and profound political consequences. Take, for example, the debate over same-sex marriage. For quite good tactical reasons, activists seeking the right to marry same-sex partners focus on the irrelevance of differences and the inherent sameness and humanity of "us" all. Gay and lesbian couples just want the same social stabilities, rights, entitlements, recognition, and legal benefits as heterosexual couples, as "the rest of us." For all the worthiness of the cause, one should note that the emphasis is on social cohesion and recognition, and on extending the notion of the citizen to all. The implication, if you like, is that gays and lesbians are people too, "just like us." They are decent and productive members of society who make an important contribution. The same is often said for other disenfranchised groups, such as illegal immigrants. They are an important part of the economy and our social fabric. That is all very well, and it is no doubt politically expedient. But what are we saying if we have to recognize someone's humanity or personhood, and especially their productivity – their contribution or active identity – before we attend to their being or life? Could we not find a way beyond recognizing someone because they are human ("just like us")? Could not their mere being or life as such, which we so want to redeem as human and personal – in all its non-productivity – not be sufficient?

Agamben wants to break away not only from Hegelian conceptions of sovereignty that privilege work, active negation, recognition, and mastery, but also from the anti-Hegelian destructions of mastery. For Agamben, the problem lies in the privilege accorded to the negative power that distances sovereignty from mere life, and then sacrificing this distance in a moment of divine abandon: "To have mistaken such a naked life separate from its form, in its abjection, for a superior principle – sovereignty or the sacred – is the limit of Bataille's thought, which makes it useless to us" (MWE: 7). Rather than accept the distance between mere life and sovereign negation or expulsion of life, and then celebrate the transgression or annihilation of that distance, Agamben wants to grant a power to potentiality before negation, and before the labor of the negative – the threshold or zone of indifference that enables negativity and the sovereign divide of language and power to emerge:

> In-difference with respect to properties is what individuates and disseminates singularities, makes them lovable (quodlibetable)…This is how we must read the theory of those medieval philosophers who held that the passage from potentiality to act, from common form to singularity, is not an event accomplished once and for all, but an infinite series of modal oscillations. The individuation of a singular existence is not a punctual fact, but a *linea generationis substantiae* that varies in every direction according to a continual gradation of growth and remission, of appropriation and impropriation. (CC: 19)

For the post-1968 generation of French thinkers that included Foucault, Bataille, Derrida, and Deleuze, the challenge of thought would be to think difference without returning difference to some ultimately *recognizing* model of philosophy: would it be possible for reason (or the logic of the self-same) to think its other? If this were so, then the revolution would not be the grasping of the process of difference by a privileged agent (the worker) and a return of all differentiating forces to some no-longer-alienated subject. Rather, analyses of power would always be consigned to thinking relations and forces while avoiding resolution or sublation: this open difference was considered in terms of play, trace, or writing (Derrida), difference in itself (Deleuze), or positive and productive power (Foucault). The project of thinking difference, un-reason, play, and even the "outside" were all ways of recognizing the limits of language and constituted systems while recognizing that any simple attempt to think outside structures and relations would itself be in relation to structure (even if that structure could never be grasped as such, always given only in its having created difference).

It is just this privileging of difference that Agamben challenges with his constant references to indifference and (more specifically) a life that might not be thought of as other than (but not opposed to) formed political life. One of Agamben's criticisms of both Foucault and Derrida is their hesitancy to think outside constituted systems of relations, and Agamben will constantly use the concept of sovereignty not to think some center for power but to rethink the emergence of difference and relations. Whereas Foucault argues that our theories of power based on sovereignty are unable to account for the distributed, positive, and productive modes of power of modernity, Agamben still sees sovereignty operating in the very conceptions of language, the individual, and art that mark the present. Even if we no longer have a centered sovereign – such as the king or even a constituted government – biopolitics, and the ways in which we manage our own biological existence, still take the form of a dualist "power over"; the managerialism of biopolitics has a simple end – life – which is organized by a series of shifting means, or a law that is nothing other than its own ongoing power to except itself from the life it controls. The only way we can escape the sovereign paradigm is not by shifting power from a transcendent power (God, the king, the human subject) to another transcendent power (humanity, democracy, individuals) but by retheorizing life as something other than that which would be abandoned or expelled by forming, governing, speaking, and personalized life. Closer to the Spinozist tradition – where Spinoza insisted that thinking could rise to the level of intuiting the absolute but would need to escape "common" notions – Agamben tirelessly makes bold claims about the possibility of thinking moments of emergence or division, even if this will not return us to a simple identity. We may only know life in each of its singular expressions (none of which can capture life itself), but what this should lead us to think about is that the life that speaks and gives itself form is an expression of an always singular potentiality, never exhausted in any of its actualizations.

There is a near mysticism in Agamben's thought that is at once messianic but also radically secular: the world might be entirely other than it is, with a blessed rather than negating, excluding, or oppositional "relation" to life, but this will not require some higher world: "Only to the extent that the Messiah renders the *nomos* inoperative, that he makes the *nomos* no-longer-at-work and thus restores it to the state of potentiality, only in this way may he represent its *telos* as both end and fulfillment" (TR: 98). Rather than maintain a division between some good form or ideal and the life that is then governed or formed, one might think of life as nothing other than a potentiality for bringing itself into form, such that form and life would be immanent to each other. Following Spinoza, God would not be a sovereign power outside of life; God *is life as such* thought in its expressive divine immanence. Spinoza's monism did not set the divine or reason outside nature, but saw nature itself as the unfolding of one divine substance. At the same time, though, there was also something absolute or outstanding that would not reduce life or exhaust life in any of its determinations. This tradition of "immanence," or refusing to see being as divided between an active forming power and a passive matter, is crucial for thinking in terms of Agamben's unique concept of power, potentiality, and profanity.

Whereas the logic of the sacred establishes the sovereign as a decisive border between a domain of life that is to be saved and an exterior that exists without force or worth, there might be another thought that refuses the constituted relation between powers. Here, Agamben draws on a long tradition running from Aristotle to Spinoza of considering potentiality, not as a *possibility* attached to an actualized body (such that what a body does or does not do does not ultimately change what it is), but as a potentiality that brings a body into being and is not always an action but equally a power not to act. It is *possible* as the being that I am to vote or not vote; possibilities can be assessed once we calculate all the relations of a situation. To think of the world as composed of actual beings allows us also to assess or calculate possibilities as what beings may or may not do. In such cases we might think of possibility as a limitation of the freedom of a being, as a choice between or among paths. Potentiality is prior to actuality, such that before there is a self who chooses among possibilities there is a potentiality for a living being who would choose. Potentiality is not added on to being; rather, there is potentiality from which some determinate, active, and identified being may emerge. This potentiality, before coming into relation, is not yet fully determined and might therefore be regarded as something like a singular "this." Considered positively, one might therefore imagine a community or polity where participants do not need to take part by way of recognition, assertion of identity, and negation, but just as this singular life as a potentiality to enter into relation.

This is why the very horror of the state of exception is also close to a realization of a messianic future. The key difference lies in whether life is conceived as the bare animal life opposed to lawful, formed, and political life, or whether we might think of life as *the potentiality for the political and the relational* (not as its expelled and abandoned outside). The same applies to law: in the current state of exception the detachment of law from a constituted legal system leads to the tyranny of a pure and immediate force, but it might also have the possibility of genuine politics: of seeing force as such, from which law would emerge (and not simply force as law's means). In the absence of a constituted and stabilized legal system, there is just a force or power for law. We currently experience this force without law in its direct and unmediated action upon bodies, but that same state of emergency also opens the thought of the pure or divine force from which all law emerges, and which might be thought of as immanent to life, rather than the force that regulates life. Here, as we have seen, Agamben draws heavily on Walter Benjamin's "Critique of Violence," where Benjamin (1996) argues that we should not see violence as some unfortunate and accidental means that is deployed by an otherwise benevolent law. Such an understanding presupposes that there would be such a thing as a non-violent law, but how could such a law come into being? To think of violence as an accident or weapon of law is only possible if we accept law as some unquestionable actuality or good. If we ask about the coming into being of law, then we are compelled to think about the force or violence that would bring law into being, and such a violence would be divine in two senses. It would be the creation of relations that did not have any basis other than itself; *and* it would not have any already existing outside. Such would be Agamben's imagined "coming community" in which relations are not fully actualized. Bodies would not be political insofar as they are identified and formed, but would be able to exist in their singularity, before all constitutions of personhood and agency. It is therefore important to go beyond thinking about power as a network of relations and forces, and instead consider the generation of force or the capacity to produce relations. Before there are differences there is a potentiality to differ, and this "before" does not simply pass away once differences are constituted, but remains. This remainder is a zone of indistinction or indifference.

7

Indifference

Here we might begin to see just what is at stake in Agamben's contribution to the present, and the untimely nature of his contribution to
new thoughts about art, politics, theology, and the relation among these
domains. Perhaps nothing is more widely accepted than the value of
difference, both at the level of high theory and of popular culture. At
an everyday level everyone assumes the right to be different, and we
celebrate multiculturalism, diversity, and – at the level of high consumer capitalism – we continue to buy and consume in order to be
different. We choose the newest products, update our looks, and are
seduced by those products and campaigns that appeal to distinction,
uniqueness, and individuality. At the level of high theory, as already
mentioned, the concept of thinking *difference as such*, without difference
being a difference between or among fairly equivalent units, has
marked the utopian project of a future liberated from the increasingly
normalized present of global capitalism. Agamben, however, poses the
question of whether we might rethink difference, and this at once
reaches back to deep theological commitments and looks forward to a
new way of thinking about futures. There is a very real sense in which
the opposition between difference and indifference has been organized
according to a notion of the good and the proper: goodness is that
which is creative, fruitful, flourishing, *always self-differing*, such that it
never remains simply in itself but comes toward what it most properly
is. Evil or the improper, by contrast, is without identity, self-formation,
or any process of becoming and distinction. The most significant
dimension of the question of indifference lies in the challenge it presents
to sovereign conceptions of difference: rather than begin from some
locus – such as the divine sovereign force that institutes a difference
between inside and outside, order and disorder, proper and improper,
or form and life – there would be a new way of thinking premised on

the potentiality of indifference that is not exhausted with the coming into being of a system of differences.

There are many respects in which we can read Agamben's project as an attempt to think beyond good and evil, but in a manner quite opposed to Nietzsche's sense of this phrase. If we were to begin our enquiry from the widespread post-Hegelian assumption that everything begins with difference and forces that produce relations, then our ethics would be beyond good and evil in the sense that whatever appears as good or original would be the outcome of a struggle among forces. The politics that would follow would be one in which there would be no transcendent term (such as God, the good, the right, the true, or the proper) that would be the basis for relations; all we would have would be the negotiation of relations. The resulting ethics and politics would not be able to distinguish between good and evil, but instead between those who have the strength to live in a world without values, and those who require some system of transcendent values because they cannot live without some foundation or ground. Rather than good and evil, this would be an ethics of authenticity and strength, with a privilege accorded to those who can face the intensity of existence, or live every "it was" as "I willed it thus." Agamben's ethics moves beyond good and evil, not by returning values to a field of forces of relations, and certainly not by affirming the will that can decide from itself without any dependence on something other than itself. Rather, and almost in opposition, his rejection of the proper and the authentic means that one cannot base ethics on a return of powers to some constituting force or even some impersonal will to power; instead there is something inauthentic or improper – something indifferent or already other than itself – at the "origin":

> For the being that is its own manner this is not, in effect, so much a property that determines and identifies it as an essence, but rather an impropriety; what makes it exemplary, however, is that impropriety is assumed and appropriated as its unique being...The impropriety, which we expose as our proper being, manner, which we *use*, engenders us. It is our second, happier, nature. (CC: 29)

There is not a self who wills, nor is there some force or will from which selves emerge; rather, there is an indistinction or indifference such that one cannot trace forces, relations, and differences back to some differentiating ground or field. Thus, confronted with what has traditionally been dismissed as evil or inauthentic – such as the human being who does not assert his will, his rights, his reason, or speech and identity – Agamben argues for this "life" as the new horizon for ethics. In terms of ethics, this might be best thought of as a relation to other persons that does not take the form of recognition, but that attends to the singularity of their being without the need for their coming to some identifying and self-differentiating willed being: "Ethics begins only when the good is revealed to consist in nothing other than a grasping of evil and when the authentic and the proper have no other content than the inauthentic and the improper" (CC: 13). Politically, the idea of thinking beyond the proper and the authentic would mark out a community that would be composed of relations that were not dependent on belonging: "These pure singularities communicate... without being tied by any common property, by any identity. They are expropriated of all identity, so as to appropriate belonging itself" (CC: 10–11).

In this thought of the improper, Agamben reformulates the problem of power and difference, yet remains subtly connected to the same domain of questions that dominated late twentieth-century theory while reconfiguring the terrain on which the problem of difference and power is posed. Modern political theory begins with the question of the emergence of sovereignty: rather than assume an already existing transcendent power (such as God or the good), we ask how the ordered polity comes into being. This is why the beginning of modern political theory might be dated from the appearance of writers, such as Hobbes, who account for the genesis of the state by way of a social contract, in which individuals renounce a degree of personal freedom for the sake of collective stability. But Hobbes, like Rousseau, Locke, and other contract theorists, assumes some basic political unit – such as the individual. Those who object to the social contract tradition argue that individuals are only possible because of social wholes, but they too assume the existence of a basic unit, such as the community. A more radical political theory asks about the emergence of these supposed basic units, and here the origin is not some already determined being but the forces from which beings are generated. From Hegel's viewpoint, as we have seen, we cannot assume a basic unit (such as an individual) who enters into the political contract; we begin with forces and struggles from which individuals are constituted.

Agamben sets himself squarely against the anti-Hegelian tradition that runs from Nietzsche to Foucault and that begins with force and power – or a pure act of difference – and then explains bodies and identities as the outcome of forces; this also means that he sets himself against a politics of agonistics. In political terms, the challenge, for Agamben, is to imagine a genuine or profound politics prior to an already constituted political field: not the law as enforced and constituted, but something like the constituting power from which any law would emerge, though without seeing that constituting power as pure decisive force. This is what is evidenced in the state of exception, which – Agamben constantly reminds us – exposes the operation of the law precisely when law ceases to operate. The state of exception is no longer politics as the war of differences and the field of contested relations, but something like a revelation of indifference, exposing sovereign power as that which is not yet, or not always, constituted within the network of relations:

> In truth, the state of exception is neither external nor internal to the juridical order, and the problem of defining it concerns precisely a threshold, or a zone of indifference, where inside and outside do not exclude each other but rather blur with each other. (SE: 23)

For Agamben, this indistinction and indifference mark an almost complete annihilation of the political; it is no longer the polity (or bodies coming together to speak and determine the good) that characterizes the contemporary milieu. This loss of the political, where speech, reason, decisions, and an ongoing order oriented to a created future break down, not only exposes the truth of politics as always harboring a logic of sovereignty; it also offers hope for a new conception of the relation between life and politics, which for Agamben would be no real relation at all. In this respect, for Agamben, there is a radicalism in what other intellectuals of Agamben's time criticized as the closure of Hegelian politics: for Agamben, there is a genuinely futural promise in a messianic version of Hegelianism where law will no longer be opposed to life, and the differences within which we live will no longer be accepted as the way of the world:

> That Hegel's dialectic is nothing more than a secularization of Christian theology comes as no surprise; however, more significant is the fact that (with a certain degree of irony) Hegel used a weapon against theology itself and that weapon is genuinely messianic. (TR: 99)

Agamben insists that the "properly political" nature of life lies in the capacity not to be political. If "man" can be reduced to bare life, then we are forced to confront a remainder of life that is not that of sovereign self-willing; what might politics be if this life were not excluded and abandoned, and not the object of biopolitical management? We might begin to discern that actual political reality unfolds from a potentiality that is at its most profound when it is fully related to impotentiality, when the political realm appears as always what might not have been, what we may not have brought into being. This means not only that politics might be different from its actual form, but – more importantly – that politics is a potentiality that is not grounded on life, but comes into being through the forming of life, establishing a relation that is not so much a secure binary or unity as a zone of indifference or indistinction. Whereas we might look nostalgically back to an age of politics where there was a clear distinction between the biological/physical/natural domain of managing life, and the human discursive deliberative space of politics, and even if it often appears as though Agamben is lamenting the increasing reduction of all life to bare life, his response is not to reassert the domain of human dignity and some proper space of sovereign decisions, but rather to emphasize an "original" indistinction. That is, it is always possible that humanity might not constitute itself in a separate and deliberative space of political community and discussion; nothing guarantees the distinction between *bios* (political, formed, deliberative life) and *zoe* (life as living substance). The condition of *homo sacer* or of not being a participant in the law, and of being abandoned to the outside of all law and decision, is a condition that haunts every political being. Rather than returning to some supposed golden age of genuine political thought and practice, Agamben focuses on how it is that the states of emergency reduce us all to possible bare life or *homo sacer*. What we know as the political might always be abandoned, and it is this absence of political relations (exposed in *homo sacer* where the human body is placed outside the law's protection and maintenance) that discloses our political potentiality by way of impotentiality.

That is, what truly needs to be questioned is the emergence of the political: how is it that humans do not exist at the level of mere life and existence but can generate a form of life and decide upon another world? In the usual sovereign situation it seems that there has been an easy passage from pre-political potential life to politically formed life. We think of humans as social, speaking, rational, and productive beings who create systems of law. In states of emergency, that natural or seemingly natural continuity is lost and the "life" that seemed to be so naturally, universally, and inevitably social and political appears as bare life: we are reduced to populations to be managed, with decisions based not on our speaking, reasoning, political nature but on the survival of the species. On the one hand, we can descry this modern condition that appears to become a permanent state of emergency: this applies not only to the "war on terror" (where democratic procedures are suspended for the sake of executive orders that reduce citizens to nothing more than mere life), but also to economic crises (where democratic local governments have been suspended and substituted by immediate managerial takeover) and the broader problem of climate change (where the imminent demise of the world's ecosystem and resources might require some form of overriding intervention, commonly referred to as "ecofascism" (Smith 2009)). On the other hand, Agamben's insistence that the current biopolitical situation is not a different logic from sovereignty precludes us from yearning for some prior notion of proper politics. This is Agamben's point: there is no proper politics. Nothing guarantees that all those factors that make politics possible – a capacity to speak, decide, create, think, enter into community relations – will emerge. To imagine that there is a proper and direct relation between life and politics, between life and community, between life and speech, or between life and art precludes a consideration of the threshold that brings relations into being.

Agamben's emphasis on sovereignty is therefore an emphasis on a splitting that brings a distinction into being but that is never fully distinct: if humans form themselves as political animals and as other than mere life, then they do so by a constant labor or anthropological machine that must mark off a distinction between animalistic biology and humanity. What Foucault sees as a historical difference between a world once subjected to a distinct sovereign power and a world now governed by the management and harnessing of forces of life is, for Agamben, a far more essential and structural difference that is articulated over and over again in a series of domains. This is why the logic of sovereignty, or the distinction between relation-generating force and force between already generated terms, appears over and over in Agamben's work. Before there can be animal rights or the consideration of the ethics of human–animal relations, we need to think of the force that divides human animality or life into the human and the non-human; before we think about the history of biopolitics, we need to think about the force that splits politics and the polity from mere *zoe*; before we think about what is required in terms of political discourse, we need to think about the split that opens humans as speaking animals from a position of silence that always haunts life as a potential (and that occurs in every event of speech where the saying is always distinct from the generality of what is said); and before we examine the work of art, we need to think about the event of the emergence of the very possibility of aesthetic practice, before there is a system of artists and spectators. The reason why Agamben so frequently talks about all these domains in terms of sovereignty – the reason why the problems of politics, art, language, animality, and theology all come down to a logic of the state of exception – has to do with his specific claim about the relation between history and thinking.

Agamben's constant references back to key texts on sovereignty, especially theological texts that concern the relation between God's being and then his governance or acting in the world, are not merely claims to textual influence and tradition, but go to a more profound problem of being, or the way the Western tradition has thought about being. As already stated, the twentieth-century French tradition with which Agamben was in constant conversation was profoundly exercised by the post-Hegelian problem of difference: is it possible to imagine difference in all its forms – sexual difference, political difference, creative difference, historical difference – without some ultimate identity that would determine and govern relations among different terms? Hegel regarded all history and reason as a process of one self-differentiating life: in the beginning is a difference, negativity, or distinction, and then finally by way of philosophy, reason, and politics "we" recognize that "we" are not beings who go through time and difference and possess reason; reason just is negativity recognizing itself. The absolute is not a self-present being, but a process of something *not* coinciding with itself, and then eventually recognizing life as non-coincidence. Humans are nothing more than aspects of one differing life, and yet it is that human moment of recognition that brings life to its proper fulfillment. In its contemporary liberal form this "end of history" has been expressed as the end of ideology: there is no political truth as such, and politics should be nothing more than the negotiation of different values without any transcendent norm (Fukuyama 1992). French intellectuals wanted to consider a more dissonant difference which did not resolve itself into one self-recognizing humanity. In many respects Foucault's critique of biopolitics was an attempt to think such a dissonance, for it was now the management and maximization of life that created one inescapable logic of modern and increasingly global political governance without any possibility for thinking otherwise.

Agamben, by contrast, argues that his own approach goes further than trying to find another space or differential power. How might we think the indifference – or pre-relational zone for potential difference – from which actual differences emerge? This question takes us back to the original ways in which this problem was expressed in the Western tradition, but for Agamben the textual tradition itself expresses a problem of human life, which is a life that is always *not itself* and yet seeks to ground this impotentiality on an actualized or exempted (transcendent) being. Agamben is committed to considering the ways in which contemporary thought is indebted to a long tradition of texts and problems which are no longer consciously present but which need to be reactivated, taking us to the problem of potentiality as such. If it is the case that we have always theorized a relation between a potentiality and its proper actualization – such as the relation between a creative God and his created world, or between a sovereign force and the law, or between humans and their political world – it is also no less true that every articulation of potentiality is haunted by the problem of impotentiality, which has never been properly confronted. If humans are essentially rational and essentially different from their animality, why does politics frequently fail to be actualized in so many instances of human life? If, today, there can be biopolitics, this is not because of some inexplicable or contingent reversal in human politics, but because that which defines the human as human – speech, politics, community, elevation above mere life – is precarious, and is always in a relation of ongoing exclusion of the supposedly non-human mere life.

Rather than simply assert the law and democracy and aim to return political practices back to due process, Agamben sees the alarming extension of biopolitics as offering a new possibility for politics. So here we can draw a distinction among three ways of theorizing the biopolitical. The first is to see biopolitics as an alarming loss of proper politics, as a historical event that reduces humans to manageable substance and forgoes the deliberative, discursive, social, historical, and cognitive powers of humans as beings never fully reducible to their biology. If we accept this account, then we would need to retrieve politics by re-invoking conditions of human self-constitution, by establishing networks of communication and reflection. This is a diagnosis and prognosis undertaken by a range of contemporary thinkers: Jürgen Habermas argues for a theory of communicative action whereby the practices of the sciences based on knowledge of humans as physical and natural beings is placed within a broader context reflecting on the ends of those scientific practices and the horizon of human meanings from which they emerge (Habermas 2003). The second approach to contemporary biopolitical reach would be to reject the notion of a retrieval of politics and instead see the twenty-first century – with its new conditions of global labor networks and immaterial labor – as releasing humans from their enslavement to material and localized production: Michael Hardt and Antonio Negri have argued that even though there has been a global intensification of the human populace as a laboring mass, these same conditions of labor create conditions in which humans can form one network of communication and self-constitution, realizing a new political sphere that will be immanent (not an imposition of power, but power as generated by human immaterial labor). A politics of immanence, in which humans are no longer subjected to an external end (whether that be the "scientific" reasoning of maximized production and life, or the sovereign reasoning of some supposed "good" of mankind), has gained widespread purchase and generally requires that politics not just be accepted as a means to some external end, but requires reflection, creation, and ongoing renewal of ends that humans create for themselves (Hardt and Negri 2000). Agamben's distinct response to biopolitics differs both from a supposed return to proper political reflection (whether that be a return to the past or a return to some implicit horizon of human meaning and production) and from some notion that man's political vocation as a productive being will be fulfilled in a future of collective self-creating labor.

For Agamben, there can be a future politics that is neither an extension of our biological/animal existence, nor a purely reflective politics that takes no account of our strange imbrication with our bare or animal existence. His approach is neither liberal in its claim that there is no foundation for law other than the law we give to ourselves as speaking, political, and rational beings, nor naturalist in its insistence that our political and communal nature follows from our specific biology or our capacity as laboring beings. This is why, for Agamben, bare life and the increasing reduction of politics to being nothing more than an immediate mastery of life, with a circumvention of deliberation and all supposedly "humanist" imperatives, is neither an accident nor a simple tragedy. Rather, if biopolitics is possible, this is because there has always been something potentially inhuman or non-human in the very constitution of the human; if all that we have come to understand as "man's" supposedly inevitable political nature has so frequently not been actualized, then this should alert us to something about the political as being a potentiality that might not eventuate. And, once this is recognized, it is possible to see that the distancing or exclusion from bare life that has constituted the political nature of man needs to be reconsidered. This returns us to both Agamben's emphasis on indifference and thresholds, as well as to the strangely theological debt of contemporary politics.

To consider indifference is to refuse that there is a simple split or binary between animality and humanity: it is not the case that there is a distinct quality of "man" that will arrive as the proper fulfillment of some human essence, so we cannot simply rest on man as a distinct political animal. Instead, the zone of indistinction or threshold is what needs to be rethought, such that politics might finally take the form not of means oriented toward some assumed end, but rather as a confrontation with a fragile and precarious potential for political being that does not offer itself as some inevitable and proper outcome of what "man" is. Strangely, this ambition for a new future of politics that would be neither the liberal freedom of the individual nor the retrieval of a self-defining and meaningful community requires, Agamben insists, a reconsideration of one of the foundational problems of theology, the distinction between being and praxis: rather than a practice or power that constitutes or *brings into being*, Agamben argues for a practice that is *destituent*, and that breaks with a long tradition of privileging creativity, act, and will:

> To think such a purely destituent power is not an easy task. Benjamin wrote once that nothing is so anarchical as the bourgeois order. In the same sense, Pasolini in his last movie has one of the four Salò masters saying to their slaves: "true anarchy is the anarchy of power." It is precisely because power constitutes itself through the inclusion and the capture of anarchy and anomy that it is so difficult to have an immediate access to these dimensions; it is so hard to think today of something as a true anarchy or a true anomy. I think that a praxis which would succeed in exposing clearly the anarchy and the anomy captured in the governmental security technologies could act as a purely destituent power. A really new political dimension becomes possible only when we grasp and depose the anarchy and the anomy of power. But this is not only a theoretical task: it means first of all the rediscovery of a form-of-life, the

access to a new figure of that political life whose memory the security state tries at any price to cancel. (SC)

If God has been defined as pure existence, bringing essences into being, then a counter-theological notion would be a power or praxis that was destituent, or de-creative. One might explain this debt to theology by arguing that our current political concepts have been derived from previous discourses, including religion. But one of the features of Agamben's most recent work has been to insist upon the inadequacy of deriving political concepts from religious discourse, as though the latter provided an unproblematic origin. Rather, the original theological problems are already paradoxical and split; this ambivalence might be thought of as accidental, as though Western culture simply inherited some rather clumsy and incoherent terms. Agamben suggests otherwise: the theological articulation of the relation between being and praxis – and its repetition in discourses of sovereignty, and finally in current discourses of law and life – expresses a problem of something like life itself which "has its roots in the fracture between being and acting in God and is, therefore, from the beginning in agreement with the theological *oikonomia*" (KG: 56).

Here, again, Agamben differs both from Foucault – for whom "life" was a modern concept, and for whom there were no essential problems outside a history of varying and reconfigured discursive distributions – and from Jacques Derrida's deconstruction, which Agamben criticized for not stepping outside the limits of language to pose the problem of the passage from silence to speech. The theological problem, one that Agamben describes as a problem of "economy," concerns how a being that is complete and self-sufficient, requiring nothing other than itself in order to be, nevertheless both creates a world and then proceeds to act in the world. For Agamben, this relates to a broader problem of the relation between potentiality and actualization (or, in Greek philosophical parlance, *dynamis* and *energeia* (HS: 31–2; Ugilt 2014: 23)).

God could not – like ordinary beings – require some passage of time in order to arrive at full potential and realization. And yet theology nevertheless needs to explain God's relation to the world, which cannot be one of necessity – for that would mean that God was constrained by something other than himself. For Agamben, this means that there must be a God of full and complete power, *and* that this power must not be diminished by God's creative and active creation and governance of the world. God's relation to the world, and his action in the world, must be at once in accord with the fullness of his power, and yet not be required by that power. Agamben notes that one explanation of this problem of economy – or the distribution and assignment of power – was explained by analogy with language. If two parties communicate, their speaking being does not lose power by conveying content to the other party; this distribution is not an economy of loss.

If we want to conceive of a truly divine power, or an absolutely sovereign decision, or a completely powerful and unconstrained God, then the force of will or decision could not be impeded by any outside essence or determination: a divine force would bear no relation to anything other than itself; it could not be the willing *of* or expression *of* a being. This pure force or absolute existence without any determining relation might be thought of in various ways: as a pure potentiality (that is not limited by anything already in existence but is a pure power to exist); as non-relational (or as a pure power *to*, without any constriction of power over); or defined as a sovereignty that is not subject to the law but generates the relation between a power to give or withhold law (a power to exempt itself or except itself from law). There would be something god-like in such a power insofar as it expressed pure freedom without reserve, limit, or subjection to any end other than its own exertion of force; at the same time, such a power might also appear – due to its freedom from any determination, essence, or end – as contingent and void of all reason, deliberation, or sense. There would be a zone of indifference or indistinction between an absolute freedom – in which action was constrained by nothing other than the exertion of pure force – and an anarchic contingency. And this is how we might conceive the ambivalence of biopolitics and the state of exception: the emergence of a force that is no longer limited by law and the conception of a life that is nothing other than substance to be managed are both nihilistic abandonments of the capacity to form and create a political space, but they are also exposures of the problem of life: nothing guarantees the emergence of humanity, law, or rights. To imagine that, by virtue of being human, we are all, always, already citizens of rights and speech is to forget the genesis of politics from a site of force that may or may not issue in the creative and practical production of a political space, of community, of art, or speech. The state of emergency of the present may be the opportunity for a new thought of politics, art, and humanity – a thought that neither assumes the inevitability of the good life on the basis of "man's" natural being, nor abandons all conceptions of political becoming by falling back on some supposed natural life that has already exhausted its potential in being nothing more than mere or bare life. For Agamben, life cannot be that which inevitably arrives at its proper expression in human reason, and so there can be no grounding of politics on naturalism. At the same time, politics as speech, freedom, and practice have always been secured by way of excluding a bare life that can never be fully mastered, captured, or evaded. It is this process of distancing and differentiation, this opening of the political field, that Agamben finds in the sovereign decision, the work of art, and the crises of contemporary states of emergency.

Animality

There has been much talk over the past few decades of an "inhuman" or "non-human" turn (Grusin 2015), and an efflorescence of animal studies. Part of this general shift has to do with various modes of post-humanism, anti-humanism, and vitalism that are increasingly offered as ways to move beyond both a liberalism that focuses on a universal subject and a focus on texts, language, and constructed social systems. For the most part, early twentieth-century European philosophy was either based on returning all formal systems to their subjective origin (phenomenology), or a refusal of any such origin or consciousness with a focus on systems (structuralism): for phenomenology, the world is given through appearances, and these appearances are always given to some lived subjectivity, while for structuralism any subject or experience is an effect of differentiating systems (Eyers 2013).

For analytic or Anglo-American philosophers who followed the "linguistic turn," philosophy could only be rigorous if it accepted the limits of language and abandoned any claims of trying to intuit a truth or absolute beyond the concepts and categories through which we know the world (Dummett 1996). In many ways, both of these maneuvers – despite their emphasis on a constituting consciousness or conceptual scheme – were the beginnings of anti-humanism, in that both continental and analytic philosophy refused any grounding of thought in something like the natural individual or "man." For a number of reasons, and across a range of disciplines and disciplinary styles, there has been a turn back to life, naturalism, and a broader context of animality, of which humans would be an instance.

Agamben's work needs to be situated both alongside, and against, this complex and confusing terrain. One of the main reasons for the general turn to naturalism, life, and animality might be attributed to a standard dialectic of intellectual trends: the focus on language and the conditions through which "we" (we humans) know the world has perhaps gone too far and led to a senseless timidity of knowledge. It is no surprise, perhaps, that a movement of "speculative realism" has set itself directly against "correlationism," or the idea that we can only know the world as it is known by the subject (Bryant, Srnicek, and Harman 2011). But there are various ways in which the limits of the knowing subject can be transcended. The first is perhaps what Foucault gestured toward in *The Order of Things*: the concept of life becomes a general substrate for knowledge and underpins a certain conception of "man" as the animal who is determined by vital forces and whose needs require him to speak and work in common. It is this conceptualization of life that, for Foucault, enables biopolitics: the governance and management of human populations proceeds by way of

knowledge practices, all the while allowing the "man" who is determined by "life" to be only dimly aware of its determining forces. Such
a determination of human beings by "life" has, if anything, intensified
since Foucault was writing, not only because various political practices
of security and population management have intervened in all levels
of bodily life but also because knowledge practices such as neuro-
science, evolutionary psychology, cognitive archaeology, and "naturalist" turns in literary theory and philosophy explain humans as a species
– a species that is an extension of a broader domain of animality. This
reaction of naturalism against human exceptionalism – or what we
might refer to as post-humanism – is quite distinct from a longer tradition of anti-humanism that runs from Friedrich Nietzsche, through
Heidegger and Sartre, to Deleuze, Derrida, and Foucault. To speak
schematically, we might say that post-humanism tries to diminish
the distinction between human and non-human, whereas anti-
humanism problematizes both the distinction and any notions of continuity or sameness. Here, rather than "man" being returned to a
broader domain of animality, there is something essentially inessential
or problematic about humans and their strange relation to animality:

> In our culture, man has always been thought of as the articulation and
> conjunction of a body and a soul, of a living thing and a *logos*, of a natural
> (or animal) element and a super-natural or social or divine element. We
> must instead learn to think of man as what results from the incongruity
> of these two elements, and investigate not the metaphysical mystery of
> conjunction, but rather the practical and political mystery of separation.
> (O: 16)

It is this anti-humanist or problematically humanist tradition that
forms the background of Agamben's work precisely because he both
refuses to return human life to some determining and illuminating life
process or vitality, at the same time as he sees all those features that
distance humans from life (language, art, work) as potentialities that
may *not* be actualized, thus leaving the human as never fully detached
from the animality against which "man" defines itself. Like Deleuze
and Derrida, whose work has played a significant part in the cultural
studies and literary critical theorization of animals, Agamben insists
neither on a simple continuity or sameness between animals and
humans, nor on an exceptionalism or distinction (unless we theorize
exception, as Agamben does, as a drawing of a distinction that remains
bound up with that from which it is distinguished). Despite the importance of animality in Agamben's work, and his continual insistence that
politics and ethics cannot rely on some actuality such as "man," he
nevertheless – and far more than Derrida, Deleuze, or Foucault –
sustains the problem of the human being at the center of his thought.

Before writing his late work that became increasingly concerned with animals (Derrida 2008), Derrida had already problematized the possibility of simply abandoning the figure and limits of "man." Responding to the anti-humanism of the second half of the twentieth century that claimed that "man" had no essence other than his existence – that he was not determined or bound by any "end" – Derrida argued that this supposed absence of ends had always been an end of man (in the sense of man's purpose, a purpose of being free from all purposes). What Derrida increasingly explored was the way a certain unavoidable figure of "man" ceaselessly invaded a supposedly pure philosophy (Derrida 1969). In his work on Heidegger, Derrida (1989a) charts the ways in which Heidegger at once wishes to escape any humanism by determining man as some special or rational animal, and yet the very means that Heidegger uses to avoid speaking of "man" nevertheless fall back upon the human body's seemingly distinct capacities (such as the difference between the human's gesturing "hand" and the animal's "merely" instrumental paw or claw). For Derrida, there can be no easy overcoming of "man" without also questioning the overly general and unreflected concept of "*the* animal" (a concept which Derrida rejects not because it discriminates against animals but because it does not discriminate enough). Derrida's project, for all its complexity, might nevertheless be characterized by two tendencies: first, like Agamben, he insists neither on a simple destruction of the human by way of a simple return to one general life of animality, but instead suggests that the border between human and animal needs to be continually renegotiated because of the complexity both of animal life and of Western thought, which cannot simply free itself from its anthropocentric determinations. Second, Derrida's approach is broadly deconstructive, and this is where he would differ from Agamben. Deconstruction is "not a method" precisely because it installs itself in a given textual complex and then exposes the mechanisms by which a text constitutes its operative differences; it then exposes those differences as both necessary and impossible. Derrida's main point of reference for his theorization of animals is therefore the Western philosophical tradition and its constant reliance on a distinction between man and animal, even if that distinction is under continual pressure from within. All those features that supposedly render man distinct – language, gesture, communication, community – are also definitive of some forms of animality; and all those features that would render the animal secondary and separate, such as a certain relationship between the animal's body and a world that is not lived as a meaningful horizon of projects, already invade the human. Derrida's engagement with animals is, by and large, deconstructive rather than speculative: that is, he installs himself within a philosophical tradition that is dependent on a constant and impossible elevation of man above animality.

In his talks on sovereignty, Derrida, unlike Agamben, focuses less on some general logic of sovereignty and more on the textual articulation of the problem of the sovereign, and the concept of sovereignty's dependence on figures of the beast or animal (Derrida 2009). While Agamben is also anchored in textual tradition, his focus is less on deconstructing texts and employing textual figures to open aporia or spaces where no determinate thought is given. The texts Agamben employs (both in his work on sovereignty and animality) suggest a speculative direction. Agamben frequently poses the possibility that for all the traditional weight of humanism, we can nevertheless think beyond the problem of animality and humanity and do so in a way that breaks away from the archive that has labored (unsuccessfully) to heal the fracture between life and its (human) articulation. In a way that is subtly different from post-humanist approaches, Agamben draws on texts that he uses positively rather than critically or by way of deconstruction. That is, whereas Derrida will install himself in Heidegger's critique of any simple natural humanism, all the while exposing the impossibility of finding a space of *Dasein* outside of man as rational animal, Agamben will not only theorize the strange life that forms the threshold of animality and humanity, he will also suggest that the witnessing of this threshold has provided and will continue to provide potential futures for thinking.

Given the significance of the problem of "life" in Agamben's thought – and the debt this concept owes to a series of other thinkers, including Hannah Arendt and Walter Benjamin – there is a sense in which all of Agamben's work concerns animality, or the ways in which humans employ a constant distancing of themselves from a silent life that nevertheless remains. Agamben's specifically sustained work on the relation between humanity and animality (*The Open*) embeds his usual attention to the history of philosophy and theology in the work of Jacob von Uexküll (2010), and Heidegger's reading of von Uexküll. The key concept in von Uexküll's work is the *Umwelt*, which if translated as "environment" maintains the sense of "environ" or surround. The key critical force of the concept of the *Umwelt* lies in the sense of the body's capacities and relations: it is not the case that there is a world that is then represented by a body. Rather, it is the body's responsive potentials that yield a specific world, or *Umwelt*. In the famous example of the tick cited by von Uexküll, the insect's world is composed of three possibilities of disturbance and response: skin, uric acid, and blood prompt the tick to fall on to a body and take in blood to the point of satiety. "Perception" or "having a world" is less akin to a camera taking a distanced snapshot of some common world, and closer to a functional coupling. This is so much so that a bee whose abdomen is cut open will continue to consume nectar, precisely because the usual bodily response of filling never arrives.

Such a theory renders problematic the notorious claim by Heidegger that an animal "has no world": for Heidegger, the human world is not some domain of objects or matter that we then choose to perceive, for the human world is given in meaningful projects. But we might say that an animal has an animal's world, made up of the animal's capacities. The world of *Dasein*, for Heidegger, is given in terms of what I can do, and this "I can" is always mine and no one else's; because of my temporal finitude I will only live to enact certain possibilities and no others, and no other person can take over this finitude for me. My world is therefore always *my world*, given to me in terms of decisions and limits, both the past that I cannot alter and a future freedom that I cannot avoid. For Heidegger, however, this horizon of meanings and projects is limited at best for animals, who are "poor in world." Non-living substances (such as a stone) are without world, or world-less. Heidegger's claim has been challenged repeatedly in the late twentieth-century interest in animals, not only because animals – it is claimed – do have a world, and that this world is given not merely in the example of an animal being nothing more than its dynamic and engaged response to its environment or *Umwelt*, but – more importantly – because the condition of animal world-loss or poverty in world cannot be clearly demarcated from the human.

If one were to identify an overarching strategy in Agamben's response to problems it would be the identification of two opposing sides of a problem, followed by a maintenance and refusal of both sides, while also avoiding some middle or compromised path. As in the case with the animal–human "divide," Agamben regards the problem as more profound and requiring less of a sense of resolution than maximized complication. Agamben's approach to the human–animal binary is neither to resolve nor deconstruct the divide, but to intensify the divide – to sharpen the difference between humanity and animality – and then to locate the problem of that difference within humanity. For Agamben, there is something distinctly human, and something that is increasingly threatened, in the biopolitical reduction of all life to bare life. What distinguishes humanity is not an actual difference from animality, but a potentiality to differentiate – a potentiality (like all potentialities) that is in part a capacity *not* to differentiate. Indeed, arguing that it is necessary to abandon the "mysterious metaphysical" conjunction of man and animal, Agamben instead offers a vision of the human as a perpetual antagonism between these two incompatible spheres, a space where "ceaseless divisions" occur (O: 16). Turning to the work of Linnaeus, Agamben locates the taxonomist's brilliance in his decision to "not record – as he does with the other species – any specific identifying characteristic next to the generic name *Homo*" outside of his "*ability* to recognize himself" (O: 25–6). Based on this insight, Agamben concludes that "*Homo sapiens*, then, is neither a clearly defined species nor a substance; it is, rather, a machine or device for producing the recognition of the human" (O: 26). He proposes the term "anthropological machine" to define the process by which the human recognizes itself by making a distinction between its animalistic and humanistic dimensions. Humanity is defined by excluding animality, but it is the ongoing "anthropological machine" of distinction and exclusion (and its failure) rather than any completed being or essence that constantly marks the human being in its humanity-animality.

Both Derrida and Agamben refuse to maintain the human–animal distinction in its simplicity, and both refuse to collapse the human into the animal altogether, but this is for quite different and significant reasons: for Derrida, this is because the animal–human difference is multiple, to the point that one could not refer simply to "the" animal, and this multiplication of differences means that even though we cannot avoid the concept of the human, every text will require a reading that exposes the dependence of the human on a series of differences that cannot be contained. By contrast, Agamben's work maintains a profound sense of the human–animal distinction outside the textual history of metaphysics. The texts he reads are not responsible for differentiating humans from animals, but they do disclose a profound problem of human life and its relation to an animality that is its most intimate truth. To this extent there is some truth to Agamben's objection to deconstruction – that it stops short at the textual traces that mark out differences, without interrogating the genesis of difference. In this case the human–animal distinction, or what Agamben refers to as the "anthropological machine," is possible because of a deeper problem of animality that might also be seen to disclose a deeper problem of potentiality.

The problem with animality lies in the concept of the *Umwelt*: what the animal *is* occurs by way of relation. One dominant response to phenomenology – both Heidegger's work, and theories of animality such as von Uexküll's – has therefore been to stress the significance and irreducibility of systems and relations, such that we do not have the world on the one hand and then living beings on the other. Rather, life just occurs as one relational system, with each living being realizing itself through relations. Agamben, however, wants to think the potentiality for relations prior to the actualization of relations. In terms of animality: if we define the human as the potential to distance oneself from animality, to take up a relation of exclusion to one's mere life, then what might be worth pondering is the coming into being of this relation, as a potential – a potential that is most exposed when it is not actualized. That is, rather than look at humans and animals in their difference, one might look at humans at the point when that difference is not achieved. This would also alter "our" relation to animality: not seeing animals as "just like us" or as worthy of rights and all the claims we attribute to humanity. If animality is a life that we know only as the most distanced and also the most intimate, then – like Derrida – there may be no such thing as "the" animal, and what we may confront when we think of animality is not a thing, nor a relation, but a potentiality for relations, a threshold. This is why Agamben's short work on the relation between man and animal is at once about relations, and yet is not about a relation between a being and its lived and meaningful world but about a capacity to enter into relation – hence the concept of "the open." At the same time, the book – though framed by the problem of a being coming into relation – is also about the non-relational, and concludes not with the animal as a silent being without world or sense, but with a human confrontation with this relation toward non-relational "silence."

It is worth noting that the conclusion of Agamben's book on animality focuses on a human-to-human relation of love, and that this human coupling is drawn from a Titian canvas (discussed earlier, but we can now turn back to this example and ask why an artwork bears such exemplarity). One could make several remarks about the force of this conclusion and what it tells us about animality for Agamben. First, Agamben's work on animals is really not so much concerned with animals as beings who are other than us, or beings with whom we have some companionship, obligation, or dependence. Rather, prior to the animal–human relation there is something like animality, and this animality in turn is something like a potential for coming into relation, a potential that is given most profoundly when that relation breaks down. Going back to the discussion of the *Umwelt*: in its everyday functioning of coupled environment, the animal's world is given not as a separate object that is then viewed or represented, but is instead nothing more than that which disturbs and elicits responses. For the most part, then, the animal is constituted as a relation to the world, and the animal's world is always the world *for* this animal. Secondly, then, animal and world are co-determining, coupled, relational, and relatively closed. Before discussion of humans' relations to their worlds, each other, and animals, Agamben cites the passage from von Uexküll of the bee whose abdomen is cut open: without the sensation of satiety – without the body's responsive mechanism – the bee continues to consume nectar (O: 52). On the one hand, this demonstrates the significance of coupling, and that – for the most part – life is relational and opens its own world; on the other hand, the bee's continued consumption and unawareness of its de-coupling from any relation of feeding or life-furtherance indicates that the potential for life is just that – a potential. The very life that had coupled the bee to the world and created an open environment and connection is the same drive that detaches the bee from any response or perception.

If one were to mark a distinction between animals and humans one might say, then, that the animal is "poor in world," for the world of the animal is always given in terms of life, drives, and the body's potentials; the animal does not take up a relation to those potentials. Yet this non-relation (or the body's continued function that closes off a recognition of a certain loss, cut, or severing) might tell us something profound about life and relations: "Not being able to have-to-do-with is not purely negative: in fact, it is in some ways a form of openness" (O: 55). Rather than see life as that which unfolds from itself and fulfills itself by way of relations and world, Agamben focuses on a life that is displayed as a potential for relation that does not arrive at relation:

> On the one hand, captivation is a more spellbinding and intense openness than any kind of human knowledge; on the other, insofar as it is not capable of disconcealing its own disinhibitor, it is closed in a total opacity. Animal captivation and the openness of the world thus seem related to one another as are negative and positive theology, and their relationship is as ambiguous as the one which simultaneously opposes and binds in a secret complicity the dark night of the mystic and the clarity of rational knowledge. (O: 59)

Animality, then, cannot be dismissed as it is by Heidegger as a poverty in world, just because the animal is nothing more than the range of responses that further its life; for in some ways the animal's captivation in the world without objectifying and cognitive relations and mastery is akin to a mystical union with life. The animal, too, can be severed from its world, exposing life as a potentiality for relation that may not yield a relation; or we might view the bee with the cut abdomen as a relation that is uncoupled, opened, exempted from the very life that is its supposedly proper potential. For Heidegger, what marks humans as having a world is to a certain extent not their potentiality for coupling but for de-coupling. In *Being and Time*, Heidegger insists that *Dasein* (or "there-being," because he does not want to use the word "human" precisely because of its connotation with man as a higher animal, or animal with the added faculty of reason) is always "thrown" into a world. That is, it is not the case that there are human subjects (as distinct beings) who then have to somehow come to know the world as a separate domain of beings; rather, there is the experience or disclosure of a world, and it is from that relation that the notion of the subject, or the separateness of human being, is derived. More importantly, though, it is only when the world breaks down that we become aware that there is anything like a world as a constituted horizon of meanings that depends upon projects, anticipated futures, and a retained past. For the most part we are connected to a world that is lived *not* as some distinct representation or separate substance, but as a series of meaningful projects – projects that are dependent upon a world of already given possibilities and anticipated outcomes (Heidegger 1996: 65). However, when something interrupts that world – when the tool or instrument we are using breaks down – we are interrupted from the flow of purposes, and from unthinking everyday-ness and become aware *that there is a world*. Heidegger insists that for the most part humans exist inauthentically; they are connected to their world and caught up in an everydayness that is unquestioned, taken for granted, and lived as simply "there." We are attuned to the world, and the world is always *our* world. If we come to live the world as blank material substance that is devoid of qualities, this too is a specific mood and mode of living the world – the detached or "mathematical" mood of modern technology. However, when that world breaks down or is interrupted, especially in moments of *Angst* or boredom where the world presents itself neither as "mine" nor as meaningful but as simply there, one is given the opportunity to live authentically or to take on one's world in a decisive and ungrounded acceptance of one's own potentiality. It is the loss of everyday givenness and simple acceptance that allows a genuine "ownness" of the world. Relations become inoperative and we become aware of the potentiality for the world as such. Agamben describes this essential disruption, but in so doing argues that it is human proximity to the animal, or human impotentiality (capacity not to be fully human), that discloses the essential:

> In being left empty by profound boredom, something vibrates like an echo of that "essential disruption" that arises in the animal from its being exposed and taken in an "other" that is, however, never revealed to it as such. For this reason the man who becomes bored finds himself in the "closest proximity" – even if it is only apparent – to animal captivation. Both are, in their most proper gesture *open to a closedness*; they are totally delivered over to something that obstinately refuses itself. (O: 65)

Two important consequences of this relation between world and meaning are important: what is the case "for the most part" does not disclose the authentic possibility of the world; even though being attuned to the world is prior to the detached scientific or technological attitude that reduces the world to so much matter to be manipulated, it is also the case that a certain loss of world by way of boredom or *Angst* allows *Dasein* to confront the potential for world disclosure from which "man" emerges. An animal is "poor in world" because an animal is nothing more than its responses; the animal cannot experience the boredom or detachment from its surroundings that would disclose the world as a world, as a "lifeworld" of possibilities that might be otherwise, and that is given through meanings and projects that are ours. This "ownness" of the world is disclosed to us only in its non-appearing.

Heidegger's use of the term *Dasein*, rather than man or human, lies in his objection to thinking of humanity as a being within the world, a being of biological life who then happens to be blessed with reason that sets him above other animals. The term *Dasein* does not signal that humans have some extra quality of reason, but that what we have thought of as humanity is better considered in terms of a specific relation. *Dasein* is not a form of biological life, nor some non-biological or mental substance such as "mind"; it is rather a way of living time in relation to life. *Dasein* is not a thing but a relation, or – more importantly – a potentiality for relation that is only disclosed when relations break down.

In many ways, Agamben's work on potentiality and relation is directly indebted to two of Heidegger's philosophical moves: a seeming accident or inessential failure for something to arrive at its potential discloses the true nature of the potential. In Heidegger's case, it is due to the *not* having of a world, or a certain loss of world in boredom and *Angst*, that one is thrown back on the relational nature of *Dasein* or being-in-the-world. Second, we cannot, then, dismiss the accident as standing outside what something is; man is distinguished from animality not by a distinct quality but by a mode of relation, a relation that appears only when actual humanity breaks down. Yet, while accepting the importance of humanity as a relation, and almost accepting the idea of animality as a poverty or absence of relation, Agamben does not seek to retheorize what has been known as humanity by distinguishing it completely from an animality or biological life against which a *Dasein* or temporal becoming would be set. Instead, Agamben seeks to interrogate humanity as a relation to animality: the human as a relation to the non-relational. If humans are defined by Heidegger as a pure relation or a pure becoming – as the time through which the world is unfolded – then Agamben sees humans as being most definitively human when they are drawn back to an animality or non-relationality that they had only seemingly excluded:

> What appears for the first time as such in the deactivation (in the *Brach-liegen*) of possibility, then, is the *very origin of potentiality* – and with it, of Dasein, that is, the being which exists in the form of potentiality-for-being [*poter-esse*]. But precisely for this reason, this potentiality or originary possibilization constitutively has the form of a potential-not-to [*potenza-di-no*], of an impotentiality, insofar as it is *able to* [*puo*] only in beginning from a *being able not to* [*poter non*], that is, from a deactivation of single, specific, factual possibilities. (O: 67)

This has direct consequences for the three major fields in which Agamben's work has had purchase: animal studies, political theory, and aesthetics. In terms of animality and humanity, we should not simply lament the biopolitical reduction of the human person to animality, but should instead think of an ethics that does not pertain to personality or humanity and that is mindful of what we might refer to as "remaining-animal" – the threshold or indistinction that provides the milieu for all human modes of taking-on-form. Heidegger had insistently emphasized that *Dasein* is absolutely singular: because I live a finite existence, and no one can die for me or substitute my life, I live at *this* moment, in this world and no other. I have only so many potentialities open to me because of the temporality and spatiality of my existence; nothing is determined in advance, but it is also the case that my death and finitude precludes me from achieving all I might imagine I could achieve "some day." This is why death at once limits but also defines potentiality. Heidegger in this respect heightens the conception of humanity by refusing *humanitas* as an essence and instead intensifying a human capacity of being thrown into a world of one's ownmost potentiality: I am not dignified because I am a member of a species, but because I am who I am, absolutely unique, decisive, and non-substitutable. By contrast, Agamben confronts the singularity (before all decisive or authentic seizing of individuation) that befalls humans in situations of exposed life: the *Muselman* of the Nazi death camps is no longer the individual of speech, reason, decision, and meaningful projects, but is reduced to bare life: "a being from whom humiliation, horror, and fear has so taken away all consciousness and all personality as to make him absolutely apathetic" (RA: 185). Such a life is singular in being irreducible to the biological life to which Nazism wanted to reduce it, and yet also not fully articulated or given meaning through testimony.

It is this life that Agamben deems to be the challenge of ethics. As long as we remain attached to the ethics of persons, and to humanity as a life-transcending being of dignity, then it would follow that mere life could be exterminated or sacrificed without any sense of violation. How might we begin to think ethically if, instead of only valuing the mode of life that is *not bare life* we were to ask about an ethics of life that does not rely on the dignity or personality of life?

For Agamben, this requires us to confront the human potential *not* to realize one's humanity that remains present in every event of speech and action, and then to respond to that exposure, which might entail the shame of confronting one's humanity-animality. Such an idea allows us to make sense of Agamben's commentary in *The Open* on a thirteenth-century Hebrew Bible where he raises the question of human redemption: would a restored heavenly humanity be free of all animality, losing all its physicality in a new heaven, or would paradise be a realm in which humanity no longer required a distance from animality, being liberated from all law, with no separate domain of sacred life? Agamben explains:

> The scene that interests us in particular here is the last in every sense, since it concludes the codex as well as the history of humanity. It represents the messianic banquet of the righteous on the last day. Under the shade of paradisiacal trees and cheered by the music of two players, the righteous, with crowned heads, sit at a richly laid table. The idea that in the days of the Messiah the righteous, who for their entire lives have observed the prescriptions of the Torah, will feast on the meat of Leviathan and Behemoth without worrying whether their slaughter has been kosher or not is perfectly familiar to the rabbinic tradition. What is surprising, however, is one detail that we have not yet mentioned: beneath the crowns, the miniaturist has represented the righteous not with human faces, but with unmistakably animal heads. Here, not only do we recognize the eschatological animals in the three figures on the right – the eagle's fierce beak, the red head of the ox, and the lion's head – but the other two righteous ones in the image also display the grotesque features of an ass and the profile of a leopard. And in turn the two musicians have animal heads as well – in particular the more visible one on the right, who plays a kind of fiddle and shows an inspired monkey's face. Why are the representatives of concluded humanity depicted with animal heads? (O: 1–2)

Going through a series of possible but unsatisfactory answers to this question, Agamben suggests that "the theriomorphous depiction of the archons refers directly back to the shadowy kinship between animal macrocosm and human microcosm" (O: 3). In terms of political theory, Agamben at once holds on to humanity as a political potential, a potential to think of a future in which a space of common speech and practice would yield a difference from the biopolitical reduction of humans to bare biological existence, and yet this community would not be based on some recognition of who "we" are, in common, as an identified nation, tradition, or culture; nor would it transcend biological or animal being.

Toward the conclusion of *The Open*, Agamben therefore departs dramatically from Heidegger's conception of authentic and decisive taking up of one's own world and instead looks to a point well beyond the language of being, and well beyond the idea of redeeming our fallen and inauthentic loss of world:

> The righteous with animal heads in the miniature in the Ambrosian do not represent a new declension of the man–animal relation so much as a figure of the "great ignorance" which lets both of them be outside of being, saved precisely in their being unsavable. (O: 92)

Agamben's political theory requires community precisely because he rejects liberal theory's and modernity's reliance on "man" as some basic political unit; there is no natural or intrinsic political relation, while there is also an excess or remainder that cannot be exhausted by political relations. Humanity is a potentiality for relation: one cannot begin either by assuming some given set of relations – a community of constituted norms and laws – nor by assuming some actualized term (such as the individual or person) from which relations unfold. Agamben suggests that we might rethink a politics *not* based on the exclusion of bare life, against which the distinct individual or person of human rights would be set; instead, the community would be based on "whatever being." This "whatever being" is not a term from which relations inevitably unfold – not the liberal political self opposed to animality. "Whatever being" signals a life that is not yet identified, dignified, or actualized into some lawful or normative self, but it is *individuated*. It is not the characterless mass of bare life that is opposed to political identity; rather, prior to identity (where I am identified *as a* male or female, Hispanic, Latino, Indigenous Australian, or "Other") there is the singularity of this being here, prior to general belonging to a named set. Politics takes place at the threshold, or in *taking place* – being "thus," allowing for a community where personhood and humanity are not the predicates through which we recognize each other. Political humanity is an exposure and living in common of a being that has no identity other than *being such*. The claim that life is attended to in its singularity when it is neither granted an individual identity, nor reduced to bare life as biological existence, takes us back to Agamben's conclusion of *The Open* where he turns to a comparison between two Titian paintings, both depicting two lovers gazing at each other's singular life. The later work, *The Nymph and the Shepherd*, depicts a scene of seemingly fallen or spent eroticism; the earlier canvas, *The Three Ages of Man* – despite the same motifs – is more serene. Agamben suggests, though, that the difference between the two works is not simply between fallen and unfallen sexuality, but an overcoming of the opposition between the tree of knowledge and the tree of life, or between the simple blessedness of mere life and being endowed with speech and humanity. It is worth recalling his discussion of the painting:

> The enigma of the sexual relationship between the man and the woman, which was already at the center of the first painting, thus receives a new and more mature formulation. Sensual pleasure and love – as the half-bloomed tree bears witness – do not prefigure only death and sin. To be sure, in their fulfillment the lovers learn something of each other that they should not have known – they have lost their mystery – and yet have not become any less impenetrable. But in this mutual

disenchantment from their secret, they enter, just as in Benjamin's apho-
rism, a new and more blessed life, one that is neither animal nor human.
It is not nature that is reached in their fulfillment, but rather (as symbol-
ized by the animal that rears up the Tree of Life and of Knowledge) a
higher stage beyond both nature and knowledge, beyond concealment
and disconcealment. These lovers have initiated each other into their
own lack of mystery as their most intimate secret; they mutually forgive
each other and expose their *vanitas*. Bare or clothed, they are no longer
either concealed or unconcealed – but rather, inapparent [*inapparenti*]. As
is clear from both the posture of the two lovers and the flute taken from
the lips, their condition is otium, it is workless [*senz'opera*]…In their
fulfillment, the lovers who have lost their mystery contemplate a human
nature rendered perfectly inoperative – the inactivity [*inoperosità*] and
desoeuvrement of the human and of the animal as the supreme and unsavable figure of life. (O: 85–6)

This is perhaps an indication that the approach to life that Agamben
indicates is not to be found in the present political terrain, but can be
intimated only in art – and in a pre-modern artwork. The Titian canvas
presents two lovers whose silent contemplation of each other exposes
them (and the viewer of the painting, presumably) to the unique relation of love, in which each body allows itself to view and be viewed
as singular life. This is not the life of the political individual or modern
person who has dignity and worth because of certain qualities, nor is
it the bodily life that is deemed to be other than, or nothing more than
the condition for, individual and rational humanity. The canvas displays the mute experience of being in relation before and outside of
constituted and formalized relations. The turn to art at the end of *The
Open* is not framed by Agamben as a specific claim about the force of
art, or the force of the image, or even the force of love; it functions as
a gesture: not yet a concept or repeatable meaning freed from the mate-
riality of its expression. The lovers offer an example of love as a singular "this here," which expresses a profound capacity to experience life
without elevating that life to some general category of personhood.
Agamben refers to art at this book's conclusion in order to indicate a
pre-political experience of life that might nevertheless point to the possibility of a new politics.

   This use of an artwork as exemplary, and as offering a reflection on
the potentiality for human relations, resonates with Agamben's more
explicit work on art, aesthetics, and images. Contemporary art,
Agamben argues, is caught up in a cult of personality or will. When I
view or purchase "a" Warhol, I am relating not to an unfolded experience of relations. I am a spectator passively viewing "a" Warhol; what
makes the work of art a work of art is not what it is, but its position in
relation to an institutional history; what we view is an act rather than
a relation or revelation of the world. The artist's signature is what sets

the work of art apart (and the signature – in turn – is not, as Agamben theorizes elsewhere, the way in which the world is revealed in its singularity, but is the repeatable mark of an identified and circulated proper name). What we view and value in the signed work is the artist's act; we are no longer in a world where art is revelation or unconcealment of what is not ourselves but empty spectacle. In the case of Duchamp and the "ready-made," for example, the urinal placed in a gallery is constituted as art precisely because of the act of refusal that it directs at the very conventions upon which it relies. It is not the artwork as singular that we are drawn toward so much as an industry of personalities, and a market of spectators:

> Christian theological thought, which conceived the supreme Being as an *actus purus*, ties to Western metaphysics the interpretation of being as actuality and act. When this process is completed in the modern era, every chance to distinguish between poiesis and praxis, pro-duction and action, is lost. Man's "doing" is determined as an activity producing a real effect (the *opus* of *operari*, the *factum* of *facere*, the *actus* of *agere*), whose worth is appreciated with respect to the will that is expressed in it, with respect to its freedom and creativity. The central experience of poiesis, pro-duction into presence, is replaced by the question of the "how," that is, of the process through which the object is produced. (MWC: 70)

The Titian, by contrast, is presented by Agamben as offering itself less as a work of a master and more as an indication of a different experience of life, a captivating experience of love as a relation that does not rely on some already constituted communicative or normative humanity:

> To render inoperative the machine that governs our conception of man will therefore mean no longer to seek new – more effective or more authentic – articulations, but rather to show the central emptiness, the hiatus that – within man – separates man and animal, and to risk ourselves in this emptiness: the suspension of the suspension, Shabbat of both animal and man. (O: 92)

In general, Agamben's turn back to the past of philosophy, theology, and art is neither straightforward nor simply nostalgic. In the case of art, though, he does recognize a loss of experience and practice in an art market of passive spectacle.

The two motifs around which Agamben's works on art are frequently structured are *poiesis* and the image, and these two motifs concern literary and visual arts respectively. Part of the importance of art for Agamben lies in the extent to which, at least in the case of poetry, the artwork renders the communicative or functional medium of language inoperative. This is an attitude toward art that characterizes the avant-garde and high modernism, and that appears at first to be similar to many of Agamben's claims regarding artworks as *poiesis*. The most significant background problem of art in the twentieth and twenty-first centuries is the relation between the artwork and the commodity. High modern artworks were avowedly and deliberately difficult to consume, precisely in response to the increasing conditions of mass literacy, mass production of artworks and reproductions, and the increasing encroachment of capitalist networks on areas of life that were once placed outside the affairs and relations of business and production. Pre-modern artworks were produced under conditions of patronage, and so artists did not need to sell their works; nor have their works been marked as original works of genius that broke away from convention.

Whereas modernist artists reacted by refusing the circulation and easy consumption of artworks, and did so by counter-institutional gestures, such as making the work itself about art as commodity, Agamben regards pure formalism or art as an artist's act of refusal and as complicit with a broader nihilism. Many of the high modernist works that were reacting against production no longer used art to convey content, and no longer strove for art to be comprehended or enjoyed.

The idea of art for art's sake, and the creation of works of art that were about nothing other than the pure capacity for there to be language, has been crucial for much of the philosophy and theory with which Agamben is engaged. Michel Foucault, for example, argued that while "man" had been formed as a being who emerges from a "life" that operates silently and governs his being, it is language – literary language – that detaches itself from some supposed ground of purposive life and seems to operate with a force of its own:

> If this same language is now emerging with greater and greater insistence in a unity that we ought to think but cannot as yet do so, is this not the sign that the whole of this configuration is about to topple, and that man is in the process of perishing as the being of language continues to shine ever brighter upon our horizon? (Foucault 1970: 385)

The emphasis on writing, text, and literature as processes that could not be grounded in knowledge and function marks both high modernist aesthetics and twentieth-century post-structuralism. Art is opposed to common sense, to shared wisdom, to enjoyment, to communication, and is certainly not a means for humans to render an unfamiliar world familiar; art is de-familiarization, detached from purposive life, and has an autonomy or force that is at odds with any recognized concept of man.

It is precisely this detachment of *poiesis* from praxis that Agamben seeks to question, while nevertheless refusing to see praxis as action grounded in life. Agamben ties modern art production to a series of shifts that include the production of art as a commodity to be bought and sold, where art becomes nothing more than a detached object for passive viewing. In the background of Agamben's broad claim regarding art and nihilism, or the reduction of the experience of art to passive spectatorship, is Walter Benjamin's claim regarding the work of art in an age of mechanical reproduction. For Benjamin, artworks originally possessed "aura," because of their singularity; the objects themselves were the object of wonder – not because of a market, culture, and institutional network of consecration, but because of the object's fragility and existence as a specific and irreplaceable "this." Once artworks can be reproduced they tend to lose their aura (Benjamin 2008).

Like Agamben after him, Benjamin does not seek to restore art to its lost original auratic condition. Instead, he looks to the future where a loss of art's distinction and separation – its sacredness – might be a way of rethinking life and escaping the exploitation of technological reproduction by fascism; rather than the loss of the sacred allowing for the nightmare condition of pure force in states of exception, there might be a different sense of art without aura. For Benjamin, fascism is more than a political system and needs to be investigated as a harnessing of a force that has unleashed itself from constituted systems of law and operates directly. Because of this, fascism operates aesthetically, through a mesmerizing force that can be deployed precisely because the earlier cults of aura that were highly charged with affect have waned:

> The increasing proletarianization of modern man and the increasing formation of masses are two sides of the same process. Fascism attempts to organize the newly proletarianized masses while leaving intact the property relations which they strive to abolish. It sees its salvation in granting expression to the masses – but on no account granting them rights. The masses have a right to changed property relations; fascism seeks to give them *expression* in keeping things unchanged. *The logical outcome of fascism is an aestheticizing of political life.* The violation of the masses, whom fascism, with its *Fuhrer* cult, forces to their knees, has its counterpart in the violation of an apparatus which is pressed into serving the production of ritual values. (Benjamin 2008: 41)

As in his arguments about law and violence, where Benjamin had regarded the onset of the police state and its use of violence outside the law as the crisis that might bring about a redeemed relation between force and life, so he regards the loss of art's aura as a possibility for thinking about the problem of the power of cults and captivation. For Benjamin, the loss of the artwork's aura is tied to a broader loss of experience. Agamben echoes this in the opening to *Infancy and History*: "The question of experience can be approached nowadays only with an acknowledgment that it is no longer

accessible to us" (IH: 15). For Benjamin, the reproduced and circulating artwork is part of a capitalist world of the seeming proliferation
of newness that is also ultimately a proliferation of the same. There
is at once nothing sacred any more because everything circulates as
the same dull round, and yet everything is sacred because it is set
apart and taken away from common use; it follows from this con-
joined dissolution of the sacred alongside the intensification of spectacle that fascism can exploit the emptiness and void of non-meaning
that marks the twentieth century. For both Agamben and Benjamin,
the response to this condition should not be a restoration of meaning,
nor a revivification or re-enchantment of the world. An art that broke
both with aura and with a society of mere spectatorship might play
a role in a future that reconfigured being and act.

What if an artwork were to display a bringing-into-being that might
also not be? Art would be neither the representation of the world, nor
the simple act of the artist, but the opening of a relation that also presented itself as the outcome of what might have remained non-relational,
a taking place of a singular "whatness" or haecceity. Most of Agamben's
work on art and images begins with a seeming lament regarding the
nihilism of the contemporary art market, and yet he also sees the current
condition, in which the artwork has become cut off from any sense of
the disclosure of the world, as a potential for destroying the sacredness
of art. The false distinction between artist and spectator, a distinction
that depends on accepting the already constituted relations of artist as
pure actor, would be displaced by an indistinction.

In terms of poetry, Agamben focuses less on what the poem says,
and more on the event *that there is saying*. At odds with the post-
humanism of his contemporaries who question the primacy accorded
to language and the privilege it grants to man as a speaking animal,
Agamben remains closer to Benjamin in thinking of language as something that remains worthy of reflection, although he rejects Benjamin's
almost mystical notion of a language of names where there might be a
direct relation between word and experience. Benjamin, reacting
against an age in which language – like art objects and political discourse – circulated without any genuine decision or thinking, raised
the possibility of thinking about the emergence of the word, as though
there might be an original act of naming before some system of differences or shared communication. Crucial to this approach to language
and poetry is the notion of the fragment: not the fragment that might,
if pieced together with other fragments, form an ultimate unity, but a
fragment that remains cut off from a whole that never arrives. (The
promised whole is intimated, but never given, almost as the fragment's
effect rather than its lost origin.) Thought of in terms of fragments,
words would be closer to gestures – indicating something other than
themselves but not yet systematized into a system of denotation. In
addition to the metaphor of the fragment, Benjamin also used the figure

of light, which is given in its effects, or which *is* its effects, and cannot be secured outside its appearing:

> The historical materialist who investigates the structure of history performs, in his way, a sort of spectrum analysis. Just as a physicist determines the presence of ultraviolet light in the solar spectrum, so the historical materialist determines the presence of a messianic force in history. Whoever wishes to know what the situation of a "redeemed humanity" might actually be, what conditions are required for the development of such a situation, and when this development can be expected to occur, poses questions to which there are no answers. He might just as well seek to know the color of ultraviolet rays. (Benjamin 2006: 402)

What this approach suggests is that one should think about the force that composes difference even if that force can only be read back from the fragments and differences that are now given. Agamben, in this respect, is at odds with both the structuralist and post-structuralist emphasis on language as a system of signs and differences, an emphasis that was essentially post-human in focusing on structures over agents and speakers. Both structuralism and post-structuralism – for all their seeming criticisms of man and the individual – nevertheless maintain a liberating notion of literature and text as practices of language that detach words from intention, sense, and speakers, and thereby expose the force of writing, text, and the traces of system. But, in doing so, these projects are complicit with sovereignty's abandonment of all that lies beyond its realm of constituted force:

> Language's sovereign claim thus consists in the attempt to make sense coincide with denotation, to stabilize a zone of indistinction between the two in which language can maintain itself in relation to its *denotata* by abandoning them and withdrawing from them into a pure *langue* (the linguistic "state of exception"). This is what deconstruction does, positing undecidables that are infinitely in excess of every possibility of signification. (HS: 21–2)

For Agamben, such projects that simply accept language as a constitutive system of differences fail to ask the question that is most important: how do we account for the emergence of difference from indifference (where indifference is *not* some plenitude or unity but a potentiality for relation)? Agamben's work on poetry is less focused on difference, text, or structure, and more on illuminating the distance between silence and speech – along with the silence of speech within language, or what cannot be captured by the linguistic system:

> In terms of human infancy, experience is the simple difference between the human and the linguistic. The individual as not already speaking, as having been and still being an infant – this is experience. But there is in

this sense an infancy of the individual, that there is a difference between the human and the linguistic, is not an event on a par with others in the realm of human history, or a simple characteristic among many that identify the species *Homo sapiens*. Infancy has its effect first and foremost on language, constituting it and conditioning it in an essential way. For the very fact that infancy exists as such – that it is, in other words, experience as the transcendental limit of language – rules out language as being in itself totality and truth. (IH: 58)

Poetry is a bringing into being of the distinction of language; it cannot be seen as an act precisely because it is in the creation of poetry or the event of speech that something like speaker and world emerge in relation. Poetry is therefore tied closely both to the problem of potentiality, insofar as it exposes an emergence of speech that is not yet one more move in an already constituted system, and also to the problem of humanity.

Agamben's approach to poetry is typical of the mode of inquiry that structures his entire corpus. At first glance it appears that his work is addressing a loss and rupture that a return to the past would repair. On this reading, we lament the fact that in modernity we no longer approach the world poetically – as a space to be brought into being – and instead we have been reduced to a single domain of manageable life. Art becomes one more circulating object, and our conception of the artist is bound up with art objects being nothing more than acts undertaken by individuals; the art object bears little if any relation to the world and is instead the fragment of an act of will. It might seem, then, that Agamben looks back to an earlier period of art as collective world creation, where the art object emerged from praxis, and where there was not yet some easy and fully actualized distinction between the general "man" who speaks and the distinct world that is spoken about. However, Agamben never regards a contemporary loss or indistinction as an occasion for returning to a richer, unified, proper, or authentic notion. There is something quasi-Christian about his approach, where it is almost fortunate that paradise be lost, precisely because a regained paradise is richer and more worthy. However, the more acute point is that there *is loss*, but there is also no simple paradise to begin with. In the beginning there is not a unity or fullness from which we are increasingly alienated. Rather, there is a journey of increasing indistinction that should lead us to turn back to an original loss or distance – a loss or distance that is original, for there is nothing that was lost, and no nearness from which we fell away. From an original indistinction, "man" generates an uneasy difference between a world of doing and then some transcendent being toward which doing ought to be directed; as history progresses, one side of the distinction falls away and all we are left with is a world of will and action, with no end other than itself.

In simpler (but not simple) terms, we can say that the present is an impoverished era for the experience of the art object and the poem. The object has lost its distinction and aura as different from everyday objects, and is only distinguished by virtue of the cult of the artist, which in turn is only possible because of an increasingly simple humanism. Humans are distinguished from the world as a different type of being – opposed to animality in their capacity to speak and create (with speaking as a simple capacity, not considered in its relation to impotentiality); the artist then becomes a particularly skilled speaker and producer. What is lost is the specialness, distinction, mystery, and enigma of the poem and art object. The world of art becomes one of consumption and spectatorship. Agamben's response, though, is not to turn back to some authentic moment, although he does refer to a past when poetry emerged from common and collective creative praxis. Rather, it is because there is today a simple and unquestioned distinction between creating/speaking humans and the world that is there to be pictured and owned that we have failed to consider the coming into being of this difference, and that it must have emerged from potential difference – a potential that is fragile and not destined to actualize itself. Even though Agamben frequently looks back to earlier works of art, such as the Titian canvas that concludes *The Open*, he is also insistent that his inquiry into zones of indistinction is oriented toward a future that would not be like the past, but would address questions that the past articulated vaguely while never fully exploring them.

For Agamben, these questions or indistinctions that were intimated but never clarified have haunted Western thought and yet remain unthought, even in the transition from a theologically dominated mode of culture and politics to an increasing secularism and disenchantment. What Agamben seeks to do is pose these questions again while neither arriving at a clear distinction nor resolving the indistinction into some unity. What is important is to consider the emergence of a relation from a potentiality: there are not humans on the one hand, and linguistic systems on the other, but a potentiality for speaking. It is from that potential for relation that humans emerge, in their distinction, as speaking beings; but this also means that – as potential for relation – the difference can also break down. Poetry, with its detachment of language from a system of relations, no longer functions as a means for humans to communicate, as though humans and language and world (as actual terms) were unproblematically distinct. It is the detachment of the word, in poetry, from functioning human life of bodies and relations that allows us once again to think the very fragile potential from which a speaking humanity emerged. There is still, for Agamben, something distinct about humans and language, but that distinction needs to be considered not in terms of actuality – two beings coming

into relation, as humans take on language as some sort of tool or technology – for the distinction is one of potentiality. Potentiality is a power
for relations and beings to emerge, but it is also a potential not to be
actualized. For this reason, Agamben's reflections on art, animality, and
politics are all united in their reference back to a time when distinctions
came into being but were never fully interrogated according to an ever-
present, ever-potential zone of indifference or impotentiality. But, as
well as being related conceptually, there is also a connection among art,
animality, and politics in terms of what we might refer to as Agamben's
theory of life, which is different from ontology.

Going back to Aristotle, ontology had always been theorized as "first
philosophy," and Aristotle is frequently cited by Agamben as the key
corpus that frames later political and theological questions (Finlayson
2010). Ontology concerns what can be said to be; the Christian tradition
of onto-theology begins with a definition that dominates later questions: if true being is that which could exist in itself, without any other
being, then there would only be one true being or substance, and that
would be God. All other beings are not truly beings but exist by analogy;
they can be said to be only insofar as they are expressions of a foundational being. To ask questions of ontology, which has been philosophy's
and theology's main task, is to ask about what it is for something to
be, and what truly and ultimately is. Are numbers, logical truths, and
rules of physics the truly real beings because they are eternal and
unchanging, or are nature and matter truly real because they exist
"concretely"? For Agamben, following Heidegger, asking questions of
ontology – or asking about what truly and ultimately is, or what
remains present – can only occur if we forget or fail to ask about how
beings emerge, or how beings come into being. That is, the question of
presence – or that which remains the same – has covered over the question of how being comes into presence; for Heidegger, this forgotten
dimension was that of time and appearing. For Agamben, the "threshold" of the dimension that gets covered over by onto-theology is not
quite time and appearing (phenomenology), but something even more
elusive, which is the potentiality for appearing and not appearing. This
is why Agamben focuses so much on the Greek distinction between
dynamis (or potentiality) and *energeia* (or actuality). For the most part,
the Western tradition has subordinated potentiality to actuality: so we
begin with actual, speaking humans and their political and artistic
productions, and we see potentiality at present as a capacity or skill
that is defined by the final action. We see potentiality as secondary or
accidental; it becomes possible for humans not to speak and create, or
possible for them to lose their humanity and become nothing more than
mere life, but this possibility is relegated to the accidental and not seen
as essential to potentiality (which is, if you like, something's essence
– or its essential inessentiality). For Agamben, though, any seeming

loss or accident – humans not speaking, humans fallen into animality, politics as mere management, art as nothing more than commodified images – discloses potentiality as impotentiality. This means that we need to rethink essence to refer not to what something always and necessarily is, but in terms of a potentiality not to be. What makes humans human is that their defining and humanizing capacities may not emerge. This is also to say that the very essence of humanity lies in a potentiality that is expressed when it does not unfold into actuality. We start to think genuinely about human–animal distinctions precisely when humans become increasingly animalized in biopolitics; only then do we become aware of the "machine" that has always – but never definitively – divided humans from their mere animality. It is when the potentiality for politics is lost that we can rethink the coming into being of the political, along with the coming into being of the human, and the emergence of poetry. This mode of questioning is not ontology; *or*, it is not ontology in its usual sense: it is not about being but about coming into being, and not about *what is* – our actual world – but about the potential for actuality *and* not being.

Agamben – though recognizing the importance of the question of essence and existence that runs from Aristotle through Marx to Heidegger – wants to question the ontological and theological posing of this question, or what he refers to as the ongoing fracture between being and act. If we think about the problem of essence and existence in terms of life (rather than ontology), then the entire mode of the question changes, and this is indeed Agamben's aim. If we take the Heideggerian (and ontological) path, then we say that humans are not defined by their biological or bodily life – the life they share with mere nature and animality – but by the free and ungrounded decisions they make, decisions that never follow automatically from their nature. Aristotle has already argued that while we have a bodily existence, we also have the defining or proper potentiality to choose the form of that existence; hence there is a distinction between *zoe* (animal, mere life) and *bios* (formed life). And even though Marxism wants to tie philosophy back to the conditions of history and man's laboring being, it does so by seeing our nature and bodily life as the outcome of a history of labor and world-making. Heidegger insisted – in the face of a twentieth century that increasingly studied humans as living beings whose needs of life would determine their politics and language – that biological life is one mode of interpreting or disclosing the world, and that prior to any such interpretation of being there would be the revealing or disclosing of beings by *Dasein*. The anti-biologism of philosophy as ontology has intensified, even as politics becomes biopolitical and only operates with a conception of life as biological substance to be managed. The split between *bios* and *zoe* becomes intensified in many of the anti-biopolitical theories that would insist upon subjectivity, performativity, or language, intensifying what Agamben refers to as the linguistic state of exception.

Given the horrors of twentieth-century eugenics, ethnic cleansing, genocide, and the specter of human genetic engineering, it is not surprising that theory of all types, but feminist theory in particular, has tended to be opposed to any form of biologism. When theory eventually turned to "the body" in the 1990s, it did so in a series of ways, though generally insisted that the body was never a mere body but always a body formed through practices, images, meanings, and political contexts of recognition. When Agamben exploded on to the anglophone theory scene, it was precisely through his theorization of *life*. Far from suggesting that democracies need to distance themselves from totalitarian regimes that had used life as a means for population management, he insisted that both democracies and totalitarian regimes were united in tying politics to life, or to the idea that the task of the polity is to maximize our life. His argument was unique precisely because he recognized that using "life" as some basis for political decisions would shut down any form of deliberation – but this was not because he did not see life as a legitimate problem. Rather, he wanted to see life neither as a being, something that simply *is* that could decide our questions of existence, nor as something that could only be known as what lies outside language – but as a potentiality for politics and language while remaining irreducible to either. And this is strangely where all of Agamben's seemingly arcane work on theology connects with his contemporary engagement with biopolitics. The traditional conception of God, as a complete Being that does not need to act or become in order to be, presupposes a norm of life – life in which the mode of existence coincides fully and without remainder with proper form, a being whose "being" or essence is nothing other than pure act. God would be a being-in-itself (absolutely complete) and a being-for-itself (absolutely self-determining). In human terms, if our proper potentiality – what distinguishes us from animals – is the capacity to decide our lives, then the perfect human life would be one of pure decision, in which we had completely transcended our non-human or merely animal being; what we are is what we would decide to be (and this is exactly what happens in sovereignty, where the law becomes nothing more than the sovereign decision, and life appears completely captured by sovereign force). Such a norm of life, which Agamben sees as ultimately theological, relies upon an opposition between a force of free, unbounded, and self-positing decision, set against a bare life in itself that – far from relating to itself and constituting itself – simply remains in its silent abandonment.

A certain theological requirement – that God be pure existence without any determination other than a divine and free act – has consequences for political history, for art, for conceptions of the human, and for our inability to understand our own life. Politically, there has always been a problem of explaining the relation between the divinely free and absolute God who creates, and the God who then has some role in the world's ongoing existence. One solution is to distinguish between God and Christ, between God as creation and Christ as incarnation in the world. But this solution sustains the problem of what Agamben refers to as "economy": if God is not involved in this world, then we are left with this world as devoid of divinity, but if God is involved in this world, then his absolute and infinite being becomes limited or relational. One "solution" to this problem is the divine economy, where the power of Christ in this world is not a lessening or weakening of God's force, but a distribution. It then comes to be increasingly important how we think about such divine governance: one model – of duty – would be to see the role of the Church as managing God's law, thereby fracturing God's being and the action or law of the world. Another model would be to see Christ's role in the world as an extension or expression of divine being, such that the order of the world would *not* be obedience to a command or rule – doing what one ought – but forming oneself *through life* in the manner of Christ. Translated away from theological terms this would yield a community that bears the structure of glory, where the community is not at odds with life, but where being *is* its declaration, appearing, or praise, and yet never exhausted in that economy:

> Philosophy and the science of politics have omitted to pose the question that appears decisive in every way, whenever the techniques and strategies of government and power are analyzed, from a genealogical and functional perspective: Where does our culture draw the criterion of politicality – mythologically and in fact? What is the substance – or the procedure, or threshold – that allows one to confer on something a properly political character? The answer that our investigation suggests is: glory, in its dual aspect, divine and human, ontological and economic, of the Father and the Son, of the people-substance and the people-communication. (KG: 259)

The force of Agamben's philosophy is, then, to shift the question of being – say, the being of God who in his absolute and infinite power must be other than any of his determined and finite creations – to the question of life; but the structure is still that of a relation between what is (divinity, the being of the world in its "thus") and what speaks or acts (the human, the way the world is). This is not because Agamben relies upon life as something that *is*, as some substance that would provide a secure material ground for law, ethics, and knowledge. Rather than resolve this problem of the relation between being and act, Agamben's work seeks to intensify this problematic by rethinking the very notion of relation. In terms of the human, this means neither asserting some continuity between humanity and animality, nor asserting the actual distinctiveness of humans, but recognizing a distinctiveness that is alongside a tendency to indistinction. Indistinction, zone of indetermination, and non-relation: these terms mark the difference between a tradition of ontology (or what something essentially is), and Agamben's emphasis on life, or the fragile potential for what might become, or emerge into distinction. A focus on ontology would be primarily theological: if we assume that the actual world unfolds from some prior conception of what it ought to be – its essence or what it truly is – then this is because there is deemed to be some prior or transcendent order which is at once outside the world but nevertheless grants this world meaning, determination, and definition. The purity or sovereignty of this prior ordering principle requires that it at once not be caught up in the actuality and determination of this world, but that it also nevertheless bears some governing relation to the world.

There is, for Agamben, a necessary problem of approaching our world, our life, and our thinking by way of this conception of being that then comes into relation or relates *to* action. We have passed from a theological order that always had difficulty in conceiving the relation between absolute divine being and the created, living, temporal, and existing world; but once we have lost that notion of a proper potentiality or world of essences toward which actuality ought to become, we only have life as other than law. The relation of law to life – if life is conceived as lawless, as bare life – becomes that of a sovereign decision that has the capacity (as sovereign) to exempt itself from the order it institutes. So there are two conceptions of life that are ultimately ontological because they have already determined what life is: the first is theological and sees life as created and determined by some divine and transcendent being (but this will always place life as other than the divine, even if properly governed by the divine); the second is the notion of life that functions in biopolitics and that has always haunted Western thought, which is the bare life that has been cast outside the law. For Agamben, that mere life without meaning, order, law, and completion is precisely where a new ethics and politics might begin. Such a politics would neither be theological by asserting some proper form of law or transcendence, nor nihilistic by abandoning all conceptions of law and resigning itself to a world of nothing more than actual life. Instead, life would be this potentiality for being mere life, which would be a forming, gestural, and *poetic* life, never coinciding absolutely with itself.

With this conception of a life that might not be abandoned and set outside the law as bare life, a life that might be redeemed or blessed immanently and on its own terms, Agamben draws on Walter Benjamin's enigmatic criticisms of messianism and divinity. What

Benjamin and Agamben want to consider is not some origin before law – some peaceful life that is extended and fulfilled by law, with law occasionally operating violently to expel a lawless outside. Instead, one might say that in the beginning is a violence that is not violence *over* or violence *by* a body so much as a violence or force that creates an inside and outside: this would then mean that the origin is not a being (such as a god who then acts), but something like an action or force from which a distinction between body and power emerges. Thus, there would be an original violence that could not be judged as either lawful or unlawful, for it is the force from which a body subject to law emerges. There is something mystical about this conception of origin precisely because it cannot be thought or known in its presence but only intuited in its having been, after the event of its fragmentation. What makes both Benjamin and Agamben radical, political, and quasi-secular in terms of this "divine" violence, as Benjamin calls it, is that their mysticism or quasi-messianism is posed in the name of life. That is, even though the structure of the critique of violence is political – for they do not see any law in this world as having an ultimate authority, and see any appeal to origin in secular terms as necessarily impossible – they do not posit an unknowable and distant God that would lie beyond knowledge and life. Instead life itself is mystical, or put differently: life is never mere life. Or, phrased differently again: it is when life is thought of as *mere* life – a life without law, form, or order – that we might start to rethink divinity. Divinity would not be some higher being that creates and orders this world and life. Life – considered not as that which is the object of law, but life as such – might bear its own blessedness and divinity, and this would occur with a rethinking of life and divinity in terms of them not existing as distinct and opposed beings.

If we consider the status of life in biopolitics – where, say, humans are granted less and less dignity as citizens and become more and more exposed to the immediate intervention of power and violence on their bodies – then it might appear that we are all being cast outside any sense of law that would protect us, and that there is widespread dehumanization. One response might be to reassert human dignity and re-establish law, insisting that we not be reduced to mere life, that we be granted the worth of personhood. But Agamben and Benjamin take a different path. The problem with asserting both the dignity of human persons, or appealing to the sanctity of the law, is that persons and law are set against life. What would be truly radical – and this is one of the distinct features of Agamben's ethics and politics – is to consider what it might be to have an ethics of humanity that was not aligned with the humanity of reason, personhood, or humanism.

Instead of seeing life as a prima facie good, worthy of dignity because it can accede to the law, one might begin from the potentiality of life without law. That is, rather than divide life between lawful life – a life that is properly and essentially rational and self-formed – and a life that is without significance and placed beyond law, Agamben redefines law by redefining force. Rather than regard force as that which is required in order to maintain a norm or law, and rather than think of law as an ideal, stable, or actual system that may or may not be attained by a good life, Agamben reconfigures the relations among law, force, and life – and he does so primarily through an attention to indistinction. This is not to reduce law to force, nor to argue for some conception of life that might be liberated from all force in order to be complete and self-sufficient. The aim of thinking about indistinction lies in allowing each of these terms to be thought not as they actually are – not the system of laws as we have it, nor the transgressions of violence that we currently recognize, nor even what we take to be living. Instead, we might think about law's emergence from a force that is not yet separated into violent or transgressive force opposed to a law-enforcing violence. Rather than sovereign force being that which acts upon life, with life being either the lawful existence of persons within the law, or the bare undignified life outside the law, life might be considered as a fragile potentiality for form, where form is not some external power. What if force were not something accidental and extraneous? We could think of force as that from which law (and all our conceptions of the proper) emerge; if this were so, then it would be radical not to try and include all life within law (granting dignity and personhood to all humans, and then perhaps also animals and maybe even plants), but to think of a life without law, and a law without force. Following Agamben, it might be possible to form an ethics of life where life is not necessarily only worthy insofar as it meets the requirements of dignity and personhood. And, rather than regulate the law's use of force, it might be possible to think of a form or rule that is not external to life.

Conclusion

The three strands that run throughout Agamben's work – art, life, sovereignty – are interrelated, and the curious mode of this interrelation provides a way of thinking about Agamben's difference in relation to the tradition of post-Heideggerian theory of which he is at once a critic and disciple. Indeed, the motif of indifference or indistinction that runs throughout Agamben's work might be applied to his own corpus: it would be easy to distinguish a post-structuralism focused on linguistic differences and relations from new vitalisms, materialisms, and realisms that privilege the life before language. Agamben's work is poised between these two tendencies, at once acknowledging the life from which relations emerge, and insisting that we consider life in its curious non-relation to language and not simply as language's negated outside. In conclusion, we would suggest that it is the concept of difference and indifference that is most useful in recognizing the distinction and resonance of Agamben's corpus (Watkin 2013).

Both Heidegger and the late twentieth-century thinkers who responded to his work accepted the Heideggerian criticism of presence: philosophy (as onto-theology) explains the difference and different beings of the world by way of referring back to a privileged Being or foundational presence (such as God, matter, substance, or life). Heidegger had argued that rather than simply accept some original presence that explains beings, some account or question needs to be given of the coming into presence or emergence of beings. Heidegger therefore rejected the metaphysical mode of beginning explanations from "man," and instead referred to the *relation* of revealing as *Da-sein* – the "there" from which being is unveiled (always as some specific being within a world toward which we are oriented in a relation of care). For most French thinkers after Heidegger there was a problem of this privilege of *Da-sein*, which was still too close to the valorized being of man. Derrida and Deleuze, for example, in different ways begin from *difference* – the difference from which relations and distinctions emerge rather than some being or substance prior to differentiation. In this vein, neither Derrida's *différance* nor Deleuze's "time in its pure state" or differentiation remain the sole terms through which they think the potential from which determined differences emerge. The tactic becomes one of finding various gestures that intimate that which cannot itself be presented precisely because it is the milieu from which distinction emerges; for this reason, both Derrida and Deleuze multiply the terms through which one might think about the differential forces (traces, stratifications, inscriptions, intensities) that precede the composition of the world as it is experienced as being, even if such terms cannot themselves be experienced. By contrast, rather than gesture toward some difference that is always other than differentiated being, Agamben presents his own work as a path toward the experience of the threshold. In this respect he is indebted to, critical of, and at odds with, the present. Several times throughout this work we have made references to various thinkers to whom Agamben is indebted, and in each case Agamben's work is *both* a future-oriented radicalization and an almost regressive retrieval. In the case of Hegel, who might be thought of as *the* philosopher of both negativity and its recuperation, all of Agamben's work might be thought of as a counter-Hegelianism: instead of thinking of what is other than thought as thought's *own outside*, Agamben accords a genuine and positive potentiality to that which does not actualize and realize itself through self-consciousness and reflection. And yet, in a manner that is almost a hyper-Hegelianism, Agamben presents his work – against his time – as *the* project that will think beyond differentiated systems to a more profound experience of the zone of indifference. In his recent work on the character of Pilate, for example, Agamben repeats the Christian notion that only with a New Testament reading of the word – the word as it makes its way into the world – will "we" approach truth; and although Agamben is mentioning this idea, he nevertheless reads this very tradition as if he were (in an almost Christlike manner) restoring the words of tradition to their life: "there is only one authentic Christian tradition: that of the 'handing over' – first on the part of the Father, then of Judas and the Jews – of Jesus to the cross, which has abolished and realized all traditions" (PJ: 10). For Agamben, reading the narrative and history of the character of Pilate is more than an act of literary hermeneutics; or, more accurately, Agamben's work of hermeneutics is, finally, an interpretation of the relation between the divine word and the life that *is divine* precisely in bearing the weight of the word and requiring no other salvation:

> To testify, here and now, to the truth of the kingdom that is not here means accepting that what we want to save will judge us. This is because

the world, in its fallenness, does not want salvation but justice. And it wants it precisely because it is not asking to be saved. As unsavable, creatures judge the eternal: this is the paradox that in the end, before Pilate, cuts Jesus short. Here is the cross; here is history. (PJ: 55)

With respect to Benjamin, Agamben seems also to render genuinely profane the thought of that life that would not be abandoned by the law, and seems to create a messianism that is profoundly of this world – if only we could experience this life as needing no divinity other than itself in order to be; and, yet, Agamben even in his most recent work sustains the need for thinking through the present by way of a history of theology, and by way of conceptions of the divine. Again, with Arendt, Agamben begins from her criticism of the ways in which what had once been seen as the condition for political life – human laboring existence – now becomes the way in which contemporary humanism conceives all political being, thereby generating the horrific managerialism and population controls of late modernity. And, while Agamben seems to problematize Arendt's opposition and *not* appeal to a retrieval of an authentic politics of reflection and collective reason, his conception of community seems oddly poised between a refusal of all humanist essentialism while nevertheless constantly articulating *man*'s unique capacity to experience the border between the political capacities of speech and the pre-political silence of animality. One might also think of Agamben's corpus in this way, as divided between his political and critical works oriented to the present – such as the first volume of *Homo Sacer*, and *The Coming Community*, where attention is focused on liberating thought from presuppositions of what counts as properly human – and his early and late works devoted to poetry and theology respectively, which are far more invested in sustaining (even while reworking) essential or foundational questions. Such divisions between forward and backward glances in Agamben's work are, however, troubled by the very indifference and indistinction that he gestures toward throughout his corpus. Indeed, one might consider one of his motifs – the gesture – as a way of thinking about the ambivalence of Agamben's thought. Gesture is at once a movement of the body that is not yet formalized into an inscribed linguistic system; it might appear to be at once highly human – such that the human hand by way of gesture becomes at once a body part but also a recognizable and repeatable sign – at the same time as gesture seems to be closer to animality, or a relation to the world that occurs through immediacy rather than the systems of language and formality that abandon the world. Agamben seems at one and the same time throughout his corpus to be gesturing, to be trying to find a way to write that would be closer, more proximate to life; and yet the means of gesturing or the way out of the empty formality of language is sometimes a painting, a photograph, or an advertisement, but also a theological, legal, or philosophical treatise. Perhaps it is not surprising that he devotes a volume to St. Paul, for whom – according to Agamben – one might speak in a certain way, live in a certain way, and yet, in so doing, gesture to one's life and world as being other than it seems: "for Paul, the messianic is not a third eon situated between two times; but rather, it is a caesura that divides the division between times and introduces a remnant, a zone of undecidability, in which the past is dislocated into the present and the present is extended into the past" (TR: 74). In the same volume on Paul, Agamben spends a great deal of time on poetry, but not because of what poetry says in its meaning, just as he says the "message" of Pauline Christianity does not consist in what it says, but – like poetry – in its capacity to take what appears as present and unified, and open the seemingly differentiated moments of past and future into a pulsation or rhythm of indifference. Time, poetry, and gesture: these are all, for Agamben, ways of taking differentiated systems and exposing a dilation or movement (an opening of relation from a potentiality):

> The poem is therefore an organism or a temporal machine that, from the very start, strains towards its end. A kind of eschatology occurs within the poem itself. But for the more or less brief time that the poem lasts, it has a specific and unmistakable temporality, it has its own *time*...By now you will have perfectly understood the hypothesis I am about to put forth, which should be taken more as an epistemological paradigm rather than as an historical-genealogical hypothesis: that rhyme issues from Christian poetry as a metrical-linguistic transcodification of messianic time. (TR: 79, 85)

Agamben repeatedly thinks of proto-linguistic movements such as gesture, rhyme, and signatures positively as something that is poised on the threshold between constituted difference and something that is singular in its difference: "the muteness inherent in humankind's very capacity for language, its speechless dwelling in language" (P: 78).

If we think about Agamben's critical motifs – art, life, sovereignty – it appears that he is thoroughly in accord with the broader post-Heideggerian criticism of a metaphysics of presence. At the same time as he rejects the positing of a foundational or sovereign being, he also sees language as one more sovereign being that determines the relations of the world, and therefore strives to think about moments, such as gesture, where language is not the sovereign force that differentiates and constitutes the world as differentiated. What if one were to read the past *not* as a system of signs that denoted a world that was silent, but as the way in which the world expressed itself, gestured toward something other than itself, or *signed itself*. Rather than see art, then, as the work that is signed by an individual whose act it incarnates, one might think of the work as a gesture or signature – as life's capacity to signal its singularity rather than its generality.

If we stay within difference (or the differential relations of language through which we speak), then we repeat the sovereign negativity of metaphysics whereby the things or beings of this world are effects of a prior ground (whether that be a ground that is present or a ground that is differential, such as the system of language). If we think about a threshold or indifference that precedes and haunts difference, we are not faced with an absence or negativity, but a potentiality for difference that needs to be conceived as singular; it positively exceeds and remains as impotentiality, or what is not actualized, in any achieved difference. There is no pure difference, difference in general, but always the singular event of emerging into difference (which is why Agamben focuses so often on the *saying* of anything "said," or its moment of bringing forth a relation). In the case of art, works are disclosive of a world, a locatedness, a coming into emergence, and therefore need to be read and perceived as singularly distinct revelations. For this reason, Agamben gives a very different account of language from that of broader twentieth-century theories of system or structure. There is something about language that is singular and that reveals the impotentiality/potentiality or threshold of human life. (When Derrida refers to writing, trace, or *écriture*, he is insistent that all the features that we think pertain to language mark all life and experience; and when Deleuze and Guattari write about the despotism of the signifier, they challenge the sovereignty of man and language, arguing for a broader conception of life that is already "semiotic" or composed of interacting differences.)

Agamben, however, wants to hold on to language *as language*, because it is at once that which makes us human – distancing us from any immediacy of life – and that which always occurs through a singular medium of sound that is still part of bodily life; language harbors the difference between differential system and the singular difference of each speaking being; it exposes a threshold or indifference that is irreducible to systems:

> The decisive element that confers on language its peculiar virtue is not in the tool itself but in the place it leaves to the speaker, in the fact that it prepares within itself a hollowed out form that the speaker must always assume in order to speak – that is to say, in the ethical relation that is established between the speaker and his language. *The human being is that living being that, in order to speak, must say "I," must "take the word," assume it and make it his own.*
>
> Western reflection on language has taken nearly two millennia to isolate, in the formal machinery of language, the enunciative function, the end, the ensemble of those indicators or *shifters* (*I, you, here, now* etc.) by means of which the one who speaks assumes language in a concrete

act of discourse. What linguistics is undoubtedly not in a position to give an account, however, is the *ethos* that is produced in this gesture and that determines the extraordinary implication of the subject in his word. (SL: 71)

If we think of language as just "a" system through which we speak and are produced as persons, then this is akin to simply accepting law or difference without questioning its emergence, or without questioning what might be otherwise and what might not have been actualized. The sovereign paradigm simply accepts that there is a system and that whatever is outside the system can only be given negatively, as the system's effected and abandoned other. If we think of language differently, in its poetic form, then the systemic dimension that posits and differentiates is split from within by language and its gestural or singular emergence. As structuralists argued, when one speaks or writes, it is the difference *between* terms that counts: I can pronounce "grass" with an English, American, Scottish, or New Zealand accent and it has the same function because English doesn't include a meaningful difference between the different ways of pronouncing the "a" for this word. However, when we pronounce "lead" differently, the word can either be a noun or a verb because English does mark this difference; what counts as a difference depends on the system, and not the isolated case. For Agamben, the differences that the system ignores expose humans uniquely to a threshold: all the singular events of language and the way every voice is at once part of a general system *and* is also this located, sonorous, accented, expressive event of emergence (an animal's cry is only the latter, whereas a sovereign conception of language is only the former).

Literary art, then, offers perhaps the clearest exposition or exposure to the threshold that would redeem us from a life that has either been subsumed by a managerial sovereignty or abandoned and set outside all systems of recognition. Literary language is not mere noise; nor is it ever close to a formal system like mathematics that suspends any concrete or specific reference. More importantly, poetic language is not *writing as writing* (nor is it art for art's sake, the pure appearance of inscription freed from all communicative, expressive, representative relations). Rather, literary art, like all art, should be considered beyond the modern paradigm of aesthetics; it is the aesthetic comportment that assumes that life is productive, operative, forceful, active, and traceable back to some power that is nothing other than a capacity to effect differences, to will itself as will. Literary writing crystallizes what Agamben wants to define as a uniquely human exposure or witnessing of the threshold of potentiality/impotentiality, even if the human "is" nothing other than that which emerges from the experience of *not* already having a world, law, system, or way of living one's life.

As Agamben's *The Open* meditates on animal life, it criticizes the notion of *a* world that is then simply doubled in representation; each animal generates a world according to its potentiality. In this respect all life is (as Agamben says of human life) essentially inessential, or able to be what it is and have the world that it has only through encounters that generate and disclose a world for a specific being. Humans, however, by way of language, are exposed to this threshold of potentiality/impotentiality and indifference. Who they are and what their world might be is not only not given in advance, but appears – especially via the contingency of language – as what might be otherwise, as potentially inoperative. Art, then, is the experience of the unfolding of the world in relation, in common, among humans – opening a political space – and this means in turn that rather than see active self-production (by way of will and self-positing) as definitive of life and humanity, where we valorize world-making, we would think of life as a potentiality for generating difference from a threshold that can never be divided securely between active and passive, between subject/agent and object. If art is best not thought of as "aesthetics" or as a product of a will that is then available for passive spectatorship, then this is because art is a form of bringing into presence from a threshold of obscurity. And this revelatory unfolding that is exposed through art would characterize all forms of human "doing," including politics. For there was, once upon a time in ancient Greece, a conception of "doing" that was inclusive of all forms of production-into-presence, and was not isolated in some distinct artistic act by some separated artist. Rather than the sovereign paradigm where *there is law* that has no world other than that effected through its operation, and that establishes relations and that might be negotiated or solicited only from within, one might think of a world not given in advance and in which each member of the polity related to every other simply in not having any pre-given identity, other than being exposed to the coming into being of a common space.

Politics would be the experience of lawlessness – a being in common without a common world. When Agamben writes about overcoming the abandonment of life (as law and as language's negative posited outside) he frequently indicates that this will be achieved by a destruction of aesthetics and the sovereign paradigm. Such destruction will also be perilously close to today's biopolitical state of exception, where there is indeed no law other than that of immediate force willed by the state, and no art other than that of a market reduced to operations. The difference between a heaven of open potentiality/impotentiality and the hell of an enclosed system of difference without positivity is itself poised on a threshold of indifference that only the annihilation of potentiality could resolve. Toward the end, *The Kingdom and the Glory* turns to the hymn to consider a form of language that is marked by an "incurable absence"; this seems to suggest an impoverished emptiness of language, and precisely in that form of language – the hymn – that bears a relation to the divine, the form of language in which humans try to move toward what is not their own life. Yet this absence and emptiness is, for Agamben, a liberation from working: "the turning in the void of language as the supreme form of glorification. The hymn is the radical deactivation of signifying language, the word rendered completely inoperative" (KG: 237).

Shortly after making this claim that ties the hymn to an emptiness that is also a purity and freedom that takes language away from all content, Agamben looks to poetry as maintaining this "postjudicial inoperativity...the eternal amen in which all works and all human words are resolved." Poetry, then, is glory, and because glory is the event of the hymn that has no other content than an address to the divine, it is also the achievement – finally, but always – of the postjudicial: "inoperativity is the name of what is most proper to God." If human words are "resolved," it is *not* because they refer, *nor* because they express a will in its pure force, but because they pass from human to divine, without that divinity being a content other than the relation from the world to what is not quite of this world:

> Poetry's bitter tendency to isolate words, which the Alexandrines used to call "free style," can be defined as "hymnical." It rests on the fact that every doxology is ultimately concerned with the celebration of the name. In hymn, all names tend to be isolated and become desemanticized in the proper names of the divine. In this sense, every poem presupposes the hymn – however distant they are – which is to say, it is only possible against the backdrop and within the horizon of the divine names. (KG: 238)

Here is Agamben at his most arcane and regressive, and at his most revolutionary. He at once refers to an original naming, an almost Adamic relation to the world liberated from the machine that organizes man in relation to a posited bare life, and yet the one who names is not man, person, or subject. The poem presupposes the hymn, which seems to tie everything back to the divine, and yet the divine is *not* the God of pure act and pure being, prior to all praxis. The divine emerges from this hymn, which is not directed *to* anything that is already different and distinct, but opens from an indistinction. In the beginning was the not-yet.

Notes

Introduction: Agamben and the Present

1 Agamben makes reference through his corpus to the ways in which Jacques
Derrida's deconstruction recognizes the extent to which language or difference operates as a force that, ultimately, cannot be grounded or stabilized
by any referent. Agamben's attitude toward Derridean deconstruction
shifts as he moves away from his early work on language as negativity, or
as ultimately ungrounded from anything other than its own event of saying,
toward an attempt to think of life beyond negativity. He remains critical of
Derrida's work throughout his career, such that his ongoing relation to
Derrida's work has been one of the key focal points in the secondary literature. Both Leland de la Durantaye and Alex Murray have commented on
Agamben's early criticism of Derrida in *Stanzas*, in which "Derrida focuses
exemplary attention on this barrier [between signifier and signified] but
becomes transfixed by what he sees" (de la Durantaye 2009: 186), or, in
Murray's words: "So where Derrida's deconstruction seeks to undermine
binary oppositions through the play of the trace, Agamben's seeks to undermine through a method of presenting the barrier or inbetween between the
binaries" (Murray 2010). Kevin Attell has devoted an entire book to explaining the ways in which Agamben traces a path beyond deconstruction (Attell
2014).
2 Agamben's diagnosis of Western thought *as negative* has been criticized by
Rosi Braidotti for being overly mournful and melancholic: "Agamben per-
petuates the philosophical habit of taking mortality and finitude as the
trans-historical horizon for discussions of 'life'" (Braidotti 2006: 39).
3 Although Agamben himself is disappointingly silent on questions of race
and colonialism, some of the most exciting work that pursues his critique
of biopolitics as characteristic of the Western tradition as a whole has
been in the area of post-colonial theory. Achille Mbembe (2003) theorized
a "necropolitics" that described the ways in which sovereignty operates by
way of the power to take and destroy life, and to do so in primarily racial

and colonizing procedures. An entire volume of essays has been devoted to the relation between Agamben's thought and colonialism (Svirsky and Bignall 2012), some theorists arguing that his theory of the "state of exception" or the biopolitical reduction of human populations to bare life is not at all exceptional in invaded territories (such as Israel's occupation of the West Bank (Svirsky 2014)), while others see his theorization of sovereignty as crucial for conceptualizing the ways in which seemingly post-colonial nations, such as Australia, continually reinscribe sovereign borders and abandon indigenous peoples to zones of indifference (Bignall 2012).

4 According to Lorenzo Chiesa, Agamben's positive task is to generate a new relation between life and the ways or forms through which life is lived (a new relation between *zoe* and *bios*), but this new politics and new relation would begin from the non-relation, because it would not assume that there are two distinct terms ("life without form" and "formed life"), and would instead think about a "cautious delineation" (Chiesa 2009: 152).

5 On the ways in which these divisions and differences are bound together by a common logic, see McLoughlin (2010). There are, then, three forms of abandonment of the living being at play in *Homo Sacer*: the distinction within political theory between politics as the good life and the simple fact of living; the juridical distinction between legally recognized life and a "bare life" that is stripped of legal recognition produced through the sovereign ban; and the ontological distinction between the living being and language at stake in the human capacity for speech, which the metaphysical tradition thinks in terms of the Voice. At stake in each of these readings is a reworking of the understanding of origin and ground as they have been thought by the philosophical tradition.

6 For a highly critical account of Agamben's retreat into gesture as a pre-political and ultimately quietist maneuver, see Morgan (2009).

7 Elizabeth Balskus compares Agamben's reading of Melville's "Bartleby, The Scrivener," with Leibniz's concept of God. For Leibniz, God actualized the best of all possible worlds and is a power of bringing potentiality into existence; Bartleby, by contrast, prefers not to act, and in so doing allows multiple potentialities to be sustained, precisely by not being actualized (Balskus 2010).

8 It is in this respect that Colby Dickinson's work on Agamben's theology does not focus on an aspect of Agamben's work so much as its overall motivation of finding a way out of the contemporary domain of language and politics that ultimately derives from theology: Agamben refuses "an 'actuality' of being which is itself overly indebted to the violent representations that have scored our political and historical landscapes and intentions. His challenge to the historical traditions of theology thereby expands upon this claim, rearticulating the way in which sin has generally been conceived – that is, as the refusal to enter into pure actuality that God has often (mistakenly) been defined as being" (Dickinson 2011: 40).

9 For a criticism of the ways in which Agamben's theory of bare life fails to deal adequately with sexual difference, see Deutscher (2008), Ziarek (2008), and Smith (2010). Agamben has also been criticized, despite his debt to Marx, from more traditionally "revolutionary" positions (Casarino 2008),

while some have argued that the key concept of "bare life" in Agamben's corpus needs to be considered as operating by racial exclusion (Weheliye 2008).

10 According to Edkins, whereas Foucault sees power in the twentieth century as no longer requiring the category of person and instead managing biological life, Agamben sees the category of person as still pertinent and defined precisely – as always – in opposition to bare life (Edkins 2013: 130).

11 For an analysis of the temporal trajectory of Agamben's work and a charting of the reversals in what counts as emancipatory, see Doussan (2013).

12 According to Leland de la Durantaye, "For Agamben, the question of potentiality is intimately linked not only to the idea of politics ... but also to concrete instances and institutions of political power.... he contends that whether we are aware of them or not, our conceptions of potentiality condition our ideas of power and its limits" (2009: 15).

13 For a criticism of Agamben, and a defense of Derrida, see Swiffen (2012) and Donahue (2013). Most work on Agamben makes some mention of the difference between Agamben's and Derrida's accounts of Kafka's parable of the law. Whereas Derrida describes the man standing before the door of the law as a way of thinking about law's necessary distance – the simple fact that there is law – Agamben sees law's distance and difference as indicative of a possible world where the door of the law will be shut. This difference between Agamben and Derrida is discussed throughout the secondary literature, and specifically by Simon Morgan Wortham (2007).

14 Although Agamben examines the threshold between human and animal, he has been criticized – most notably by Cary Wolfe – for "a dismissal and disavowal of the embodied existence that we share with nonhuman animals" (Wolfe 2013: 24).

15 According to Jeffrey Librett (2007), Agamben fails to confront the concept of sacrifice and remains problematically with a Christian Heideggerian privilege of the spirit over letter: "In the light of these basic aspects of Nazi ideology, when millions of Jews are murdered by the Nazis, one must understand this as a scapegoating sacrifice of the dead letter (or the law) of the antinatural race to the living voice and immediacy of the race of races, the naturally supernatural as such. The Aryan race thus tries to purify itself of all mediation and representation in favor of immediacy and pure presence. Nazi anti-Semites destroy the Jews for the sake of the Leader, but the Leader is a transcendent version of themselves of the people, race, and state without any significant internal differentiation whatsoever: all henceforth 'sacred'" (Librett 2007: 27).

Chapter 2   Sovereignty, State of Exception, and Biopolitics

1 Despite his criticism of rights insofar as they are based on a normative conception of the human that is tied to a constitutive exclusion of the inhuman, or bare life, his work has been taken up by theorists keen to generate more fruitful conceptions of rights. See Gündoğdu (2012), and Lechte and Newman (2013).

2 For an in-depth account of the sacred and profane ("as the most profound intentions of Agamben's philosophy") throughout Agamben's corpus, going back to his earliest work on language, see de la Durantaye (2008).
3 See: <http://www.fhi.ox.ac.uk>.

Chapter 3   *Homo Sacer*, Sacred Life, and Bare Life

1 "Lengthy Arizona Execution Heightens Lethal-Injection Questions," *Wall Street Journal*, July 25, 2014: <http://online.wsj.com/articles/lengthy -arizona-execution-heightens-lethalinjection-questions-1406213831>.

Chapter 4   New Ethics, New Politics

1 Justin Clemens (2010) has provided an original and singular account of the importance of psychoanalysis and melancholy in Agamben's work. Freud's theory of mourning an object that never was, and that disturbs the borders of the desiring subject, is – argues Clemens – crucial to Agamben's entire corpus, including the early work on the thresholds of language and later work on the borders of the political.

References

Works by Agamben

CC: *The Coming Community*. Trans. Michael Hardt. Minneapolis, MN: University of Minnesota Press, 1993.

CK: *The Church and the Kingdom*. Trans. Leland de la Durantaye. Chicago, IL: Seagull Books, 2012.

DP: "What is a Destituent Power?" Trans. Stephanie Wakefield. *Environment and Planning D: Society and Space* (2014) 32: 65–74.

EC: "For an Ethics of the Cinema." In Henrik Gustafsson and Asbjørn Grønstad (eds.), *Cinema and Agamben: Ethics, Biopolitics and the Moving Image*. London: Bloomsbury, 2014, pp. 19–24.

EP: *The End of the Poem: Studies in Poetics*. Trans. Daniel Heller-Roazen. Stanford, CA: Stanford University Press, 1999.

ER: "The Eternal Return and the Paradox of Passion." *Stanford Italian Review* (1986) 6/1–2: 9–17.

HP: *The Highest Poverty: Monastic Rules and Form-of-Life*. Trans. Adam Kotsko. Stanford, CA: Stanford University Press, 2013.

HS: *Homo Sacer: Sovereign Power and Bare Life*. Trans. Daniel Heller-Roazen. Stanford, CA: Stanford University Press, 1998.

I: "I Am Sure That You Are More Pessimistic Than I Am...": An Interview with Giorgio Agamben. Vacarme. Trans. Jason Smith. *Rethinking Marxism* 16/2 (April 2004): 115–24.

IH: *Infancy and History: Essays on the Destruction of Experience*. Trans. Liz Heron. London: Verso, 1993.

K: "K." In Justin Clemens, Nicholas Heron, and Alex Murray (eds.), *The Work of Giorgio Agamben: Law, Literature, Life*. Edinburgh: Edinburgh University Press, 2008, pp. 13–27.

KG: *The Kingdom and the Glory: For a Theological Genealogy of Economy and Government*. Trans. Lorenzo Chiesa and Matteo Mandarini. Stanford, CA: Stanford University Press, 2011.

LD: *Language and Death: The Place of Negativity*. Trans. Karen E. Pinkus with Michael Hardt. Minneapolis, MN: University of Minnesota Press, 1991.

MWC: *Man Without Content*. Trans. Georgia Albert. Stanford, CA: Stanford University Press, 1999.

MWE: *Means Without Ends: Notes on Politics*. Trans. Vincenzo Binetti and Cesare Casarino. Minneapolis, MN: University of Minnesota Press, 2000.

N: "Nymphs." In Jacques Khalip and Robert Mitchell (eds.), *Releasing the Image: From Literature to New Media*. Stanford, CA: Stanford University Press, 2011, pp. 60–80.

NP: "No to Bio-Political Tattooing." *Le Monde* (January 10, 2004). At: <http://www.ratical.org/ratville/CAH/totalControl.html>.

O: *The Open: Man and Animal*. Trans. Kevin Attell. Stanford, CA: Stanford University Press, 2003.

OD: *Opus Dei*. Trans. Adam Kotsko. Stanford, CA: Stanford University Press, 2013.

P: *Potentialities: Collected Essays in Philosophy*. Ed. and trans. Daniel Heller-Roazen. Stanford, CA: Stanford University Press, 1999.

PJ: *Pilate and Jesus*. Trans. Adam Kotsko. Stanford, CA: Stanford University Press, 2015.

PT: "The Power of Thought." Trans. Kalpana Seshadri. *Critical Inquiry* 40/2 (winter 2014): 480–91.

RA: *Remnants of Auschwitz*. Trans. Daniel Heller-Roazen. New York: Zone Books, 1999.

S: *Stanzas: Word and Phantasm in Western Culture*. Trans. Ronald L. Martinez. Minneapolis, MN: University of Minnesota Press, 1992.

SC: "For a Theory of Destituent Power." 2014. At: <http://www.chronosmag.eu/index.php/g-agamben-for-a-theory-of-destituent-power.html>.

SE: *State of Exception*. Trans. Kevin Attell. Chicago, IL: University of Chicago Press, 2005.

SL: *The Sacrament of Language: An Archeology of the Oath*. Trans. Adam Kotsko. Stanford, CA: Stanford University Press, 2010.

ST: *The Signature of All Things: On Method*. Trans. Luca D'Isanto with Kevin Attell. New York: Zone Books, 2009.

TC: "Thought is the Courage of Hopelessness." An Interview with Giorgio Agamben. Trans. Jordan Skinner. At: <http://www.versobooks.com/blogs/1612-thought-is-the-courage-of-hopelessness-an-interview-with-philosopher-giorgio-agamben?>. Interviewed in French by Juliette Cerf. At: <http://www.telerama.fr/idees/le-philosophe-giorgio-agamben-la-pensee-c-est-le-courage-du-desespoir,78653.php>.

TR: *The Time That Remains: A Commentary on the Letter to the Romans*. Trans. Patricia Dailey. Stanford, CA: Stanford University Press, 2005.

WM: "The Work of Man." Trans. Kevin Attell. In Matthew Calarco and Steven DeCaroli (eds.), *Giorgio Agamben: Sovereignty and Life*. Stanford, CA: Stanford University Press, 2007, pp. 1–10.

Other Works

Abbott, Mathew. 2014. *The Figure of this World: Agamben and the Question of Political Ontology*. Edinburgh: Edinburgh University Press.

Adler, Anthony Curtis. 2014. "Fractured Life and the Ambiguity of Historical Time: Biopolitics in Agamben and Arendt." *Cultural Critique* 86: 1–30.

Arendt, Hannah. 1958. *The Human Condition*. Chicago, IL: University of Chicago Press.

Attell, Kevin. 2009. "An Esoteric Dossier: Agamben and Derrida Read Saussure." *ELH* 76/4: 821–46.

Attell, Kevin. 2014. *Giorgio Agamben: Beyond the Threshold of Deconstruction*. New York: Fordham University Press.

Bailey, Richard, Daniel McLoughlin, and Jessica Whyte. 2010. "Editors' Introduction: Form-of-Life: Giorgio Agamben, Ontology and Politics." *Theory & Event* 13/1. At: <http://muse.jhu.edu.ezaccess.libraries.psu.edu/journals/theory_and_event/v013/13.1.bailey.html> and <http://muse.jhu.edu/journals/theory_and_event/v013/13.1.bailey.html>.

Balskus, Elizabeth. 2010. "Examining Potentiality in the Philosophy of Giorgio Agamben." *Macalester Journal of Philosophy* 19/1: 158–80.

Bataille, Georges. 1990. "Hegel, Death and Sacrifice." *Yale French Studies* 78: 9–28.

Bataille, Georges. 2001. *Literature and Evil*. Trans. Alastair Hamilton. London: Marion Boyars.

Baugh, Bruce. 2003. *French Hegel: From Surrealism to Postmodernism*. New York: Routledge.

Benjamin, Walter. 1996. "Critique of Violence." *Selected Writings: 1913–1926, Volume 1*. Cambridge, MA: Harvard University Press, pp. 236–53.

Benjamin, Walter. 2006. *Walter Benjamin: Selected Writings*, vol. 4. Ed. Marcus Bollock and Michael W. Jennings. Cambridge, MA: Belknap Press of Harvard University Press.

Benjamin, Walter. 2008. *The Work of Art in the Age of Its Technological Reproducibility, and Other Writings on Media*. Trans. E. F. N. Jephcott, ed. Michael William Jennings, Brigid Doherty, and Thomas Y. Levin. Cambridge, MA: Harvard University Press.

Bignall, Simone. 2012. "Potential Postcoloniality: Sacred Life, Profanation and the Coming Community." In Marcelo Svirsky and Simone

Bignall (eds.), *Agamben and Colonialism*. Edinburgh: Edinburgh University Press, pp. 261–84.

Blencowe, Claire. 2010. "Foucault and Arendt's 'Insider View' of Biopolitics: A Critique of Agamben." *History of the Human Sciences* 23/5: 113–30.

Braidotti, Rosi. 2006. *Transpositions: On Nomadic Ethics*. Cambridge: Polity.

Brennan, John. 2012. "Speech on Drone Ethics." NPR, May 2012. At: <http://www.npr.org/2012/05/01/151778804/john-brennan -delivers-speech-on-drone-ethics>.

Britt, Brian. 2010. "The Schmittian Messiah in Agamben's *The Time That Remains*." *Critical Inquiry* 36 (winter): 262–87.

Bryant, Levi, Nick Srnicek, and Graham Harman (eds.). 2011. *The Speculative Turn: Continental Materialism and Realism*. Melbourne: re.press.

Butler, Judith. 1987. *Subjects of Desire: Hegelian Reflections in Twentieth-Century France*. New York: Routledge.

Butler, Judith. 1990. *Gender Trouble*. New York: Routledge.

Butler, Judith. 2013. *Parting Ways: Jewishness and the Critique of Zionism*. New York: Columbia.

Campbell, Timothy. 2011. *Improper Life: Technology and Biopolitics from Heidegger to Agamben*. Minneapolis, MN: University of Minnesota Press.

Campbell, Timothy and Federico Luisetti. 2010. "On Contemporary French and Italian Political Philosophy: An Interview with Roberto Esposito." *Minnesota Review* 75: 109–18.

Casarino, Cesare. 2008. "Time Matters: Marx, Negri, Agamben, and the Corporeal." In Cesare Cesarino and Antonio Negri, *In Praise of the Common*. Minneapolis, MN: University of Minnesota Press, pp. 219–93.

Chiesa, Lorenzo. 2009. "Giorgio Agamben's Franciscan Ontology." *Cosmos and History: The Journal of Natural and Social Philosophy* 5/1: 105–16.

Clemens, Justin. 2010. "The Abandonment of Sex: Giorgio Agamben, Psychoanalysis and Melancholia." *Theory & Event* 13/1. At: <http:// muse.jhu.edu.ezaccess.libraries.psu.edu/journals/theory_and _event/v013/13.1.clemens.html> and <https://muse.jhu.edu/ login?auth=0&type=summary&url=/journals/theory_and_event/ v013/13.1.clemens.html>.

Clough, Patricia Ticineto and Jean Halley (eds.). 2007. *The Affective Turn: Theorizing the Social*. Durham, NC: Duke University Press.

Coleman, Mathew and Kevin Grove. 2009. "Biopolitics, Biopower, and the Return of Sovereignty." *Environment and Planning D: Society and Space* 27/3: 489–507.

Coole, Diana and Samantha Frost (eds.). 2010. *New Materialisms: Ontology, Agency and Politics*. Durham, NC: Duke University Press.

Cornell, Drucilla, Michel Rosenfeld, and David Gray Carlson (eds.). 1992. *Deconstruction and the Possibility of Justice*. New York: Routledge.

Crockett, Clayton. 2011. *Radical Political Theology: Religion and Politics After Liberalism*. New York: Columbia University Press.

Culler, Jonathan. 2008. "'The Most Interesting Thing in the World.'" *Diacritics* 38/1–2: 7–16.

De Boever, Arne. 2009. "Agamben and Marx: Sovereignty, Governmentality and Economy." *Law Critique* 20: 259–70.

Deleuze, Gilles. 1983. *Nietzsche and Philosophy*. Trans. Janis Tomlinson. London: Athlone.

Deleuze, Gilles. 1994. *Difference and Repetition*. Trans. Paul Patton. New York: Columbia University Press.

Derrida, Jacques. 1969. "The Ends of Man." *Philosophy and Phenomenological Research* 30/1 (September): 31–57.

Derrida, Jacques. 1978. *Writing and Difference*. Trans. Alan Bass. London: Routledge.

Derrida, Jacques. 1989a. "Geschlecht II: Heidegger's Hand." In John Sallis (ed.), *Deconstruction and Philosophy*. Chicago, IL: University of Chicago Press, pp. 161–97.

Derrida, Jacques. 1989b. *Of Spirit: Heidegger and the Question*. Trans. Geoffrey Bennington and Rachel Bowlby. Chicago, IL: University of Chicago Press.

Derrida, Jacques. 1992. *Acts of Literature*, ed. Derek Attridge. London: Routledge.

Derrida, Jacques. 2008. *The Animal That Therefore I Am*. Trans. Marie-Louise Mallet. Stanford, CA: Stanford University Press.

Derrida, Jacques. 2009. *The Beast and the Sovereign*. Trans. Geoffrey Bennington. Chicago, IL: University of Chicago Press.

Descombes, Vincent. 1980. *Modern French Philosophy*. Cambridge: Cambridge University Press.

Deutscher, Penelope. 2008. "The Inversion of Exceptionality: Foucault, Agamben and Reproductive Rights." *South Atlantic Quarterly* 107/1: 55–70.

Dickinson, Colby. 2011. *Agamben and Theology*. London: T&T Clark International.

Dickinson, Colby. 2012. "The Poetic Atheology of Giorgio Agamben: Defining the Scission Between Poetry and Philosophy." *Mosaic: A Journal for the Interdisciplinary Study of Literature* 45/1: 203–18.

Docherty, Thomas. 2002. "Potential European Democracy." *Paragraph* 25/2: 16–35.

Dolphijn, Rick and Iris van der Tuin. 2012. *New Materialism: Interviews and Cartographies*. Michigan: University of Michigan Library.

Donahue, Luke. 2013. "Erasing Differences between Derrida and Agamben." *Oxford Literary Review* 35/1: 25–45.

Doussan, Jenny. 2013. *Time, Language, and Visuality in Agamben's Philosophy*. London: Palgrave.

Dummett, Michael. 1996. *Origins of Analytical Philosophy*. Cambridge, MA: Harvard University Press.

Durantaye, Leland de la. 2008. "*Homo profanus:* Giorgio Agamben's Profane Philosophy." *boundary* 2 35/3: 27–62.

Durantaye, Leland de la. 2009. *Giorgio Agamben: A Critical Introduction*. Stanford, CA: Stanford University Press.

Duttmann, Alexander. 2008. "Integral Actuality: On Giorgio Agamben's *The Idea of Prose*." In Justin Clemens, Nicholas Heron, and Alex Murray (eds.), *The Work of Giorgio Agamben: Law, Literature, Life*. Edinburgh: Edinburgh University Press, pp. 28–42.

Eaglestone, Robert. 2002. "On Giorgio Agamben's Holocaust." *Paragraph* 25/2: 52–67.

Edkins, Jenny. 2000. "Sovereign Power, Bare Life, and the Camp." *Alternatives* 24/3–4: 3–25.

Edkins, Jenny. 2013. "Time, Person, Politics." In Gert Buelens, Samuel Durrant, and Robert Eaglestone (eds.), *The Future of Trauma Theory: Contemporary Literary and Cultural Criticism*. London: Routledge, pp. 127–40.

Esposito, Roberto. 2008. *Bíos: Biopolitics and Philosophy*. Trans. Timothy Campbell. Minneapolis, MN: University of Minnesota Press.

Esposito, Roberto. 2012. *Third Person: Politics of Life and Philosophy of the Impersonal*. Trans. Zakiya Hanafi. Cambridge: Polity.

Eyers, Tom. 2013. *Post-Rationalism: Psychoanalysis, Epistemology and Marxism in Post-War France*. London: Bloomsbury.

Finlayson, James Gordon. 2010. " 'Bare Life' and Politics in Agamben's Reading of Aristotle." *The Review of Politics* 72: 97–126.

Fiovoranti, David. 2010. "Language, Exception, Messianism: The Thematics of Agamben on Derrida." *The Bible and Critical Theory* 6/1. At: <http://novaojs.newcastle.edu.au/ojsbct/index.php/bct/article/view/289>.

Foucault, Michel. 1970. *The Order of Things*. London: Routledge.

Foucault, Michel. 1977. *Discipline and Punish: The Birth of the Prison*. Trans. Alan Sheridan. New York: Pantheon.

Foucault, Michel. 1978. *The History of Sexuality: Volume One, An Introduction*. Trans. Robert Hurley. New York: Random House.

Foucault, Michel. 2006. *History of Madness*. Trans. Jean Khalfa. London: Routledge.

Frost, Tom. 2010. "Agamben's Sovereign Legalization of Foucault." *Oxford Journal of Legal Studies* 30/3: 545–77.

Fukuyama, Francis. 1992. *The End of History and the Last Man*. New York: Free Press.

Gatens, Moira. 2004. "Can Human Rights Accommodate Women's Rights? Towards an Embodied Account of Social Norms, Social Meaning, and Cultural Change." *Contemporary Political Theory* 2: 275–99.

Goldberg, Shari. 2013. *Quiet Testimony: A Theory of Witnessing from Nineteenth-Century American Literature*. Oxford: Oxford University Press.

Grusin, Richard (ed.). 2015. *The Nonhuman*. Minneapolis, MN: University of Minnesota Press.

Gündoğdu, Ayten. 2012. "Potentialities of Human Rights: Agamben and the Narrative of Fated Necessity." *Contemporary Political Theory* 11/1: 2–22.

Habermas, Jürgen. 2003. *Future of Human Nature*. Cambridge: Polity.

Habermas, Jürgen. 2006. *Time of Transitions*. Ed. and trans. Ciaran Cronin and Max Pensky. Cambridge: Polity.

Hardt, Michael and Antonio Negri. 2000. *Empire*. Cambridge, MA: Harvard University Press.

Heidegger, Martin. 1995. *Aristotle's Metaphysics Theta, 1–3: On the Essence and Actuality of Force*. Trans. Walter Brogen and Peter Warnek. Bloomington, IN: Indiana University Press.

Heidegger, Martin. 1996. *Being and Time*. Trans. Joan Stambaugh. Albany, NY: SUNY Press.

Heidegger, Martin. 1998. *Pathmarks*. Ed. William McNeil. Cambridge: Cambridge University Press.

Jarvis, Jill. 2014. "Remnants of Muslims: Reading Agamben's Silence." *New Literary History* 45/4: 707–28.

Kant, Immanuel. 1965. *Critique of Pure Reason*. Trans. Norman Kemp Smith. New York: St. Martin's Press.

Laforteza, Elaine Marie Carbonell. 2015. *The Somatechnics of Whiteness and Race: Colonialism and Mestiza Privilege*. London: Ashgate.

Lechte, John. 2012. "Agamben, Arendt and Human Rights: Bearing Witness to the Human." *European Journal of Social Theory* 15/4: 522–36.

Lechte, John and Saul Newman. 2013. *Agamben and the Politics of Human Rights: Statelessness, Images, Violence*. Oxford: Oxford University Press.

Levinas, Emmanuel. 1969. *Totality and Infinity: An Essay on Exteriority*. Trans. Alphonso Lingis. Dordrecht: Kluwer.

Librett, Jeffrey S. 2007. "From the Sacrifice of the Letter to the Voice of Testimony: Giorgio Agamben's Fulfillment of Metaphysics." *Diacritics: A Review of Contemporary Criticism* 37/2–3: 11–33.

MacIntyre, Alastair. 1981. *After Virtue: A Study in Moral Theory*. Notre Dame: University of Notre Dame Press.

McLoughlin, Daniel. 2010. "The Sacred and the Unspeakable: Giorgio Agamben's Ontological Politics." *Theory & Event* 13/1. At: <http://muse.jhu.edu.ezaccess.libraries.psu.edu/journals/theory_and_event/v013/13.1.mcloughlin.html> and <https://muse.jhu.edu/login?auth=0&type=summary&url=/journals/theory_and_event/v013/13.1.mcloughlin.html>.

McQuillan, Colin. 2005. "The Political Life in Giorgio Agamben." *Kritikos: An International and Interdisciplinary Journal of Postmodern Cultural Sound, Text and Image* 2 (July): 1–13.

McQuillan, Colin. 2012. "Agamben's Fictions." *Philosophy Compass* 7: 376–87.

Mbembe, Achille. 2003. "Necropolitics." Trans. Libby Meintjes. *Public Culture* 15/1: 11–40.

Mills, Catherine. 2005. "Linguistic Survival and Ethicality: Biopolitics, Subjectivation and Testimony in *Remnants of Auschwitz*." In Andrew Norris (ed.), *Politics, Metaphysics and Death: Essays on Giorgio Agamben's Homo Sacer*. Durham, NC: Duke University Press, pp. 198–221.

Mills, Catherine. 2014. *The Philosophy of Agamben*. London: Routledge.

Morgan, Alastair. 2009. "'A Figure of Annihilated Human Existence': Agamben and Adorno on Gesture." *Law Critique* 20: 299–307.

Murray, Alex. 2010. *Giorgio Agamben*. London: Routledge.

Negri, Antonio. 1991. *The Savage Anomaly: The Power of Spinoza's Metaphysics and Politics*. Trans. Michael Hardt. Minneapolis, MN: University of Minnesota Press.

Negri, Antonio. 2008. "Sovereignty: That Divine Ministry of the Affairs of Earthly Life." *Journal for Cultural and Religious Theory* 9/1 (winter): 96–100.

Oliver, Kelly. 2013. *Animal Lessons: How They Teach Us To Be Human*. New York: Columbia University Press.

Power, Nina. 2010. "Potentiality or Capacity? – Agamben's Missing Subjects." *Theory & Event* 13/1. At: <http://muse.jhu.edu.ezaccess .libraries.psu.edu/journals/theory_and_event/v013/13.1.power .html> and <http://muse.jhu.edu/login?auth=0&type=summary &url=/journals/theory_and_event/v013/13.1.power.html>.

Protevi, John. 2009. *Political Affect: Connecting the Social and the Somatic*. Minneapolis, MN: University of Minnesota Press.

Prozorov, Sergei. 2014. *Agamben and Politics: A Critical Introduction*. Oxford: Oxford University Press.

Rabinow, Paul and Nicholas Rose. 2006. "Biopower Today." *BioSocieties: An Interdisciplinary Journal for the Social Study of the Life Sciences* 1/2: 195–218.

Rawls, John. 1972. *A Theory of Justice*. Oxford: Clarendon Press.

Ricciardi, Alessia. 2009. "From Decreation to Bare Life: Weil, Agamben, and the Impolitical." *diacritics* 39/2: 75–93.

Rushdie, Salman. 1990. *Is Nothing Sacred* (Herbert Read Memorial Lecture, February 6, 1990). London: Granta.

Sartre, Jean-Paul. 2001. *Being and Nothingness*. Trans. Hazel Barnes. New York: Citadel Press.

Sayeau, Michael. 2013. *Against the Event: The Everyday and Evolution of Modernist Narrative*. Oxford: Oxford University Press.

Schmitt, Carl. 2006. *Political Theology*. Trans. George Schwab. Chicago, IL: University of Chicago Press.

Sexton, Jared. 2010. "People-of-Color-Blindness: Notes on the Afterlife of Slavery." *Social Text* 28/2 (103): 31–56.

Singer, Peter. 1993. *Practical Ethics*, 2nd edition. Cambridge: Cambridge University Press.

Smith, Anne-Marie. 2010. "Neo-eugenics: A Feminist Critique of Agamben." *Occasion: Interdisciplinary Study in the Humanities* V/2 (December 20, 2010). At: <http://occasion.stanford.edu/node/59>.

Smith, Mick. 2009. "Against Ecological Sovereignty: Agamben, Politics and Globalization." *Environmental Politics* 18/1: 99–116.

Svirsky, Marcelo. 2014. *After Israel: Towards Cultural Transformation*. London: Zed Books.

Svirsky, Marcelo and Simone Bignall (eds.). 2012. *Agamben and Colonialism*. Edinburgh: Edinburgh University Press.

Swiffen, Amy. 2012. "Derrida Contra Agamben: Sovereignty, Biopower, History." *Societies* 2/4: 345–56.

Taylor, Charles. 1991. "Being, Person, Community." In *Hegel and Legal Theory*. London: Routledge, pp. 71–2.

Terada, Rei. 2002. "The Life Process and Forgettable Living: Arendt and Agamben." *New Formations* 71 (spring 2011): 95–109.

Thurschwell, Adam. 2004. "Specters of Nietzsche: Potential Futures for the Concept of the Political in Agamben and Derrida." At: <http://papers.ssrn.com/sol3/papers.cfm?abstract_id=969055>.

Uexküll, Jakob von. 2010. *A Foray into the Worlds of Animals and Humans*. Trans. Joseph D. O'Neil. Minneapolis, MN: University of Minnesota Press.

Ugilt, Rasmus. 2014. *Giorgio Agamben: Political Philosophy*. Ann Arbor, MI: humanities-ebooks. At: <http://www.humanities-ebooks.co.uk/book/Agamben>.

Watkin, William. 2013. *Agamben and Indifference: A Critical Overview*. London: Rowman and Littlefield.

Weheliye, Alexander G. 2008. "Pornotropes." *Journal of Visual Culture* 7/1: 65–81.

Whyte, Jessica. 2013. *Catastrophe and Redemption: The Political Thought of Giorgio Agamben*. Albany, NY: State University of New York Press.

Wolfe, Cary. 2010. *What is Posthumanism?* Minneapolis, MN: University of Minnesota Press.

Wolfe, Cary. 2013. *Before the Law: Humans and Other Animals in a Biopolitical Frame*. Chicago, IL: University of Chicago Press.

Wortham, Simon Morgan. 2007. "Law of Friendship: Agamben and Derrida." *New Formations* 62 (autumn): 89–105.

Zartaloudis, Thanos. 2010. *Giorgio Agamben: Power, Law and the Uses of Criticism*. New York: Routledge.

Ziarek, Ewa Plonowska. 2008. "Bare Life on Strike: Notes on the Bio-politics of Race and Gender." *South Atlantic Quarterly* 107/1: 89–105.

Žižek, Slavoj. 1993. *Tarrying with the Negative: Kant, Hegel and the Critique of Ideology*. Durham, NC: Duke University Press.

Index